KU-168-449

ON THE TRAIL OF THE YORKSHIRE RIPPER

LIBRARIES NI
WITHDRAWN FROM STOCK

On the Trail of the Yorkshire Ripper

His Final Secrets Revealed

RICHARD CHARLES COBB

PEN & SWORD
TRUE CRIME

First published in Great Britain in 2019 by
Pen & Sword True Crime
An imprint of
Pen & Sword Books Ltd
Yorkshire – Philadelphia

Copyright © Richard Charles Cobb 2019

ISBN 978 1 52674 876 8

The right of Richard Charles Cobb to be identified as Author of this
work has been asserted by him in accordance with the Copyright,
Designs and Patents Act 1988.

A CIP catalogue record for this book is
available from the British Library.

All rights reserved. No part of this book may be reproduced or
transmitted in any form or by any means, electronic or mechanical
including photocopying, recording or by any information storage and
retrieval system, without permission from the Publisher in writing.

Printed and bound in the UK by TJ International Ltd, Padstow,
Cornwall.

Pen & Sword Books Limited incorporates the imprints of Atlas,
Archaeology, Aviation, Discovery, Family History, Fiction, History,
Maritime, Military, Military Classics, Politics, Select, Transport, True
Crime, Air World, Frontline Publishing, Leo Cooper, Remember
When, Seaforth Publishing, The Praetorian Press, Wharncliffe Local
History, Wharncliffe Transport, Wharncliffe True Crime
and White Owl.

For a complete list of Pen & Sword titles please contact

PEN & SWORD BOOKS LIMITED
47 Church Street, Barnsley, South Yorkshire, S70 2AS, England
E-mail: enquiries@pen-and-sword.co.uk
Website: www.pen-and-sword.co.uk

Or

PEN AND SWORD BOOKS
1950 Lawrence Rd, Havertown, PA 19083, USA
E-mail: Uspen-and-sword@casematepublishers.com
Website: www.penandswordbooks.com

For my children,
Brandon, Michael and Hannah

Contents

Acknowledgements

My parents Philip and Roberta Cobb who have always supported and encouraged my work and endured my endless discussions on the subject. My brothers Colin and Michael. The late great David Jones, who took me around several of the Yorkshire Ripper sites when I first arrived in Bradford, and his wife Rhonda who helped me search the archives during my research.

I'd also like to thank all those true crime enthusiasts, authors and close personal friends who have always been there for advice and support. Neil Storey, Fiona Kay, Lyndsey Jones, Scott Nichol, Joanna Connor, Dean Garth, Prof David Wilson, Ashlin Orrell, Carol Ann Lee, Jackie Murphy, Anjum Fi, Darren Field, Paul Harrison, Stuart Evans, Martin Fido, Rob Clack, Lindsay Siviter, Trish Routh, Lauren Davies, Andrew Laptew, Nicky Latz, Amanda Spencer, John Holloway, Johanne Edgington, Vicky Roberts, Kirsty Giles, Jackie Beck, David Beck, Martin and Karen Trueman, Tania Simpson, Steve Blomer, David Jones Jr, Luka Hirst and my long suffering crime scene tour buddy, Elizabeth Blakemore.

A special thanks to the East End crew: Mick Priestley, John Chambers, Lizzie Quinn, Greg Baldock, Jamie Biddle, Sinead O'Leary, Amy Harper and Andre Price.

Mr Colin Farr, who I promised to acknowledge if I ever wrote a true crime book. A promise made thirty-one years ago whilst a pupil in his superb history class. Well sir, better late than never.

Finally, I'd like to thank three people without whose enthusiasm, guidance and knowledge this book simply wouldn't have been possible: Mr Chris Clark for writing the foreword and sharing his in-depth knowledge of the case with me, Mr Chris Routh for the maps and diagrams and Mr Mark Davis for the photography.

I couldn't have asked for a better team.

Richard Charles Cobb

Foreword

I joined the police force to make a difference. My first real job was that of gardener. Not just any gardener, as my boss was not just any employer. Between 1964 and 1966, I worked at Sandringham House, an enormous country pile set in 20,000 acres of beautiful Norfolk countryside. My job was to tend the kitchen gardens on behalf of the owner: Her Majesty the Queen. But I knew I wanted to do something more, something different – something that involved service to the public rather than its head of state. And so, on Thursday, 10 March 1966, I found myself boarding the train at King's Lynn for the 50-mile journey to Norwich. There, in the city's Shirehall Magistrates' Court, I was sworn in as an officer for the Norfolk Constabulary.

When the ceremony was over I was Constable 409, Clark C: 'A citizen locally appointed but having authority under the Crown for the protection of life and property, the maintenance of order, the prevention and detection of crime and the prosecution of offenders against the Peace.' I collected my warrant card, uniform and the tools of my new trade: one set of handcuffs, a whistle and a truncheon. After a thirteen-week training course in Oxfordshire I was ready to pound the beat as a probationary constable. I was sent to an urban district on the fringes of Norwich, which at that time had its own separate police force. I was 20 years old, rather shy and distinctly introverted. But the job – as all coppers call it – was no place for shrinking violets.

By the mid-1960s, crime was growing and changing fast. The immediate post-war years had seen an explosion in robberies – many of them carried out with the glut of weapons brought home from the fight against Hitler – in cities up and down the country. But throughout the 1940s and 1950s there was still strong respect for the law and particularly for those who upheld it: attacks on policemen were rare and shocking. However, shortly after I began patrolling my beat – often at night, always alone, unarmed (of course) and with no means of communication other than the traditional whistle and any public telephone that happened to be nearby – the police and the country itself received a wake-up call.

The summer of 1966 had, by and large, been a good one: England was swinging (not that we saw much of this in Norfolk) and the national football team had just won the World Cup. But within a fortnight the news would be dominated by what became known as the Massacre of Braybrook Street. Harry Roberts – a 30-year-old petty criminal who had learned his trade as a child black marketer during the war, before learning how to kill during two years' National Service – shot dead three unarmed police officers in broad daylight in a residential street in London's Shepherd's Bush. He and his accomplices then went on the run: using his military training, Roberts evaded capture for almost three months. If any one crime symbolized the transformation coming over Britain, it was the cold-blooded murder of those three police officers.

The world we had known was changing – and not for the better. By the time I'd finished policing, the police force itself had changed. Like other forces up and down the country, the old city, county and borough constabularies were merged into new organizations. This was, I think, the beginning of the end for much that had been traditional: the bobby on the beat was losing out to the patrol car and the hierarchy was changing too. The bosses and management we had worked under were solid Second World War veterans who had grafted their way to the top and had both real experience and the ability to deal with their staff in a fatherly way that got the best out of them. Gradually, they were squeezed out by high-flyers who came into the job with higher education qualifications – no bad thing of course – but more worryingly with old-school ties and memberships of secretive masonic lodges. But there was, at least, one change for the better. It was during this time that divisional intelligence officers – collators as they became known – were introduced, and I was instrumental in setting up the office for the King's Lynn district in 1968.

A similar system would have been set up in the former West Riding Police and West Riding Criminal Records Office (CRO) at Wakefield, which existed under that title until 1969, the very year that Peter Sutcliffe was arrested on two occasions. Firstly the 'stone in the sock' episode and secondly the 'going equipped with a hammer' episode.

It would also have been set up in Bradford covering Bingley, the home and workplace of Peter Sutcliffe. Had the Bradford collator done his job, there should have been a card raised during 1968 from back record converting in the nominal index filed under Peter William Sutcliffe, date of birth 2 June 1946, and a CRO number and CRO 74 antecedent history and associates for his previous convictions gained in 1965 for attempted theft. On a Sunday night in March 1965 when he was aged 19, Sutcliffe was seen with another person trying door handles of several unattended motor vehicles in Old Main Street, Bingley, beside the River Aire. Both were arrested for attempting to steal from an unattended motor vehicle and appeared at Bingley West Riding Magistrates' Court on 17 May 1965. His address was 57 Cornwall Road, Bingley, which was his parents' address, and he was fined five pounds. His fingerprints would have been taken then. His descriptive form included that he had black curly hair, brown eyes and (at that time) a fresh, clean-shaven complexion.

Before this, in 1963, aged 17, Sutcliffe had obtained a learner driver licence and was stopped and reported by Keighley Police for driving a car unaccompanied and failing to display L-plates. There was a similar case against him in May 1964. Sutcliffe gained more motoring convictions during 1965 and 1966. All of these offences should have been on his nominal record index card.

Each time that Sutcliffe came to the notice of a police officer anywhere in the United Kingdom, a copy of that information should have been forwarded to the Bradford collator for updating on his record card and also forwarded to the central West Yorkshire Intelligence Bureau and combined CRO.

The West Yorkshire Constabulary was, from 1968 to 1974, the statutory police force for the West Riding of Yorkshire in northern England. It was formed under the Police Act 1964, and was a merger of the previous West Riding Constabulary along with six borough forces for the county boroughs of Barnsley, Dewsbury, Doncaster, Halifax, Huddersfield and Wakefield.

The other four West Riding county boroughs – Bradford, Leeds, Sheffield and Rotherham – retained independent police forces (a merged force for Sheffield and Rotherham) until 1974. In 1974 the force was split under the Local Government Act 1972. The bulk of the force went to form the new West Yorkshire Police (with Bradford and Leeds) and South Yorkshire Police (with Sheffield and Rotherham Constabulary, the former Barnsley and Doncaster County Borough forces and the interlinked county areas), with other parts coming under the North Yorkshire Police, Cumbria Constabulary, Humberside Police and Lancashire Police forces. The subdivision of Saddleworth, part of the Huddersfield division of the West Yorkshire Constabulary, was taken into the new Greater Manchester Police.

During July and August of 1975 there were three hammer attacks, which occurred on unaccompanied women in quick succession within the new West Yorkshire Metropolitan Police District. These were at Keighley on 5 July (Anna Rogulskyj), Halifax on 15 August (Olive Smelt) and Silsden on 27 August (Tracy Browne).

Keighley is just 12 miles north of Halifax and both would have had a collator; Silsden is just 4 miles from Keighley and would have been in the same subdivision.

By the end of August 1975, someone from West Yorkshire Metropolitan Police Intelligence section should have joined up the dots that three attempted murders had been committed, all with injuries to the back of the skull that left a crescent-shape mark (hammer being the most likely weapon) and all, more than likely, the work of one person. With the combined witness recollection concluding that a local, shortish man with black curly hair, a black beard and moustache and local accent to Bradford was responsible. This should have been passed to the Bradford collator who should have been able to say that he had one man in his nominal index who fitted the description of the assailant.

Furthermore, the description and any photofits obtained should have gone out to all stations and surrounding force areas via a crime bulletin, similar to the *Police Gazette*.

At this stage, with local investigation and public appeals in Bradford, the sifted intelligence both from his own nominal index card and public investigation, Peter Sutcliffe's fate would have been sealed and he would have been arrested and charged before Wilma McCann's murder on 29 October 1975.

Sadly, this did not happen, hence Richard C. Cobb's excellent offer *On The Trail Of The Yorkshire Ripper*, which I fully endorse.

Retired police intelligence officer Chris Clark,
December 2018.

Introduction

History will brand the Yorkshire Ripper as one of the most feared and callous killers of all time; his crimes surpassing the original Jack the Ripper of Whitechapel infamy, the Moors murderers and the Black Panther.

No detective could have predicted that a single murder in the 1970s would herald one of the most notorious and long-lasting series of sadistic killings Britain has ever endured. Nor could anyone have envisaged the fear it would engender in Northern women and their families by the man the newspapers first dubbed the 'Leeds Jack the Ripper Killer', or that he would remain free for so long.

His trial in 1981 attracted vast crowds. The gallery was packed, the seats in court were packed and the press benches were packed; even seats that were normally allocated to relatives of victims went to reporters. Outside the doors of the Old Bailey in London, people slept in the street to be able to get a chance to get in to see the most infamous monster since Jack the Ripper face justice for his appalling crimes. It was a media circus.

Most national newspapers had sent two or three staff each and, including international reporters, there were thirty or forty journalists in court at any one time.

Sutcliffe himself was a sorrowful figure in many ways – not very well built and towered over by four prison guards. His wife, Sonia, turned up quite a lot of times to lend what support she could, but it all relied on the medical and mental problems he may or may not have had. He really showed no emotion, no smiling, and no laughing. The crowd expected a monster but instead they got a nobody, a small, insignificant man with a softly spoken voice. He was the most unlikely killer you've ever seen. He didn't fit the bill, but they say you never can tell.

Sutcliffe had pleaded not guilty to thirteen counts of murder, but guilty to manslaughter on the grounds of diminished responsibility. The basis of this defence was that he had heard 'voices from God' telling him to go on a mission to rid the streets of prostitutes. He claimed he heard these voices back as far as the late 1960s, coming from one of the gravestones while working as gravedigger in Bingley Cemetery. Doctors for the defence claimed Sutcliffe was showing clear signs of someone suffering from schizophrenia, but as the details of the crimes were presented it would become apparent to all in the jury that these were the acts of an evil and distorted man.

There was a certain inevitability about the verdict because of the number of victims involved. It was over pretty quickly for a trial of that magnitude. They had to agree thirteen victims had been murdered by someone and he was the only candidate.

Sutcliffe was found guilty of murder on all counts and sentenced to twenty life sentences with a recommendation he serve a minimum of thirty years before he be considered for parole. The judge said he was beyond redemption and hoped he would never leave prison. With thirty-eight years now served, the 73-year-old killer would have been eligible to apply for parole had the terms of his sentence not been changed. However, in 2002 the High Court ruled he must serve a 'whole life' tariff which means he will die in jail, along with a small but exclusive club of three dozen or so other violent inmates.

For nearly four decades, the murderous onslaught and afterlife of Peter William Sutcliffe has filled miles of newsprint, numerous books and days of television, securing his place as one of the most notorious serial killers in criminal history. But the vital statistics are human – the thirteen women he is known to have brutally murdered and the seven he failed to kill. Their lives and those of thousands of others, including dozens of children and hundreds of relatives and friends, are marred forever by his legacy.

He struck in a time unacquainted with serial killers. It was an era when police systems were incapable of connecting the masses of information they accumulated. Ultimately the largest manhunt in British criminal history was flawed with bad decisions, missed clues and opportunities. Endless paperwork, thousands of statements and a puzzle wrapped in an enigma proved too much for an out-of-date police force using out-of-date investigation techniques.

If the Yorkshire Ripper were at large today, DNA and databases would soon nail him, but that's little consolation to Sutcliffe's victims. In the north of England, the Ripper years were dark and terrible and some of the scars have yet to heal.

This book revisits those dark days and lays out the real story behind the Yorkshire Ripper murders. It re-examines the crime scenes as they were then and how they are now, reintroducing key witnesses and uncovering new information, which is published here for the first time. It highlights the fatal mistakes made by the investigators and lays bare the circumstances of how this case changed the way murder investigations are handled today. After thirty-eight years we are finally back on the trail of the Yorkshire Ripper.

Chapter 1

Peter

'What has happened does not alter the fact that he is still my son and always will be as long as I live. What upsets me is that there were no signs early on to give us a warning about Peter. If there had have been, it could have saved some poor girl's life.'

John Sutcliffe, 23 May 1981

H e did not stand out in a crowd, and the crowd never noticed him. He was a dull young man, the 'man next door', just as many had suspected. Dull but deadly. Something inside him had snapped, maybe long years before. But it did not show. All that showed was an inconspicuous personality, a usually agreeable demeanour and every now and then a sly smile. That, and the beard of course. Most people remember the beard even if they do not remember him. If some men are said to be low profile in their introversion, then Peter William Sutcliffe was positively underground. Even his own father did not know him properly.

After a five-year reign of terror and the largest, most expensive and most protracted manhunt ever mounted by a police force in this country, the career of the Yorkshire Ripper was brought to an end by sheer luck when two police officers did a routine check of his car – although they had no idea at the time.

The Sutcliffe home was no place for the likes of Peter. His father, John, was a dominant extrovert and his brothers shared many of their father's manly characteristics. John Sutcliffe was a self-proclaimed man's man, a local boy-about-town, as well as a famed footballer, cricketer and actor – a man for all seasons.

Peter, by contrast, was small and weedy from the start. He weighed in at just 2.3 kilos (5 pounds) when he was born on 2 June 1946. His parents, John and Kathleen, were living in a row of terraced cottages: 2 Heaton Royd, Ferncliffe, Bingley. The cottages are still there, hemmed in by blackened stone houses peering out across the Gilstead estate where Peter would spend much of his childhood. (Number 2 has since been renamed 4 Heaton Royd). John Sutcliffe was a journeyman baker in those days. Peter's mother Kathleen Sutcliffe (nee Coonan), was of Irish extraction;

her family hailing originally from Connemara. She is still fondly remembered in Bingley and the local area as a woman who was kind, decent, honest and good-looking.

As their family started to grow, the Sutcliffes moved out of their tiny stone cottage on the sprawling council estate and moved to 70 Manor Road. There, John and Kathleen went on to have more children – Anne, Michael, Maureen, Jayne and Carl – before moving one last time to a four-bedroomed, semi-detached property at 57 Cornwall Road. All the Sutcliffe children went to the same Roman Catholic schools, St Joseph's and Cottingley Manor School, but although bright and quick-witted, Peter did not excel academically. He didn't adjust well to school and was detached from other children of his age. He would spend playtimes on his own and was never involved in the normal rough and tumble of the playground. At home, he was also quiet and loved reading and being at his mother's side.

Unlike his brothers, Peter was socially awkward and never quite managed the art of surviving daily life comfortably in the council-estate world of Bingley, a somewhat dour town just 6 miles north of Bradford along the Aire Valley. His weak build and shyness made him an easy target for school bullies and by the time he moved to Cottingley Manor Secondary School in 1957, the bullying became so bad he played truant sometimes for weeks on end, hiding all alone in the attic with just his thoughts for company. To the rest of his family he was seen as a puny and introverted boy who clung to his mother's skirts, following her everywhere.

As he entered his teenage years, he didn't take any interest in girls and his thoughts were focused on motorbikes and cars. As a schoolboy, he was always fascinated by anything mechanical. When he reached 15, he left school and, on 17 August 1961, he began a £2.50-a-week job as an apprentice engineer at a local firm, Fairbank Brearley. However, he left less than a year later never completing his apprenticeship and the reasons are unknown.

At 16, he bought his first motorcycle and began to assert himself a bit more confidently. He quickly gained a reputation as reckless on two wheels. According to his father, it was as if he had at last found something he was good at. He also started going out more with boys of his own age. Once, three or four of his male friends got together to try and form a pop group and he also became keen on shooting rats with an air gun. As his confidence grew, he took an interest in bodybuilding and would spend hours alone training with a bullworker, gaining upper arm and chest strength.

On 27 May 1962, he went to work in a fibre factory for about two years, but during this time he started to develop a habit of being late for work, which would eventually lose him the job. In fact, over the next couple of years it would cost him around eleven jobs. For a man who must later have used a near-phenomenal sense of split-second timing, his timeless approach to life in his youth seems odd.

For the next couple of years, Peter drifted through a variety of undistinguished, dead-end jobs, going from one to another seemingly rudderless and without ambition, yet oddly never short of money.

In 1963, aged 17, he obtained a learner driver licence and was stopped and reported by Keighley Police for driving a car unaccompanied, and failing to display L-plates. There would be a similar case against him in May 1964.

That same year, he took a job that marked an important milestone in the making of the Yorkshire Ripper. He went to work as a gravedigger at Bingley Cemetery, and it was there that we find the first signs of a flawed mind; a man who was slowly falling in love with death. He actually worked two stints at the cemetery, as he left for a while to work for the water board at Gilstead filter beds but was sacked for bad timekeeping. He returned to gravedigging in June 1965 and stayed there until November 1967 before he was sacked once more for bad timekeeping. His boss at that time, Douglas McTavish, recalled later: 'I had to sack him. He should have started work at 8am but kept arriving at 8.30am and 8.45am. When the other men started arriving late as well, I gave him his last chance but he was late again.' Mr McTavish was adamant that this was the only reason for Sutcliffe's dismissal.

But there are rumours that bad timekeeping was not the only problem at the cemetery in those days. The rumours, which have never been officially proved, are horrific.

Sutcliffe's two spells as a gravedigger are littered with revolting stories of desecration and grave-robbing that tell of ghastly, dark shadows that had been gathering in his mind even in his late teens.

A former work colleague, Tom Nixon, said: 'It was about 1965 when I started work at Bingley Cemetery. At first everything was fine and we all worked together quite well. But it soon became obvious what was going on. Someone was having a look inside the coffins when the relatives had gone.' Mr Nixon resigned in disgust.

Sutcliffe's job at Bingley Cemetery gave him ample opportunity to indulge in his macabre fantasies, and showed his greed for rings and other gold trinkets that had been laid to rest with their owners.

Another work colleague, Steve Close recalled the lengths he would go to get them:

> 'If Peter couldn't get a ring off, he would take the finger. He used to go down to the tool shed and get a pair of really sharp hedging shears – and snip. I have seen him do it, though I wasn't involved myself. If he was lucky he would get two or three valuable pieces of jewellery a week. He always had plenty of money. When we were all spent up, he was never short.
>
> 'Peter seemed to get a real kick out of death. He would look at a corpse, touch it and then eat his sandwiches without even washing his hands. He was a really creepy sort of guy. I have never seen anyone so morbid. I'm not exaggerating when I say that he examined nine out of ten bodies he buried. He did it because he wanted to see if there were any valuables – but also because he liked it. I have seen him look at the most gruesome things which would turn any other man's stomach. But Peter just wasn't bothered – he got his thrills from death.
>
> 'One time he opened a coffin whose occupant had been mangled by a train. It wasn't a body – just two plastic bags of flesh. But he got the bags out and started to look inside. I just walked away. But no one reported him. I suppose we all thought our job was pretty rotten and that was Peter's way of letting off steam.
>
> 'Perhaps we were all as twisted as Peter because sometimes we thought him a real scream. He would turn up in a black frock-coat carrying a prayer book. Then he would stand over the grave and come up with all the "ashes to ashes" stuff. As soon as he got going for a few minutes he would begin speaking the foulest four-letter words and the most horrible oaths.
>
> 'One day the body of a female magistrate came in. Peter had known her and took delight in opening her coffin. I remember to this day that he grabbed a hold of her face as hard as he could and said: "You won't be putting anyone else away now, will you, you bitch?"'

Other colleagues recall that he prised open the mouths of fresh corpses and yanked teeth with gold fillings out with pliers. He jumped into freshly dug graves and pulled out bones and skulls from other graves that he had disturbed in the process. He would use the bones to frighten passing schoolgirls by the cemetery wall, all the while laughing hysterically at the shock he caused. Another unsavoury aspect of his character was his habit of discussing necrophilia (having sex with dead bodies). Although we don't know for sure if Sutcliffe sexually interfered with the dead bodies, he had plenty of opportunity to do so.

When a vacancy opened up to work in the mortuary, Sutcliffe jumped at the chance. The mortuary was based in Croft Road, Bingley and was eventually demolished to make way for the five-storey Bradford and Bingley Building Society offices in 1972.

Here he could spend time alone with the bodies, washing them down and preparing them for burial. He would often comment to others about how he particularly enjoyed working with the bodies that had been involved in car accidents or had been opened up for autopsies.

On a Sunday night in March 1965, when he was 19, he was seen with another youth trying door handles of several unattended motor vehicles in Old Main Street, Bingley, beside the River Aire. Both were arrested for attempting to steal from an unattended car and appeared at the Bingley West Riding Magistrates' Court on 17 May. His address was 57 Cornwall Road, Bingley – his parents address – he was fined five pounds and his fingerprints were taken. His descriptive form included that he had black curly hair, brown eyes and a fresh, clean-shaven complexion.

Shortly after this conviction, Sutcliffe began sporting a neatly trimmed beard and was nicknamed 'Jesus' by his workmates. Friends and family noted that he became withdrawn from conversations and when he did talk, he would discuss death or his job digging graves. Curiously, he also spoke of his sisters' moral welfare. He preferred the solitude of his own bedroom, in which his family were not allowed, and would become agitated when his sisters' boyfriends came round for dinner.

He would frequent several pubs with his work colleagues but would always bring the conversation back to his fascination with death. Another gravedigger at that time, Lawrie Ashton, recalled: 'I know that he told a friend he could come up to the mortuary and see two death crash victims if he wanted.' On another occasion, when Sutcliffe was out drinking with pal Eric Robinson, he mentioned that he had the keys to the mortuary and said he could 'come and see a couple of ripe ones' if he wanted to.

Sutcliffe took a robust attitude to the job, according to Lawrie Ashton: 'I used to pull his leg about washing and cleaning the bodies and say I could not stand that sort of thing. But he just used to laugh and say that he enjoyed it.'

The revolting stories of Sutcliffe's career in the graveyard and mortuary come from virtually everyone who ever worked with him, yet it would seem nobody reported him to the authorities for grave-robbing. They may have reported him to the boss and it's possible he was sacked for this reason but, quite understandably, and no doubt wanting to maintain the reputation of his business,

Douglas McTavish was quick to criticize rumours about Sutcliffe interfering with the bodies. 'All he did was bury a box as far as I can remember. He had nothing to do with bodies in the Chapel of Rest,' he said.

Officially Sutcliffe was dismissed for bad timekeeping.

As well as a dark, morbid side to his nature, other acquaintances remember him as having an unpredictable sense of humour which kept asserting itself. According to Eric Robinson, Sutcliffe 'got very excited about people who looked funny, and once he started laughing he would go into hysterics.' And Paul Carter, a drinking acquaintance in younger days, recalled how 'he had a dry sense of humour and a very strange laugh. Sometimes he would shave off one sideburn, and sometimes half his moustache, apparently to attract people's notice.'

Even during the height of his reign of terror, he would chillingly play up to his hidden alter ego. When he knocked on a female family friend's door in Bingley, she asked who was outside and got the reply, whispered through the letterbox: 'It's Jack the Ripper.' She opened the door to admit Sutcliffe who, in her mind, was making a little joke. This story, perhaps the most macabre but by no means the only example of Sutcliffe's odd sense of humour, illustrates a significant streak of perverse vanity in his nature. For a man who was thought to maintain a low profile socially, he had a penchant for attracting attention to himself in the most peculiar ways, as we have seen with his half-shaven moustache.

Certainly, Sutcliffe gave the impression of trying to mark himself out from his companions, even when he was a member of a teenage Teddy Boy-type gang frequenting pubs in Bingley. Although Teddy Boy clothes were still in vogue, Sutcliffe was invariably more smartly dressed than the average youth and had a strong tendency to wear black.

Later on, still a natty dresser ('fussy as a woman' according to one acquaintance) he would wear dark, sober suits and a shoestring tie in contrast to the flamboyant kipper ties which others favoured. Right up to his arrest he retained the 'man in black' image, always dressing in black clothing of some sort – jackets, pullovers and jeans.

In 1966, when Sutcliffe was 20, he met two people that were to play a major part in his later life. Trevor Birdsall, an 18-year-old Bingley lad, became his best friend and would be the person who came closest to witnessing first-hand the beginning of Sutcliffe's reign of terror, and 16-year-old Sonia Szurma – the first girl he ever took home to meet his mother. Sonia seemed to understand him. He met her when he was frequenting the Royal

Standard pub, one of his favourite haunts on Manningham Lane in Bradford. She was a quiet schoolgirl, whose family had left Czechoslovakia and moved to the area.

They were an odd couple; Sonia had seven O Levels, plus piano qualifications, Peter had left school at 15. She had ambitions to become a teacher and he was an ex-gravedigger, but they seemed to hit it off and were often seen kissing and cuddling in the corner of a bar.

For the next few years, life seemed to be going well for the young Peter, with a steady job and a girlfriend he thought the world of. However, the events of 1969 were about to bring his world crashing down. It soon became apparent that his mother, Kathleen, was having an affair with a neighbour, a local policeman. His father arranged for his children, and Sonia, to be present at a Bingley hotel for a grand and humiliating confrontation. Kathleen arrived at the bar believing she was meeting her boyfriend, only to find her entire family waiting. In an act of vengeance, her husband degraded her in front of them by forcing her to show the whole family the new nightdress she had bought for the secret occasion. It destroyed the innocent image Peter always held for his mother.

A further devastating blow was his discovery that, in late July of the same year, Sonia had been secretly meeting with another boyfriend, a local Italian ice-cream salesman named Antonio. She had been spotted by Peter's brother Mick, who promptly told Peter what was going on. Peter decided to confront her, but she refused to answer any of his questions or tell him whether their relationship was over.

That night a bitter and wounded Sutcliffe decided he would take revenge by going with a prostitute. Taking his car, he patrolled the red-light district of Manningham Lane, an area he knew well from drinking at the Royal Standard. Approaching a service station located between Valley Parade and Burlington Street, he spotted a prostitute clearly waiting for customers. He drew alongside her and after confirming that she was 'doing business' they agreed on a price of five pounds.

This, in his own words, is how he justified his later actions against prostitutes and women he thought were ladies of the night:

'I thought that I would have intercourse with the prostitute but changed my mind when it got to the stage where we had got to do it. We were on the way to her place and were talking and I realized what a coarse and vulgar person she was. We were practically there and I realized that I did not want to do anything with her. Before getting out of the car I was trying to wriggle out of the situation but I felt stupid as well. I picked up the girl outside a garage and I realized later that the men who worked there were her protectors. I'd given her a ten pound note and she said she'd give me my change later. We got to her house and went inside. There was a huge Alsatian dog on a mat in front of the fire downstairs. She started going upstairs and I realized I just didn't want to go through with it. The whole thing was awful. I felt disgusted with her and myself. I went upstairs behind her and into the bedroom. I even unzipped her dress, but I told her straight out I didn't want to do anything with her. She could keep the money, just give me my change. She said she'd have to go back to the garage where I'd picked her up, to get some change, so I drove her there. I just wanted to get away. I felt worse than ever about Sonia and everything.

'We went back to the garage by car and she went inside and there were two chaps in there. I don't know whether she did this regularly, but she wouldn't come back out. One of the men came banging on the car roof when I refused to go away. He said, "If I were you I wouldn't get out of that car. You'd better get going." I would have had a go at him, but he was holding the wrench in a menacing sort of way. Then I saw the girl come out with another big-built bloke. They walked off together, having a laugh. I just felt stupid, I drove home angrier than ever. I felt outraged and humiliated and embarrassed. I felt a hatred for the prostitute and her kind.'

Three weeks later, Sutcliffe saw the same prostitute in a pub in Bradford's Lumb Lane. He said:

'I went and approached the one I had been with three weeks previously and told her I hadn't forgotten about the incident and that she could put things right so there would be no hard feelings. I was giving her the opportunity to put things right and give back the payment I had made to her. She thought this was a huge joke and, as luck would have it, she knew everybody else in the place and went round telling them about our encounter. Before I knew what was happening, most of the people were having a good laugh.'

It was here Sutcliffe reached his lowest point and, reading through the circumstances of his crimes and how they happened, there are signs that one of his many underlying issues involved being impotent. A strong indicator of Sutcliffe's impotency and frustration about his ineffective bodily functions manifested itself when he was 18 and on holiday with a male friend in the Lake District. As they were getting ready for bed, his friend made a joke about sex and Sutcliffe's inability to perform, sending Peter mad with anger and, slashing at his friend's private parts, he raged: 'I'm going to cut your dick off you bastard!' His friend had to go to hospital for stitches.

After the embarrassing pub episode, Sutcliffe started to develop an unhealthy interest in prostitution and he would spend a great deal of time cruising the red-light districts and pubs of Leeds and Bradford, often in the company of his friend Trevor Birdsall. In male company, he would continuously boast of having sex with prostitutes, which was almost certainly a fantasy. He was clearly fascinated by the idea of women selling their bodies for money, and found it hard to believe they charged so little for an act that he held in such awe. His behaviour was also becoming more erratic. One incident was recalled vividly by his friend, Cath Ashton, when she was with a crowd from work drinking in the Royal Standard. She said:

> 'One Friday night when everybody was in a happy, carefree mood, Peter just picked up his pint of beer and smashed it on to a table, with broken glass and beer splashing about. He didn't say anything and just sat there. Sonia looked amazed. Then another friend who was sitting nearby lifted his pint and threw it over Peter's head. But Peter just sat there and didn't wipe it off. It was very strange and made everybody feel a bit creepy.'

After pub closing times, Sutcliffe would drop his friends home and stalk out the red-light areas alone, obviously gaining pleasure by watching prostitutes with their clients. But soon his voyeurism entered a new dimension and his desire to inflict physical injury started taking over.

CHAPTER 2

A Build Up To Murder

'I'm coming to finish you off Olive, I dint do a good enough job last time.'

Phone call to Ripper survivor, Olive Smelt, 1978

Trevor Birdsall would become a key player in the evolvement of Britain's most notorious serial killer, and in 1981 would be telling his story to a hushed court at the Old Bailey. If only he had told his story to the police a decade earlier there may never have been a Yorkshire Ripper.

Sutcliffe's friendship with Birdsall had blossomed by 1969 and they were regular drinking partners. On the nights when he did not see Sonia, Sutcliffe would call at Birdsall's home in his car (cars had replaced motorcycles in his affections and he would continually change vehicles over the next ten years) and they would go out to Bradford, Keighley, Halifax, even as far as Manchester or York on occasions.

Trevor Birdsall would be present at three of Sutcliffe's early attacks on women, yet remained strangely silent when the whole world was later asking what kind of man the police could be looking for. An article in *The Sun* on 8 May 1981, during Sutcliffe's trial, saw Birdsall recall how, around the late 1960s (it's unknown which month or year he was referring to as the question was, surprisingly, never asked in court), he and Sutcliffe were out touring the red-light district (area unknown) in Birdsall's car. Sutcliffe told his friend to stop and, explained Birdsall, 'He got out of the car and followed a woman who was staggering about. When he returned he said he had made love to the woman and beaten her up.' Birdsall didn't elaborate and without a precise date or year it's difficult to pin down who it may have been. Most research conducted on the Yorkshire Ripper fails to mention this attack but it's a vital piece of information, because it predates the most well-known and first recorded attack on a prostitute, which has become known as the 'stone-in-the-sock' attack.

That notorious incident happened in September 1969, shortly after Birdsall celebrated his 21st birthday. He and Sutcliffe had been out in several of the bars and clubs along Manningham Lane. Later, as they drove back towards Bingley in Birdsall's Austin Mini, Sutcliffe ordered his friend to stop the car at the junction of St Paul's Road and Manningham Lane. He had spotted a woman walking along the pavement and, as she turned right into St Paul's Road, he got out of the car and proceeded to follow her, disappearing out of view. Twenty minutes went by before Sutcliffe came running back to the car, flung open the door, jumped in and told his friend to drive off quickly. According to Birdsall, 'He was clearly out of breath.'

As they headed towards Bingley, Sutcliffe was muttering about how he followed an 'old cow to a house somewhere' and 'hit her on the back of her head with a stone in a sock.' He then removed the sock from his pocket and dumped its contents out of the window. Sutcliffe would later confess that it was part of a brick and when he struck the woman, a piece of the brick tore out of the sock.

There are not many details of this attack. The file seems to have been misplaced or simply binned in a weeding process.

So, who was the woman? A random stranger, or did Sutcliffe know her?

In an interview with *The Yorkshire Post* on 23 May 1981, Birdsall recalled part of the conversation in the car following the attack: 'Pete said she had screamed and I asked if she was alright. He said, "Of course she is, the old cow. I just wanted the money."' It would appear, from these words, that the woman he had beaten over the head was the prostitute who had conned him out of his five-pound change, and who would later mock him in the pub. This would explain why he insisted Birdsall stopped the car when he saw her.

It's unknown if her screams had scared Sutcliffe away, or perhaps attracted others who chased him from the scene, but he didn't stick around for long. Surprisingly, someone managed to take a note of Birdsall's registration plate as the pair drove off. This could have been the woman he attacked or perhaps someone who had given chase following the assault.

A few days later, two police officers knocked on Birdsall's door and he promptly gave them Sutcliffe's details and address at 57 Cornwall Road, Bingley. Sutcliffe admitted hitting the woman but failed to reveal he used the makeshift cosh as a weapon, instead saying he hit her with his hand. Luckily for Sutcliffe, the woman probably did not want to draw attention to her lifestyle so she did not press charges. Her identity, just like the woman he claimed to have 'beaten up' in the late 1960s, remains unknown to this day.

It's a shame Sutcliffe was not charged with aggravated assault as it would have made him stand out as a person of interest to detectives later on, during the Ripper manhunt.

The circumstances of the next known incident involving Sutcliffe could well have saved the lives of many women, had the correct police procedures been followed.

During the early hours of Tuesday, 30 September 1969, Sutcliffe was once again in the Manningham area of Bradford, this time on his own and armed with a hammer and a knife. He was spotted by a police officer on routine patrol sitting in an old Morris Minor at the side of the road. The engine was running but the lights were off. As the officer, PC Bland, approached the car, Sutcliffe put it into gear and sped off down the road. A short while later the same officer noticed the car in the Manningham area again, parked up next to a row of terraced houses. This time there was no occupant in the vehicle. PC Bland started to check the gardens of the nearby houses and found Sutcliffe hunched behind a privet hedge with a hammer in his hand. He told the officer that a hubcap had flown off his front wheel and he was looking for it. When quizzed about the hammer he claimed it was to help him secure it in place.

Quite rightly the policeman thought 'what a load of bull' and arrested him for being in charge of an offensive weapon. However, he arrested him on the charge of going equipped for burglary or theft and not for being in possession of an offensive weapon. A police van was summoned to come and collect Sutcliffe but, shamefully, he was never searched before getting into the van.

Searching a suspect at the scene of a suspected crime would have been a routine task and this was instilled into officers at training school. He should have been searched to obtain evidence of a crime and prevent injury to the officer or offender.

Had such a search taken place, the officer would have revealed the presence of a knife. Twelve years later, Sutcliffe would claim that he slipped the long-bladed knife down a gap between the side of the police vehicle and the wheel arch cover inside the police van that came to collect him.

At Bradford Police Station, he was photographed and finger-printed and appeared at the magistrates' court two weeks later. He was fined twenty-five pounds.

As is routine, a local and national check should have been made to see if there was anything known about him, and that should have thrown up the local caution for assault a couple of weeks earlier. A huge opportunity was missed to link him to the caution for the stone-in-the-sock assault, especially as both offences were committed in areas well-known for street girls and that the caution for assault involved a prostitute.

If the two cases had been linked, and he was charged with carrying an offensive weapon, then Sutcliffe would have been viewed as a possible danger to women and recorded at force headquarters, which would have catapulted him to the top of any suspects list in 1975 when the first recorded Yorkshire Ripper murders began. This could have saved a lot of women's lives, countless enquiries, mountains of paperwork as well as ridicule from the public.

Sutcliffe's conviction for this offence was recorded both at West Riding Criminal Records Office and by the Bradford City Police collator but sadly with no reference to a hammer – a blunder that would save him from detection during his later questioning. However, it was recorded at New Scotland Yard's method index as 'going equipped with a hammer.'

Between 1969 and 1975 there is a curious lull in Sutcliffe's criminal activities but there is a very real possibility that he may have carried out further attacks on prostitutes or unaccompanied women during this time. These crimes, if he did commit them, may have gone unreported or simply not been linked by the police at the time to the later Ripper murders. There was also a lot going on in Sutcliffe's life which may explain this temporary respite.

In 1970, after four years of being courted attentively by Sutcliffe, Sonia moved to London to attend a teacher training course at a college in Greenwich, staying with her sister Marianne and her Jamaican husband, Haleem Hasani. Sutcliffe visited often. But around Easter 1972, Sonia suffered a nervous breakdown and was diagnosed with schizophrenia. She heard voices and believed she was the second Christ. She thought she had stigmata – the marks of the crucifixion nails – on her hands.

She was taken back to Bradford for compulsory treatment in a psychiatric hospital which lasted three weeks, followed by a period as a voluntary outpatient. Sutcliffe took care of her. But she was never the same again. She became reserved, tense, highly strung and obsessed with cleanliness. It was this strict hygiene code that would hinder any chance of Sonia becoming suspicious of Peter's activities in later years. He was forbidden to wash his work clothes with hers and she insisted he did all his washing out in the garage. A black bin liner was kept in the corner where only his clothes could go. Never once did she look inside the bag and, had she done so, she may have seen the bloodstained garments waiting to be washed.

Another interesting aspect of the symptoms and struggles that Sonia had to endure was the fact they were all witnessed by Sutcliffe and would later play a significant role in his future trial.

In November 1971, Sutcliffe started work on the packaging line at the factory of Baird Television, but in April 1973 he took up employment at Anderton International, an engineering firm located at the Britannia Works on Ferncliffe Road in Bingley.

On 10 August 1974, Sonia Szurma celebrated her 24th birthday by becoming became Mrs Sonia Sutcliffe at Clayton Baptist Church on School Street, Clayton in Bradford. The wedding was performed in front of fifty guests by Reverend William Nelson. The marriage certificate got Sutcliffe's age wrong – it said he was 29 but he had only celebrated his 28th birthday two months earlier. Sutcliffe chose, as his best man, an old school friend from Cottingley Manor School, Ron Wilson, but only after two other friends had turned down the offer. Recalling the events leading up to the wedding Ron said:

'I hadn't seen much of him for a long time since we used to tinker with cars together. He had other friends closer than me and he asked them to be best man, but they all gave some kind of excuse. He asked me to do it as a favour a few days before the wedding. He said he was stuck.'

Ron never saw him again after the wedding. The reception was held at the Quarry Arms pub at 158 Bradford Road in Clayton, which has since closed down and been turned into a residential property. The church were Peter and Sonia married was demolished in 2002 and replaced by a slightly less atmospheric modern house of worship.

The decision to marry had followed long and serious talks with Sonia's father who was assured they planned to save every penny they could for a deposit on a house of their own. So, after a honeymoon in Paris, it was back to live with Sonia's parents at Tanton Crescent. Sonia had finally regained enough mental health to return to college, but it wouldn't be in London. Instead, a place was chosen at Margaret McMillan College in Bradford.

But as she returned to teaching, her husband also returned to the red-light districts.

In the early hours of Saturday morning, 5 July 1975, Sutcliffe decided to take a drive to the centre of Keighley as he had heard it was a popular area for prostitutes. He loitered around the area of the Ritz Cinema on Alice Street. If you decide to go there today you won't find it under its original name; however this classic old building still stands although the last film played here in the late 1970s. It's just far enough off the beaten track to not yet attract developers. Today it houses the Gala Bingo club. It's doubtful the current owners or the majority of people who go there know of the terrible events that took place just outside its doors in the summer of '75.

That night, 36-year-old Irish-born Anna Patricia Rogulskyj had gone out drinking, taking the bus from Keighley to Bradford, and by midnight she was in Bibby's club, not far from Manningham Lane. Later that night she managed to hitch a ride with two Jamaicans who drove her back to her home in Highfield Lane around 1am.

Probably worse for drink, she then decided to call on her boyfriend, Geoff Hughes, with whom she had a stormy relationship, at his home a short walk away in North Queen Street. To get there her route took her down Alice Street and around the back of the Ritz Cinema where she cut directly into North Queen Street.

As she approached the cinema, she heard a man in a darkened doorway ask if she 'fancied it'. Quite startled, she replied, 'Not on your life' and quickened her pace towards the safety of her boyfriend's house, arriving around 1.30am.

But despite shouting and pounding on the front door, she could not raise him. Finally, in a fit of drunken anger she removed her shoe and put it through a ground-floor window.

She stormed off in the direction she had come but with all the commotion she had probably forgotten about the strange man who still loitered close by. As she turned back onto the main street, he emerged from the shadows and again asked the same question. Anna ignored him and kept walking.

He followed her a few paces before producing a ball-pein hammer from his coat and smashing it onto her skull. Anna, who died in 2008, could never remember the attack and Sutcliffe's later confessions are vague, but hospital examinations showed bruising on her hands and right forearm, which suggests she must have put up some kind of struggle.

In all likelihood, the initial assault took place out on the street with one hammer blow to the back of the head, followed by a struggle and the victim dragged out of sight into the closest alleyway, which runs directly behind the cinema. Then her attacker hit her twice more on the head with the hammer, rendering the poor woman unconscious.

Sutcliffe had probably raised her blouse before this and, at some stage, produced a knife and slashed her across her abdomen. In all probability, he was about to stab deeper into her stomach

21

Freepost Plus RTKE-RGRJ-KTTX
Pen & Sword Books Ltd
47 Church Street
BARNSLEY
S70 2AS

✂ DISCOVER MORE ABOUT PEN & SWORD BOOKS

Pen & Sword Books have over 4000 books currently available, our imprints include: Aviation, Naval, Military, Archaeology, Transport, Frontline, Seaforth and the Battleground series, and we cover all periods of history on land, sea and air.

Can we stay in touch? From time to time we'd like to send you our latest catalogues, promotions and special offers by post. If you would prefer not to receive these, please tick this box. ❑

We also think you'd enjoy some of the latest products and offers by post from our trusted partners: companies operating in the clothing, collectables, food & wine, gardening, gadgets & entertainment, health & beauty, household goods, and home interiors categories. If you would like to receive these by post, please tick this box. ❑

We respect your privacy. We use personal information you provide us with to send you information about our products, maintain records and for marketing purposes. For more information explaining how we use your information please see our privacy policy at www.pen-and-sword.co.uk/privacy. You can opt out of our mailing list at any time via our website or by calling 01226 734222.

Mr/Mrs/Ms ....

Address..

Postcode...................................... Email address..

Website: www.pen-and-sword.co.uk Email: enquiries@pen-and-sword.co.uk
Telephone: 01226 734555   Fax: 01226 734438
Stay in touch: facebook.com/penandswordbooks or follow us on Twitter @penswordbooks

when a resident living at 10 Lord Street, which overlooked the alleyway, heard the commotion and decided to take a look. He called out and asked what was happening, causing Sutcliffe to flee and leaving his victim alive. Hearing no answer, the resident went back inside the house and went to bed.

Anna lay unconscious on the ground for around forty minutes until she was found by a passer-by at 2.20am. She was lying on her back, fully clothed with three severe crescent-shaped lacerations to her fractured skull. Part of her clothing had been disturbed and her handbag lay close by but nothing was stolen. On her abdomen were several cut marks, 7 inches (ins) long below the navel and above this a further seven deeper cuts. She was only 50 yards from her boyfriend's house. She was rushed to the casualty department at Airedale Hospital and then transferred to Leeds General Infirmary where she underwent a twelve-hour operation, which included the removal of splinters of bone from her brain. At one point she was given the last rites.

A forensic examination of her clothing revealed the presence of semen. It was apparent that her attacker – Sutcliffe – had masturbated over her body.

When she came round, she had no idea what had happened to her and out of confusion came to the conclusion it must have been her boyfriend who attacked her after she smashed his window. It would be a further three years before she would discover she had survived an attack by the Yorkshire Ripper. This was later confirmed by Sutcliffe in his confessions to the police:

> 'Yes, that was me. She had a funny name and I asked her if she fancied it. She said, "not on your life" and went to try and get into a house. When she came back, I tapped her up again and she elbowed me. I followed her and hit her with the hammer and she fell down. I intended to kill her but I was disturbed.'

Just over a month later, Sutcliffe would strike again and once more he was out with his friend Trevor Birdsall.

On Friday, 15 August 1975, 46-year-old Olive Smelt left her small terraced house at 16 Woodside Mount, Halifax for a night out in Halifax town centre with her friends, having a few drinks in several pubs, including the Royal Oak at 3 Clare Road.

Sutcliffe and Birdsall were also out drinking in Halifax that night and ended up at the Royal Oak. Sutcliffe launched a tirade against some of the women in the bar, saying it was a prostitutes' bar and, as he glanced over at Olive Smelt, said to Birdsall: 'I bet she's on the game.' He said something similar to her face as he passed by her on the way to the toilet. Sutcliffe was on the losing end of the exchange as he was put in his place by an angry Olive Smelt.

Just before closing time, Olive and one of her friends met two men that they knew who offered to give them a lift home. Olive was let out of the car in a lay-by in Hayley Hill just before the Boothtown Road next to a fish and chip shop. She was hoping to get a late supper for her and her husband Harry and their family. From here she could nip round the back of the shops and cut through the dividing alleyways, which ran from Woodside Grove to the rear door of her house in Woodside Mount.

Sutcliffe and Birdsall had also left the Royal Oak and were driving back to Bradford via the Boothtown Road when Sutcliffe spotted Olive coming out of the fish and chip shop and going into Woodside Grove.

'That's the prostitute we saw in the public house,' shouted Sutcliffe and pulled his car over to the lay-by. Birdsall noticed Sutcliffe reach his hand down the side of the seat before getting out, saying he was going to speak to somebody. He went round the back of the car but didn't appear to go in the same direction as the woman. In fact he ran down the parallel Woodside Road and cut into the side alley just as Olive was coming down.

When he caught up with her, she had almost reached the end of the alley, about 20 yards from her door. He slowed down but carried on walking. 'Weather letting us down' or 'weather been playing us up' he said as he got close to her. Then he pulled out a ball-pein hammer and struck her on the head. She collapsed to the floor and with her body half in and half out of the alleyway, he bent down and struck her fiercely a second time. He pulled down her knickers and made two slash marks about 6-8ins long, just at the top of her buttocks. No doubt he would have cut more, had it not been for a courting couple sitting in their car at the near end of Woodside Road. They had caught a glimpse of the woman falling half out onto the road and, after a short pause to consider what they had seen, decided to turn the car headlights on. Sutcliffe stopped what he was doing and fled back to the safety of his car.

Olive was rushed first to Halifax Infirmary and later to Leeds General Infirmary, where she had brain surgery and spent the next ten days under medical care. The infirmary more or less told her husband Harry that they didn't expect her to survive as her 'skull had been crushed like a coconut shell.'

But survive she did and she was able to give a description of her attacker. She described him as about 30, 5ft 10ins in height, slightly built, with dark hair and some beard or growth on his face.

Trevor Birdsall would later read in his local paper, the *Telegraph & Argus,* about the apparently motiveless attack on Olive Smelt. She hadn't been sexually assaulted or had anything stolen and it did cross his mind that his friend might be responsible for the attack, but he did nothing about his suspicions.

Tragically the torture that Olive went through didn't end there. It would be a further two years before the police would consider her to be a victim of the man known as the Yorkshire Ripper, and when they did she would be subjected to several crank calls taunting her about her experience. One such caller said: 'I'm coming to finish you off Olive, I dint do a good enough job last time.' Sceptics and police put the call down to a cruel hoaxer but unfortunately Olive believed it came from the man who attacked her. She had heard his voice and was convinced it was him. She became a recluse and a virtual prisoner in her own home. When she did dare to venture out, she would have to stop to glance behind her every few minutes.

Years later, her daughter Julie Lowry would say: 'She never did get over that night. She did well to survive and had to learn to accept what happened mentally. But physically her mobility was never the same.'

Even while Olive was recovering in hospital, Sutcliffe was looking for another victim. With research carried out over the last forty years it's almost a certainty that he struck again less than two weeks after the attack in Halifax.

Vivid memories of a vicious late-night attack by a dark-haired, bearded man are still to this day with Tracy Browne. She was only 14 years old when, on Wednesday, 27 August 1975, she was attacked on a dark country road.

Tracy and her twin sister, Mandy, had been out at a friend's house in Silsden, near Keighley (where Anna Rogulskyj had been attacked). They were to be back to their home at Upper Hayhills Farm, South Craven at 10.30pm. That night Mandy left to go home earlier than Tracy. This left the teenager to walk the 1 mile along the Bradley Road by herself.

As she made her way along the road, she stopped briefly and saw a man in his late twenties or earlier thirties loitering in front of her. He stopped to look at her and claimed he had lost his driving licence somewhere in the area. He then joined her, chatting to her along the way, as she recalled later:

> 'I talked to the man for about thirty minutes. We chatted as we walked together along the Bradley Road. He talked in a soft Yorkshire accent, about what it was like to live in Silsden,

whether I had a boyfriend and how he had lost his driving licence. I remember he kept blowing his nose because he had hay fever. Then he fell behind as we walked as he had to stop and tie his shoelaces.'

As Tracy reached the gate to her house, the stranger attacked. 'I thought I would stop and say goodnight and thank him for talking to me,' she said, but as she began to turn around she felt a terrific blow to the back of her head and saw the ground coming up to meet her. He continued to rain blows on top of her as she tried desperately to protect herself while screaming, 'Don't hit me! Don't hit me!' She was still conscious and remembered what happened next:

> 'I fell into a ditch and he threw me over a fence when a car came round the corner. I remember scrambling around in a field and that I was blind. I felt no pain but there was blood pouring out of my head. I managed to get to a nearby caravan about 400 yards from the attack.'

It would seem that once again Sutcliffe had been foiled by a motorist.

Tracy was taken to Chapel Allerton Hospital in Leeds where she was found to have two fractures of the skull and a piece of bone lodged in her brain. Neurosurgeons battled for four hours to save her life. The bone was removed, and she had fourteen stitches. Thankfully, the young girl recovered well.

Because Tracy Browne had spent such a long time in her attacker's company she remembered everything about him, from his height – around 5ft 10ins – to the fact he had a moustache, beard, frizzy hairstyle, staring eyes and thin face. She also said he had hay fever and that he spoke with a soft Yorkshire accent.

Looking at the photofit she gave the police, it's hard to not immediately consider it the work of Peter Sutcliffe. The likeness is uncanny and perhaps the most accurate photofit in the entire investigation. Her description of the attacker was confirmed by a witness who came forward and provided a photofit of a dark-haired, bearded man, who had been noticed in the neighbourhood that night, and had been seen standing near what was described as a white Ford car (Sutcliffe, at the time, owned a lime green Ford Capri).

Found near the scene of the attack was a distinctive hippy-style bracelet of wooden beads and a paper handkerchief (the police said the attacker suffered from hay fever, which Sutcliffe did).

The photofit was also used in local 'wanted' posters. Unfortunately, after this attack the Yorkshire Ripper murders officially began and diverted attention away from the Tracy Browne assault, and the search was called off and the photofit no longer issued. It's incredible to think her attack was not linked to the murders at the time. If it had been, her description was so good, Sutcliffe would have been caught sooner.

It wouldn't be until much later in the investigation, when a similar-looking photofit was published in *The Yorkshire Post*, following the attack on Marilyn Moore in 1977, that Tracy and her mother, Nora Browne, told Keighley Police that they believed she may have been attacked by the same man. Shockingly, they were ignored.

Nora Browne remembers it well:

'We spoke to a young policeman at the desk who seemed to treat the whole thing like a joke and asked us to fill in a form. He obviously did not take us seriously and I became so angry I decided we should leave to give me time to calm down. We went for a coffee and I knew we had to go back to the police station.'

This time they managed to speak to a senior officer who treated them with more respect but nevertheless did not connect the attack with the Ripper murders. As far as the police were concerned, the Ripper only attacked prostitutes.

In her frustration, Nora Browne called her uncle, local magistrate Monty Featherman, but no progress was made to link this attack with the Ripper series. Tragically Tracy's photofit was never reissued during the manhunt and, in an article in *The Mail On Sunday* in May 1981, her father, Anthony Browne, said: 'If they had taken my daughter's account seriously – and released the photofit – some of the Ripper's victims would be alive.' Eventually the attack would be confirmed as the Ripper's but only after Sutcliffe had been caught. He was not questioned about the attack on Tracy until after his conviction and initially he refused to take responsibility for it and challenged officers to prove it. Finally, in 1992, Sutcliffe admitted it to Chief Constable Keith Hellawell.

They say hindsight is a wonderful thing, but I can't help but feel there were too many missed opportunities in those early days to apprehend Sutcliffe and lock him away before he became a killer. His friend, Trevor Birdsall, could have gone to the police sooner and that is something he has had to live with every day since. Likewise, the victims who survived were all valuable witnesses and many of them were ignored. The process of compiling an offender criminal record was seriously lacking and the failure to write down the basic details of a crime, namely the hammer found with Sutcliffe in 1969, enabled him to remain at large for so many years.

When he struck next it would be considered the first official murder committed by the Yorkshire Ripper.

CHAPTER 3

Wilma McCann

Murder in the fog

'A young Leeds mother of four was stabbed to death in a brutal sex attack following a night out in the city centre on Wednesday night. The woman named locally as 28-year-old Wilma McCann was found 100 yards from her family home on Scott Hall Avenue in the early hours of this morning with multiple stab wounds to the body.'

Daily Express, 31 October 1975

An eerie atmosphere descended upon the city of Leeds in the early hours of Thursday, 30 October 1975. The early morning fog and mist had swirled and settled across the grass when Alan Routledge, a milkman of Prince Edward Grove, Leeds, drove his milk float up Scott Hall Road, the main artery into the city centre, and turned left into Scott Hall Avenue, a narrow street aligned on both sides by well-to-do-suburban houses. Half way up the street he took another left and found himself in the rectangular car park of Prince Philip Playing Fields. This community centre on the edge of the fields was one of the many drop-off points on his daily rounds.

This morning he was accompanied by his 10-year-old brother Paul who, while unloading the bottles from the van that would be drunk by the infants attending the centre's nursery school, was first to spot something lying on the grass verge to the right. It was close to the rear of the caretaker's house and community centre club house.

Being less than a week away until Bonfire Night, his first thought was that it must be a discarded Guy left by some of the children from the nearby houses.

As the two brothers cautiously approached the object, they could make out the shape of a woman, lying on her back. Her pale, white body was exposed to the world, her strawberry blonde hair matted with blood and trails of blood were running down her partly stripped body from a series of savage stab wounds on the breasts and abdomen.

'It's a body!' cried the younger brother in fright, and they ran over to the caretaker's house and banged on the door.

John Bauld, the caretaker, answered and forced himself to go and see what lay on the grass behind his house. It was nearly 8am and he could see the body lying in the field was 28-year-old Wilma McCann.

'I recognized her straight away,' he would recall later. 'Both my wife and I knew her because she used to bring her kids to the nursery school. It was a terrible sight. She was lying on her back with her eyes staring, her clothes open, her body covered in blood. I told the milkman to get on the phone and dial 999.'

On hearing the commotion, John's wife, Margaret, drew back her bedroom curtains. 'I'll never forget the awful shock of what I saw,' she said. 'Those staring eyes just seemed to be looking in through the window at me. Ever since that morning I've tried to forget about the injuries I saw on her body and the blood.' Later she would say:

> 'What I couldn't get over – still can't – is that we never heard anything. We always sleep with the window open and we used to have a big South African Ridgeback called Butch who used to bark if anyone came anywhere near the house. It always used to wake me up, but he didn't bark that night, yet this terrible thing was happening only a few feet from our window.'

Before long, the sound of a police siren cut through the air. Close on its heels came Dennis Hoban, one of the most respected and best-liked detectives in the West Yorkshire Police. Hoban was, at 48, a detective chief superintendent (DCS) and head of Leeds CID. Born of Irish-Yorkshire stock, he started out as an electrician until his career was interrupted by war service in the Royal Navy. After demob, he decided he wanted more out of life than repairing fuses and became a policeman.

The job suited him and in no time at all he had risen through the ranks and gained a reputation as a top plain-clothes man and thief-taker. Described as a tenacious and tireless copper who knew the ins and outs of Leeds like the back of his hand, he had become the youngest detective superintendent (DSI) in the north of England by the age of 31.

Within a short time, more officers arrived on the scene and arrangements were made to have the body covered from public view, using a large screen which was placed around the corpse. But that was not before a newspaper photographer captured the now infamous image of Wilma McCann lying dead on the grass. It was an image that would mark the start of a five-year reign of terror.

Only eleven hours earlier and less than 150 yards away at 65 Scott Hall Avenue, Wilma was getting ready for a night on the town. At 7.30pm, sporting slack white trousers, a pink blouse, a dark blue bolero jacket and her hair fashioned up in a beehive, she was ready to leave the house. She said goodnight to her four children: Sonia 9, Richard 7, Donna 6 and 5-year-old Angela. Leaving Sonia in charge, she slipped out the back of the house, as she always did and went down the side of the playing fields. She was spotted leaving by 14-year-old Jayne Macdonald (a later victim) of nearby 77 Scott Hall Avenue, and her friend 13-year-old Irene Bransberg, who lived on the same street at Number 40. Both kids were playing hide-and-seek at the time in the field.

Wilma didn't like the neighbours knowing she went drinking practically every night but it was the worst kept secret on the street.

Heavy drinking had become an everyday norm for the fiery Scots woman from Inverness, following her separation from husband Gerald a few months earlier. Although she'd always had a fondness for the nightlife, with convictions for drunkenness, theft, anti-social behaviour and rumours that she worked as a prostitute, her life bore all the hallmarks of spiralling out of control. She had agreed to a divorce on the grounds of her continued adultery which she admitted, but had never bothered to turn up for the appointments that Gerry had fixed with a solicitor.

The one thing Wilma McCann liked most of all was her freedom to go and do as she liked without any tiresome restrictions.

Tonight would be no different. Whisky and beer would be on the menu for Wilma as she drank primarily in the Kirkgate area of Leeds – in the Regent Inn at 109 Kirkgate, the Scotsman at 106 Kirkgate, the White Swan at 37 Call Lane and eventually the Royal Oak at 29 Kirkgate. There she got chatting to two friends before closing time forced her to head north along Vicar Lane and towards the Room At The Top Club, located at 215–219 North Street, Sheepscar.

She stayed there until 1am before deciding to call it a night. Around this time, about 50 yards from the club, she was seen near Rakusen's food warehouse in Meanwood Road. She was clearly drunk and holding a white plastic container of curry and chips, while trying to thumb a lift. She had done this 100 times before and was an expert in persuading lorry drivers to drop her off at her house or even, as she had done before, take her all the way to Scotland, on impulse, to see her parents or friends. A friend or relation could always pop round to watch the kids until she returned.

Wilma McCann continued to stagger around recklessly and in front of traffic in the hope of getting a lift home. She managed to flag down a lorry heading towards the M62, but when greeted by an incoherent mixture of instructions and abuse, the driver declined to pick her up, and drove on.

Unfortunately, this was the night Peter Sutcliffe was driving through Leeds in his lime green Ford Capri GT after having a few pints, and he saw her thumbing a lift. He pulled over, rolled down the window and asked if she had far to go. She said, 'Not far, thanks for stopping' and jumped in.

Within twenty minutes she would be dead, her body left on the playing fields directly behind her house.

At around 8am the following morning, 11-year-old Tracey Attram left her home at 59 Scott Hall Avenue to make the short journey across Scott Hall Road to collect her mum's morning papers. Glancing over at the bus stop, she noticed two other children whom she recognized as being the eldest kids of Wilma McCann. Sonia (who was known as Sonja) and Richard were huddled together, shivering in the cold with just their pyjamas and school coats on. She was surprised to see them up so early for it was the half-term holidays. 'Hello, Sonja,' said Tracey. 'What are you doing here at this time?' 'We're waiting for mummy to come home,' replied the 9 year old, who had been waiting there with her brother since 6am. 'Perhaps she's gone shopping.' Tracey said: 'Well, if you come over to the shop with me, I'll take you home and we'll see if your mum's come back.' Sonia slipped her right hand into Tracey's and held her brother with the left. The three children crossed to the newsagents then retraced their steps back to their home at 65 Scott Hall Avenue. Tracey waited on the top step by the front door as Sonia and Richard went inside where their sisters, Donna and Angela were warming themselves in front of the gas fire. After a moment, Sonia came back to the door, a worried frown on her small face. 'Mummy's not been back,' she told Tracey. 'We'll just wait here for her.' But they waited in vain. Wilma McCann never came home again. If they had glanced out of their back window they would have seen her corpse lying on the field outside. Perhaps it's some small comfort that they didn't.

Visiting the scene today, Prince Philip Playing Fields lies just off the Scott Hall Road in Leeds. It is less than a five-minute drive from the town centre and access can be gained by turning off the road and into Scott Hall Avenue. As you turn to enter the street and glance to the right you see the bus stop where Wilma's two young children waited for her to return. Further up the avenue is the main entrance to the fields, leading up to a large stone community and sports centre. Here, on any given weekend, you will see the local teams carrying out football practice along with young sports enthusiasts having a leisurely kick around. During the week, the area is quiet and peaceful. Very few realize that this is where the biggest criminal manhunt in British history began.

What we know is that sometime after 1.30am on 30 October 1975, Peter Sutcliffe and Wilma McCann arrived in Scott Hall Avenue. According to Sutcliffe's later confessions, on the way to her home, Wilma had asked him if he 'wanted business'. He asked her to explain what she meant to which she replied, 'Bloody hell, do I have to spell it out?'

She told him where to park the car. It was just off the avenue to the left, in the car park of the playing fields, next to the community centre.

They sat for a minute talking and Wilma said sex would be a fiver. Although Sutcliffe has never admitted as much, it was fairly obvious that there was some attempt to have sex in the car and that he was having difficulty gaining an erection. By this point Wilma had opened the car door and got out. She slammed the door and shouted, 'I'm going. It's going to take you all fucking day. You're fucking useless.'

Sutcliffe shouted back to her: 'Hang on a minute, don't go off like that.'

'Oh you can fucking manage it now, can you?' she replied.

'There's not much room in the car,' answered Sutcliffe. 'Can we do it on the grass?'

She stormed up the hill into the field, waiting for Sutcliffe to follow her, which he did, but unbeknown to her, he had retrieved a hammer from the toolbox in the back seat of his car. He got out the car, took his coat off and carried it over his arm, concealing the weapon in his right hand. He placed the coat on the grass, turning his body in a way that hid the hammer. Wilma most probably sat down on the coat. She unfastened her trousers and said, 'Come on then, get it over with.' Sutcliffe replied, 'Don't worry, I will.'

He swung the hammer down on top of her head. She slumped forward and, according to Sutcliffe's later confessions, started 'making a horrible noise like a moaning gurgling noise.' He hit her once more on the head and then exposed her body, which he stabbed at repeatedly. Later he claimed he went back to the car after striking her with the hammer, sat for a while and then decided to grab a knife and go back to finish her off. There is evidence to support this, as we will see with the attack on Marcella Claxton later in the book.

After he was finished, and he was quite sure she was dead, he climbed into his car and drove back to his mother-in-law's house.

He quietly let himself in, went to the bathroom to wash his hands and went to bed.

Six hours later when her lifeless body was found, Wilma was lying face upwards on the sloping grass just to the right of the old stone sports club. She was positioned with her head pointing uphill and her feet towards the car park. Her blue jacket and pink blouse had been ripped open and her bra pushed up exposing her breasts. Her white trousers had been dragged down to her knees. Her underwear was still in the correct position. Six buttons lay on the grass next to the body; five of these were torn off her blouse and one was from her jacket. Her red handbag strap was still looped around her left wrist.

If you go to the crime scene today, a metal gate and fence separate the playing field from the car park. There was no such barrier back in 1975 but, as a marker, the body was found on the sloping bank just in front of the gate that is now the entrance to the field.

It was clear from the start of the investigation that this was an horrific murder. Stab wounds to the neck, chest and abdomen had resulted in blood oozing out across the body, staining the grass where Wilma lay. In total, fifteen stab wounds had penetrated the victim. There was a deep stab wound to her throat, two stab wounds under her right breast, three stab wounds below the left breast and nine stab wounds around the abdomen.

Examining the crime scene was Professor David Gee, head of forensic medicine at Leeds University and one of the top pathologists in the north. He noted the angle and position of the body and concluded, correctly, that the way the blood had trickled down across the right side of the body showed that the victim had been stabbed as she lay on the ground. Blood had also oozed down onto the victim's knickers but not under them, suggesting that any sexual intercourse, if it had occurred, had probably taken place prior to the stabbings.

Later forensic tests and a vaginal swab would confirm that no sexual intercourse had taken place at all. However there were semen stains on the back of Wilma's trousers and underwear. Forensic scientists at a Harrogate laboratory were unable to identify a blood group from the semen, most likely because the attacker did not secrete his blood cells in his bodily fluid.

Further examination at the mortuary found that the back of Wilma's head had been smashed in by two deep blows from a blunt instrument (most likely a hammer) which penetrated the full thickness of the skull.

From here a clear and accurate picture emerged. Wilma had been in an upright or sitting position when struck from behind with a hammer or other blunt instrument more than 3ins long and ¼ins broad. She fell face forward onto the grass before her killer pulled her trousers down. The semen stains found on the back of the underwear and trousers suggests that at some point the killer masturbated over her.

Wilma was then turned over onto her back, her bra lifted to expose the breasts before the fifteen stab wounds were inflicted on her body.

Officers soon discovered the family home and went about making sure the McCann children were taken into care at a nearby children's home run by Leeds County Council. It would fall to Dennis Hoban to perform the grim task of informing them that their mother had died. Later that day, he gathered them together in one room, knelt down to speak to them and said, 'I'm sorry, but your mum has been taken to heaven. You won't be meeting her again.' He then gently asked them to help identify some of the belongings that Wilma had on her when she was found and asked if anything was missing. Everything was there but for a small white plastic purse. The purse had been a gift from Sonia, on which the little girl had scrawled the word 'MUMIY'. The purse has never been found. I've often wondered what happened to it.

For the next few weeks, the investigation traced the final hours of Wilma's life and details emerged of the pubs and club she had attended prior to her death. Apart from this, there was no other information for the police to work on. The killer had simply come and gone in the night. Regulars at the Scott Hall Hotel, a 1930s Whitbread house which Wilma frequented, denied that she was ever a prostitute but did admit that she had an unusually large number of boyfriends. In fact, Wilma McCann had never been charged with a prostitution offence and never came to the attention of the authorities for working as a prostitute. This idea seems to have been exaggerated because of her promiscuous lifestyle and the myth that surrounded the Yorkshire Ripper about only targeting working girls. On the night she was murdered she wasn't out working the streets, she was out drinking in the pubs around town and trying to thumb a lift back home.

In his confessions to the police, Sutcliffe claimed that Wilma tried to charge him for sex, and we only have his word for it that she did. However, it's worth pointing out that at the time of his confessions it was in his interests to make the world think he was on a mission from God to rid the streets of prostitutes. All we really know is on that night Wilma was thumbing a lift and Sutcliffe picked her up, took her where she wanted to go and murdered her. What happened inside the car will never be known.

By mid-December the police announced that they had interviewed over twenty-nine boyfriends linked to Wilma McCann, but this would help little with their enquiries. Sutcliffe did not know Wilma; he had only met her the night he killed her. There was nothing but bad luck that connected them.

An extensive inquiry involving 150 police officers and 11,000 interviews, failed to find the culprit. As Wilma had been seen trying to hitch lifts from lorry drivers, 6,000 were interviewed. A further 7,000 interviews were processed, including those with residents along her route home, associates, friends and family. It amounted to nothing. The coroner's verdict was 'Murder by person or persons unknown'.

It would take another three months and another murder before investigators realized that a monster was on the loose in Leeds.

CHAPTER 4

Emily Jackson

'The man we are looking for seems to have a pathological hatred of prostitutes and good time girls…there is little doubt that he will strike again.'

Detective Chief Superintendent Dennis Hoban

By the end of 1975, Peter and Sonia Sutcliffe's prospects of buying their own home were boosted when he eagerly accepted the offer of £400 redundancy at Anderton International and used £200 of that to pay for lorry driving lessons at Apex Driving School in Cullingworth. From here Sutcliffe found a job as a long-distance driver with a Bradford firm, T. & W.H. Clark (Holdings) Limited of Canal Street in Shipley. Tom Clark and his son, William, were soon impressed by the conscientious and meticulous new driver. His log books reflected the care he took for his lorry. In their eyes, the quiet and shy young man was a model employee. They had no way of knowing their star worker had already killed one women and was about to kill again.

The Roundhay Road is a main ring road in and out of the city of Leeds, which is known today as 'curry mile' and is home to a variety of nationalities. It borders the area known as Harehills, which in all honesty has always had a poor reputation, as does neighbouring Chapeltown and most of East Leeds. Having attracted undesirables from the 1960s until the early '90s, this busy road has seen its fair share of dodgy pubs and seedy drinking dens. However, as time has gone on and it has become a predominately Muslim area, these characteristic venues have faded away.

One of its most notorious pubs was the Gaiety, once located at 89 Roundhay Road at the junction of Gathorne Terrace and surrounded on three sides by small Victorian terraced houses, some of which still stand to this day. Despite its later reputation, it had a very promising start when it first opened its doors on 7 December 1972. A massive pub that could accommodate 350 to 400 people on the ground floor, the second floor housed the famous Carousel Bar with a dancefloor, jukebox and 17-metre circular bar. It also had the Variety Room, which provided live entertainment at weekends and offered room hire for private parties and weddings. The décor was traditionally Edwardian and legend has it that on opening night, actor Stephen Lewis – 'Blakey' from the TV sitcom *On The Buses* – pulled the first pint. It was a place where well-dressed West Indians mingled with Poles, Irishmen, Jews – all representatives of the waves of immigration that had entered the city – as well as Yorkshire men and women.

It was a hit with all the locals, especially the ones that worked late at night in Chapeltown's red-light district.

Chapeltown was the city's main prostitution area so it's not surprising that within four years the Gaiety had gained a reputation for attracting working girls. It probably didn't help that the owners decided to have female strippers on during the day to entertain the male clientele – local office workers, businessmen and labourers from nearby Manor Street Industrial Estate. At lunchtime, the prostitutes would come to the pub in the hope of picking up a client, and at night they would stand on the crossroads outside trying to attract the regular kerb crawlers. Outraged local residents complained bitterly about the 'square mile of vice' on their doorstep. Women walking home, and even teenage schoolgirls had been propositioned by men looking for sex. The police had blitzed the area many times, but even they accepted it was a losing battle against the world's oldest trade.

By mid-1975 the Gaiety had acquired two new regulars, Sydney and Emily Jackson, a married couple since 1953 with three children, Neil 18, Christopher 10 and 7-year-old Angela. A fourth, Derek, had died tragically five years earlier at the age of 14 when he fell out his bedroom window and onto the pavement.

The Jacksons lived nearby in a neat semi-detached house at 18 Back Green, Churwell. Sydney was a local roofing contractor, Emily was 41 and slightly overweight, which made her look older than her years. She helped with the paperwork and drove him from job to job in the old blue Commer van, since he did not drive.

To the outside world everything about the Jacksons appeared to be normal. However, they were leading a strange double life. Emily was a nymphomaniac; she had an insatiable sexual appetite, which created serious problems in the marriage at the beginning but as time had gone on Sydney had accepted the way things were. He would often accompany her to pubs and clubs and wait patiently at the bar while she took strangers out to the car park and into the back of the van, which had become a makeshift love nest to satisfy her sexual cravings.

In the autumn of 1975, financial pressures meant Emily and Sydney decided that they might as well start making money from Emily's night-time activities and so a life of prostitution began. Now the men she picked up on their almost nightly excursions to the pubs would be charged for her time, and if customers could not be found in the pubs, she would step outside to take part in the more lucrative business of attracting kerb crawlers. Although she had never been arrested or charged with prostitution, she was a well-known figure to both the vice squad and the working girls of Chapeltown Road.

The night of Tuesday, 20 January 1976 started like any other for the Jacksons. They left their house at 6pm, with Emily driving the van into the car park of the Gaiety fifteen minutes later. She was wearing a blue and white striped dress, white cardigan, strappy heeled shoes and a green, blue and red chequered overcoat. As soon as they arrived, Sydney went to the bar and Emily looked around to see what business could be had.

For the next four hours, Sydney waited for his wife to return, but by 10.30pm he decided to call it a night. Stepping out into the car park he could see the van was still there but there was no sign of Emily.

After waiting a short while longer he decided that she had probably gone to another pub so he took a taxi back home. Little did he realize his wife was now lying dead, less than 600 yards away, another victim of the Yorkshire Ripper.

Manor Street Industrial Estate lies just off the Roundhay Road and covers a wide area of land. Only a stone's throw from where Wilma McCann was last seen alive after visiting the Room At The Top nightclub, it is now home to modern factories and business units with big, crisp, fancy advertising signs. Its roads are clean and tarmacked, there are planted trees and greenery with big, bright street lamps on every corner to illuminate the area at night. On any given day, you can see young businessmen in sharp suits mixing with labourers with hard hats and hi-vis jackets. Truck drivers and smartly dressed women dart back and forth during lunch-hour breaks. It really is a million miles away from what it looked like forty years ago. Back then it was a very rough, dirty area consisting of dilapidated buildings and factories, many of which stood boarded up on the cobbled streets. Waste ground, burning tyre yards, dark cul-de-sacs, tiny alleyways and courtyards were littered with rubbish and discarded office furniture.

During the hours of darkness, it became a hangout for prostitutes who found the deserted side streets and waste ground perfect sites for alone time with their clients. With the busy Gaiety pub just 400 yards up the road it was the nearest spot away from the public gaze and it was where Emily Jackson would bring Peter Sutcliffe at about 8.30pm that night.

Sutcliffe had driven to Leeds in his lime green Ford Capri and spotted Emily in her overcoat by the phone boxes, close to the Gaiety. She was attempting to flag down would-be punters who were cruising round the area. He watched her for a while before pulling up. Rolling down the window he asked, 'How much?' She said, 'Five pounds' and Sutcliffe agreed. She quickly got into his car and they travelled along the Roundhay Road and into the seclusion of the industrial estate. They parked up in one of the small cul-de-sacs.

Later Sutcliffe would recall: 'I remember when she got in, there was an overpowering smell of cheap perfume and sweat. This served all the more for me to hate this woman even though I didn't even know her.'

We don't know what happened in the car while it was parked up, but we do know that when it was time to leave, Sutcliffe pretended the car wasn't working. He turned the ignition slightly so only the red warning light came on. He exited the car and lifted up the front bonnet, pretending to have a look. He then asked Emily to give him a hand as he couldn't see the engine in the dark without a torch. She got out of the car and offered to use her cigarette lighter to shine under the bonnet. She ignited the lighter, cupped her hand over the flame to protect it from the draft and peered into the engine. Sutcliffe then took a step back, produced a ball-pein hammer, which he had hidden in his coat, and hit her on the back of the head. She fell onto the road. He hit her once more, fracturing her skull, then grabbed her wrists and dragged her into the darkness.

At 8.10am the next morning, a workman drove his car into the industrial park and to the far end of Manor Street where he turned right into an unnamed, cobblestoned cul-de-sac.

A large brick wall lay at the far end, on the right-hand side was a flat-roofed factory building belonging to Hollingworth & Moss bookbinders, and on the left-hand side was a row of scruffy, red-brick buildings, which were boarded up and awaiting demolition. Running between these was a narrow alleyway and, despite being littered with rubbish, scrap metal and burnt wooden timber, it made an ideal short cut onto what is now Enfield Terrace.

It was near the entrance to this alleyway that the workman parked his car and, after stepping out from the driver's side, glanced to his right and noticed something unusual. Two legs were protruding from the rubble which lay about 15ft inside the alleyway. Thinking it was a discarded mannequin, he went in for a closer look only to reel back in horror.

The attack on Emily Jackson had been so horrific and merciless that hardened detectives froze at the sight that greeted them.

She was lying on her back and her legs had been pushed wide apart, with her right leg bent upwards and outwards and her left leg bent at the knee. To crime scene investigators it looked as though she had been deliberately posed in a lewd manner. She was still wearing her red, blue and green overcoat but her striped dress had been pushed up. Her tights, which were torn at the knee, were crudely pulled down on the left side revealing black knickers. This suggested that an attempt was made to pull the tights down or they were pulled down and an attempt was made to put them back into position.

Emily was barefoot, with one shoe lying next to her right foot and the other a few feet away against the wall. Her light yellow handbag lay open close to her head (its contents helped detectives identify her). There were blood stains on her right arm and hands, along with a larger pool of blood above and beneath her head, some of which had already congealed into clumps.

The front of her body, including her face and thighs, were scratched and heavily soiled by mud and dirt. There were also marks on the ground leading from the street into the passageway, showing how the killer had dragged her body to the spot where it was found. At the front entrance of the alleyway were more drag marks in the gravel. There were blood spatters on the cobblestones and a noticeable shoe impression in the mud, probably from a size 7 heavy-ribbed wellington boot. A similar boot print was also found on Emily's inner thigh, which her killer more than likely stepped on as he leaned over her in the dark.

Further examination would need to take place in the mortuary so, at the request of the pathologist David Gee, the body was wrapped carefully in plastic sheets to protect any vital evidence. As it was taken away, a dozen officers on hands and knees began searching the alleyway and cul-de-sac in which Emily had been murdered, picking their way through the coarse grass and placing any likely clue – a cigarette butt, scrap of paper, blood-slashed pebble – into individual envelopes for minute examination later.

During the formal autopsy, the clothing was removed from the body and the extent of the horrific injuries became apparent.

Emily was 5ft 6ins and had sustained a total of fifty-two stab wounds to the torso, neck and back, clustered together in separate small areas, giving an almost 'pepperpot' look to the injuries. There were thirty stab wounds to the back, twelve to the abdomen, eight to the neck and the heart had been penetrated twice from the front and the back.

The weapon was considered to be around 2-4ins in length and had left a curious X-shaped wound on the skin. This caused great confusion at the time and only later was it suggested that a Phillips crosshead screwdriver was the most likely instrument. However, with so many wounds close together it would prove impossible to follow the wound track with 100 per cent certainty.

Upon examining the fractured skull, it was apparent that the two savage blows to the head – one on top and the other at the back of the skull – were caused by a flat-surfaced weapon, more than likely a hammer.

A vaginal swab did yield a sample of semen, but the laboratory felt this was from sexual activity prior to the attack.

The investigation concluded that the victim had been in an upright position when struck on the head and the killer had dragged her face down from the street into the alleyway. Here, her dress was lifted up to expose her back where she was stabbed multiple times. She was then turned over and her bra pushed up above her breasts. She was stabbed in the torso and neck multiple times and at some point the killer stood on her thigh before pulling her clothes back down over her body.

Despite a thorough examination of the body and a fingertip search of the crime scene, no useful information could be found that might lead detectives to the killer.

Eye witness testimony came from a prostitute who claimed to have chatted with Emily outside the Gaiety the night of the murder. Maria Sellars told the police her conversation took place shortly before 7pm, and that Emily had spotted a possible client, gone over to talk to him and got in his Land Rover. She watched them drive off along Gledhow Road. Her descriptions of the Land Rover and its driver were very detailed. Further questioning of prostitutes in the area helped to build up more details of the man, including the fact he was believed to be Irish.

Neither the vehicle, nor the Irish suspect, who was probably Emily's last customer before accepting a ride from Sutcliffe, was ever traced.

A month after the murder, on 19 February 1976, West Yorkshire Police issued a crime intelligence bulletin to all police forces officially linking the Wilma McCann and Emily Jackson murders. The head of Leeds CID, DCS Dennis Hoban, who made the connection following the pathology report from David Gee, issued a stark warning to the public:

> 'I believe the man we are looking for is the type who could kill again. He is a sadistic killer and may well be a sexual pervert. I cannot stress strongly enough that it is vital we catch this brutal killer before he brings tragedy to another family.'

An incident room was opened at nearby Millgarth Police Station as the biggest manhunt the country had ever seen was about to begin. As the press dubbed the killer 'The Ripper', posters of Emily appeared in shop windows, on buildings and on the sides of police cars touring the streets. Appeals were made over tannoy systems at cinemas, bingo halls and football and rugby matches. Over the course of a year police checked thousands of vehicles, made almost 4,000 door-to-door enquiries and took over 800 statements. Hoban even spoke to doctors about any suspect patients who could have done such a thing.

No stone was left unturned, but despite Hoban's extraordinary clear-up rate, the Ripper still eluded him.

The left-hand side of the cul-de-sac where Emily Jackson met her death no longer exists. The dilapidated buildings and narrow passageway which concealed the murder were demolished shortly afterwards and the old, cobblestoned street now lies beneath the car park of Hollingworth & Moss bookbinders, which is the only building remaining on the street.

In 1990, the Gaiety closed its doors for the last time but stood derelict for many years before it was demolished and Archway, a resource centre for 16–25 year olds, was built on the site. Set up in 2001 by Leeds City Council, its services include housing support, counselling and advice on education, work, drugs and mental health issues.

In mid-1976 Hoban was promoted to Deputy Assistant Chief Constable for Crime and was replaced by James 'Jim' Hobson as head of Leeds CID. Hoban, who was a diabetic and suffered from asthma, died suddenly in 1978.

CHAPTER 5

Marcella Claxton

'She went behind some trees to urinate and suggested that we "start the ball rolling on the grass". I hit her once on the head with the hammer.'

Peter Sutcliffe, 1981

Marcella Claxton aged 20 was attacked in Leeds in the early hours of Sunday, 9 May 1976. Her description of the assailant matched perfectly with that of the Tracy Browne assault case in Silsden ten months earlier. Again, the police did not link the attack to the Yorkshire Ripper series, though they did re-examine the file after the next murder in February 1977. With Sutcliffe's previous warning for assault and going equipped with a hammer, plus the similar description, one can only imagine how quickly he would have been arrested had the authorities back in the 1970s had the computerized database that we use today.

Marcella lived in one of the many terraces of back-to-back houses off the Roundhay Road in the red-light district of Leeds. She was a West Indian single mother-of-two but her children had been placed in care the year before. She was now expecting a third child as she was three months pregnant.

On Saturday, 8 May, Marcella had been at a late night party in Chapeltown, not far from her home and, rather worse for drink, had set off for home at around 5am.

Earlier that night, Sutcliffe had been cruising through Chapeltown in his white Ford Corsair. He was now parked up on Spencer Place with the lights turned off and the engine running. Marcella Claxton has always maintained that she was not a prostitute and much about what has been written differs, depending on what story you read. For the purposes of this chapter, I have relied on interviews given by Marcella over the years, and the later confessions of Peter Sutcliffe. I'm hopeful that somewhere in this account lies the truth.

According to Sutcliffe:

'I picked her up in the Chapeltown area. She asked me if I was the police, I said, "No, do I really look like a policeman?"

> She decided to get into the car, and suggested where we go.
> We ended up in what I knew later as Soldiers Field. We got out
> of the car at my suggestion and she took off her trousers whilst
> leaning against a tree, and she sat down on the grass.'

According to Marcella, she knocked on the car door and asked him for a lift. She got in the car with him and Sutcliffe drove into Roundhay Park and to Soldiers Field. When he stopped the car, he offered her five pounds to take her clothes off and have sex on the grass. She said she did not want to, and got out of the car saying she needed to urinate. She hid behind a bush until she thought he had gone away. Then she emerged back out into the open again.

Regardless of which version is correct, both of them ended up in Soldiers Field, a section of Roundhay Park, which is considered to be a more affluent part of Leeds. It was a perfect quiet spot for courting couples and, of course, prostitutes with clients. A much more detailed description is given later in this book when dealing with the murder of Irene Richardson.

At some point, Marcella left the car, whether to urinate or undress and when she did, Sutcliffe followed. He may have dropped his hammer, as Marcella claims to have heard a clunk noise. She said, 'I hope that isn't a knife' and he may have replied, 'It's my wallet.' He then walked over and struck her eight or nine times on the head with his ball-pein hammer. She collapsed, stunned but not unconscious. She would later claim she had only pretended to pass out but she lay there without moving as Sutcliffe stood over her, masturbating. When he was finished he wiped himself with a tissue and threw it on the grass, then he pushed a five pound note into her hand and told her not to call the police. He then casually walked back to his car and drove up back towards the Roundhay Road, leaving Marcella sprawled out on the grass.

Marcella's statement is of paramount importance in the Yorkshire Ripper case as it clearly shows the driving force of Sutcliffe's actions. Semen stains found on the clothing of his other victims suggests that he masturbated at those scenes as well. We will also learn later how he came to fashion a bizarre set of trousers, with padded knees and exposed crotch for easy access to his genitals. If we look back at his time as a gravedigger and the rumours and discussions about his interests in necrophilia, it's perfectly plausible that he was now recreating his sexual fantasy of having a lifeless or motionless body to excite him. If we also take into consideration his issues involving impotency, the desire to kill or render his victims immobile or unconscious was based on the need to ejaculate, and his climax could only happen if it coincided with his victim's demise.

If this truly was the case, the chances he attacked and killed far more than we know about really does become a frightening reality.

Luckily for Marcella, Sutcliffe had not gone for the kill and seemed to have left her alone. Remarkably, she still had enough strength to get herself back on her feet and, using her knickers, managed to stem the flow of blood from her head. She staggered to a nearby phone box to call for help. But to her horror she noticed Sutcliffe's car returning up the road. She said later: 'After I had dialled 999 and was sat on the floor of the telephone box, a man in a white car kept driving past. He seemed to be staring and looking for me. It was the man that hurt me.' She watched him as he stopped the car: 'He got out and began searching the spot where he had left me. He must have come back to finish me off.'

Sutcliffe may have decided to finish her off, just like he did with Wilma McCann in 1975. On that occasion, he claimed to have struck Wilma with a hammer then gone back to the car where he contemplated what to do next. He decided to return with a knife and kill her. Fortunately, Marcella had managed to move from where he'd left her.

The phone box was south of Soldiers Field at the junction of Glenhow Lane, Princes Way and Roundhay Road. In the 1970s there were no trees and it was a flat, grassy area with streetlights on Princes Avenue and Old Park Road. There was nowhere to hide and he would have easily been seen by any passing motorist or pedestrian. So, in all probability, he knew where she was, he just didn't feel safe going in to finish her. Instead he drove back to the spot where he had attacked her and got out of the car. I believe he went back to retrieve the incriminating semen-stained tissue he had wiped himself with, before driving off for good.

When the ambulance finally arrived, 'after what seemed like ages', according to Marcella, she required extensive brain surgery and fifty-two stitches to close the eight laceration wounds in her head. She contacted the police frequently to offer further clues from her memory, and was convinced her attacker would strike again. Despite her appalling injuries, her description of Sutcliffe was fairly accurate; she said he was a young, white man with crinkly black hair and beard, a Yorkshire accent, who said he didn't live in Leeds and was driving a white car with red upholstery.

Marcella believes to this day that the trauma and stress of what happened to her that night made her miscarry as she tragically lost her unborn baby.

Her attack would not be conclusively linked to the Yorkshire Ripper case until after Sutcliffe's arrest and confession. It had been one of several attacks that had been looked at but no connection was made. After the Irene Richardson murder in February 1977, in almost the same spot, DCS James Hobson said after talking to Marcella and examining the file: 'We have an open mind on this girl's story.'

However, this conflicted with an internal West Yorkshire Police report which said:

> 'Although she had been struck about the head with an unknown instrument there were factors that were dissimilar to previous "Ripper" attacks. Most significant was the absence of stabbing to the body and there was the motive of taking the money and running away… . Officers were aware of the dangers of including details of an incident that was not part of the series because it would mislead the investigation as a whole.'

After the attack on Marcella Claxton, the Yorkshire Ripper appeared to enter a period of inactivity for 271 days. When he did return, he would take his victim to the same spot on Soldiers Field and this time he would make sure she would not be alive to tell anyone.

CHAPTER 6

Irene Richardson

'I said, "What's the matter luv?" and I bent down and brushed her hair to the side. Then I saw blood on her neck and her eyes were glazed over and staring.'

Jogger John Bolton

Today Roundhay Park in Leeds is one of the biggest city parks in Europe. It has more than 700 acres of parkland, lakes, woodland and gardens, which are owned by Leeds City Council.

Situated on the north-east edge of the city and bordered by the suburb of Roundhay to the west and Oakwood to the south, it is visited by nearly a million people a year. In 1891, an electric tram with overhead power (trolley system) linked Roundhay Park with Leeds city centre 3 miles away. The tram terminus is now a car park but some of the trolley poles remain.

The area around the park is considered to be one of the richer and more cultured parts of Leeds, even though it does share a border with the slightly more run-down areas of Chapeltown and Harehills. Among the trees that line its route you can see many of the Victorian mansions and luxurious flats that overlook it.

Located at its southern end is Soldiers Field, a recreation area for organized sport and so called because the Army used to train there in the 1890s. Today, amateur football teams play here on weekends and the visiting teams get to use the flat-roofed stone pavilion as their changing rooms. The easiest way to get there from the city centre is by following the Roundhay Road onto Park Avenue then turning left onto West Avenue.

The stone pavilion is at the far end of West Avenue on the left-hand side. It's a secluded spot, surrounded by beech trees. It's much the same as it would have been back in 1977.

It was here at 7.40am on Sunday, 6 February 1977 that John Bolton, a 47-year-old accountant from nearby Gledhow Lane, was passing on his pre-breakfast jog.

As he neared the rear of the pavilion, he noticed a woman lying face down in the grass. At first, he thought she may be ill or in need of help so he crouched down to look closer and asked her what the matter was. When he received no answer, he brushed her hair to one side and noticed blood on her neck. Then he glanced up and saw her eyes staring back at him and glazed over. Suspecting the woman was dead, he ran across to one of the nearby houses to alert the police.

Irene Richardson, 28, was like Wilma McCann, in that she had not found much luck in her short life. Originally from Glasgow, she had run away from home in 1965 to live in London, and over the next five years had two children – a boy and a girl – who ended up being given to foster parents. By 1971 she had married 31-year-old plasterer, George Richardson, and had two more children, Amanda and Irene. By this time the family was living in Balmer Grove, Blackpool. Not long after the children's birth, Irene moved out of the family home and went to London. George would find her and move in with her around June 1975 but in April 1976, she would run away again.

Eventually the marriage ran into difficulty and Irene ran away once and for all. She was reported missing. George would recall the day it happened: 'I went out to work one morning and when I came back, she was gone. I never saw her again.'

By October 1976, Irene's youngest children were also living with foster parents. She had no proper accommodation and moved between various boarding houses. She had resided at 82a Harehills Avenue and then moved to 35 Mexborough Drive in Chapeltown. Occasionally, she was found sleeping in public toilets and with a lack of money and food, she turned to prostitution in an effort to survive. She would now be seen on the corners of Chapeltown looking for customers.

By Saturday, 5 February 1977, Irene Richardson had spent the last week homeless and was almost penniless. Luckily, she managed to get herself into a lodging house located at 1 Cowper Street, a large Victorian mansion that had been converted into bedsits. It's worth noting that Cowper Street is only a three-minute walk from the Gaiety where Emily Jackson had last been seen on the night she died.

At 11.15pm, Irene mentioned to a fellow resident that she was going to Tiffany's nightclub, located at the Merrion Centre in Leeds. Being a 'no denims' venue, she had dressed up as best she could and had on a yellow skirt and brown jacket, blue and white checked blouse, brown cardigan and imitation suede coat. She brushed her shoulder-length brown hair and left the house at around 11.30pm.

Within thirty minutes she would be lying dead in Roundhay Park.

By 9am on Sunday the crime scene in Soldiers Field had been sealed off. Wooden duckboards had been placed on the ground leading up to where the body lay and a 35 foot (ft) plastic screen concealed the body from public eyes.

Suspecting this could be the same person who killed Wilma McCann and Emily Jackson, Professor David Gee was once again brought in to examine the murder scene. He arrived shortly after 10am and was followed fifteen minutes later by Edward Mitchell, one of the forensic scientists from the Harrogate laboratory. Investigating the case from the police side was DCS Jim Hobson. A Leeds man born and bred, Hobson joined the force in 1951 and was promoted to sergeant by 1958. He became DCS in 1975.

Irene Richardson lay face down in the shaded grass area at the rear of the sports pavilion, just hidden from view of the road. Her hands were under her stomach and her head was turned to the left. She was positioned with her head in the southern direction of the park while her feet pointed uphill towards the end of West Avenue. The brown hair she had taken great care to brush the night before was matted with thick blood. Go to the park today and you can clearly pinpoint the exact murder site. This is due largely to one of the trees, located at the rear of the pavilion, having an unusual diamond shape break in its trunk. The same diamond shape is visible in the original crime scene photos.

Irene still wore her brown cardigan which, along with the leaves and grass around her head, was stained heavily with blood.

Her three-quarter length imitation suede coat with fur trimming had been draped over the lower half of her body, leaving only her feet showing. There was a sock on her left foot but her right foot was bare. Beside her was a soiled tampon lying in the grass. Later tests would show that Irene Richardson had been menstruating at the time of her death.

A handbag lay 4ft away from the body in the direction of the pavilion. It was open, with a cosmetics bag and lipstick next to it and there was no indication that anything was missing. There was, however, a trail of blood lead from the handbag to the body.

Irene had been struck violently on the head with three blows from a hammer. This time the pathologist could be more precise in his opinion of the type of weapon used. The force of the attack had been so powerful that parts of her skull were driven nearly an inch into her brain. The hammer had actually got stuck in the skull with the force of one blow and marks in the bone showed it had to be levered out to remove it. Measuring the circular fracture, it was 1½ins in diameter, the precise dimension of a hammer head. Death would have occurred in seconds.

Her calf-length boots had been placed over the back of her thighs and were covered with her coat.

Her skirt had been pushed up and her tights had been pulled off her right leg. It was also discovered she had been wearing two pairs of knickers, one red and one brown. The brown nylon knickers were still in the correct position; however the red pair had been removed and were now stuffed inside the tights along with her missing sock.

When the body was turned over, more horrific injuries were revealed. She had been viciously stabbed in the side of the neck and front of the throat, causing a gaping wound which exposed the larynx.

She had also been stabbed three times in the left-hand side of the abdomen. All of these cuts were downward strokes 6-7ins long, which had caused her intestines to spill out of her body and onto the muddy grass.

Unlike the previous two victims, her bra had not been pushed up or removed. However, as with Wilma McCann, semen stains were found on her knickers and tights. An examination later showed she had sexual intercourse in the twenty-four hours up to her death.

Time of death was estimated to be around midnight.

With the murders of Wilma McCann and Emily Jackson there had been very little evidence left at the crime scene to help investigators, but with the Irene Richardson murder the police discovered an important clue.

Fresh tyre marks discovered close to the body revealed the killer had driven his car onto the soft ground of Soldiers Field. The police were able to determine the tyre marks as being two India Autoway tyres and a Pneumant on the rear offside, all crossply. DCS Jim Hobson decided to concentrate the bulk of the investigation into finding the car that made the prints. Provided the killer didn't change the tyres, he felt confident that a thorough search of vehicles using the same tyres would bring results.

A picture now emerged of Irene Richardson's final hours. It was almost certain she had been picked up, by car, around the streets close to her home shortly before midnight on Saturday and driven by her killer up to Roundhay Park.

This was correct.

Sutcliffe had picked Irene up in his white Ford Corsair, registration plate KWT 721D, not far from the Gaiety on Roundhay Road. He'd spent quite a while cruising around looking for a suitable victim. He had either been turned down or turned down those who approached him.

When he saw Irene, he stopped his car a few yards ahead of her. She jumped in without a word and when Sutcliffe said that he might not want her, she replied that she would show him a good time. He drove a mile along Roundhay Road and into Roundhay Park, and continued onto Soldiers Field, almost to the exact spot he attacked Marcella Claxton in May 1976.

He turned left off the road and drove onto the grass in front of the sports pavilion. When Irene got out of the passenger's seat, Sutcliffe put a hammer and Stanley knife into his pocket. She wanted to go to the toilet inside the pavilion, but finding it locked, decided to crouch beside the car to urinate. As she did, Sutcliffe hit her once on the back of her head and twice more as she fell onto the grass. He then dragged her out of sight behind the pavilion. Here, he slashed at her throat with the Stanley knife, pushed up her skirt and slashed at her abdomen causing her intestines to fall out. He then stabbed her twice more in the stomach. He turned her over onto her front and pulled down her tights and knickers, at which point one sock came off.

Due to the presence of semen on the back of her knickers and tights, similar to the Wilma McCann murder, it's highly likely that Sutcliffe masturbated and ejaculated at some point during this attack.

Stuffing her knickers and sock into the tights, he placed her boots on the back of her thighs before covering her with her coat and leaving the scene.

Although police were careful not to disclose exact details of the horrific injuries, it didn't take long for the press to learn about their severity. It was a news editor's dream – prostitutes were being stalked on the dark, foggy streets of Yorkshire by an unknown killer who cut their throats and ripped open their stomachs.

The legend of a new 'Jack the Ripper' took root, as bigger and bolder headlines graced newspaper stands up and down the country. And this was just the beginning.

The comparisons between Sutcliffe and Jack the Ripper, who terrorized the streets of London in 1888 and butchered five East End prostitutes, were inevitable. Like Sutcliffe, Jack knew his territory, lured his victims into quiet traps and killed them quickly. His signature was to slit his victims' throats and most were mutilated, with intestines pulled out and body parts cut off. He was never caught. The press of 1888 had a field day with stories of the Victorian Ripper and, ninety years on, it looked like history was repeating itself.

When Irene Richardson's body was found in February 1977, DCS Jim Hobson took charge of the investigation. Hobson had taken over as head of Leeds CID when Dennis Hoban had been promoted seven months earlier. However, DCS Hobson's initial dealings with the Yorkshire Ripper came in August 1975, although he didn't know it at the time. The investigation into the attack on Tracy Browne was Hobson's responsibility. But in the five years that followed, no attempt was ever made to link that attack to the Yorkshire Ripper. So the best description and photofit of the Yorkshire Ripper, given by Tracy Browne, was never widely circulated, as her attacker was considered to be 'local' to her in Silsden, just 23 miles from Leeds.

A link between the murders of Irene Richardson, Emily Jackson and Wilma McCann was not even made until 9 May 1977 when a 'special notice' was issued to all forces.

Officers who interviewed Sutcliffe in November 1977 failed to examine his red Ford Corsair, the tyres of which he changed from his white Corsair. This would have linked him with the murder of Irene Richardson nine months earlier. According to a report by Chief Inspector of Constabulary Sir Lawrence Byford, this was a 'vital error', which gave Sutcliffe the opportunity to commit a further seven murders before his arrest in January 1981.

CHAPTER 7

Patricia Atkinson

'All I could see was her head, an arm and blood on the pillow, but I knew she was dead.'

Caretaker Jack Robinson

The murder of Patricia Atkinson was unusual in the Yorkshire Ripper case for it was the first and only time Sutcliffe would kill indoors. All murders before and after would be committed outside, either on the streets, in back alleys or on waste ground.

It was also his first murder in Bradford, which threw more strain on the fledgling police investigation which, until this date, had only been concerned with Leeds. This time the Yorkshire Ripper had moved his operation to the seedy red-light area of Manningham.

The area, which includes Lumb Lane, Gracechurch Street, Oak Avenue, Hanover Square and Bowland Street, just north of Bradford's city centre, is still as run down and grimy as it was in the late 1970s, despite numerous operations to try to clear up the problems of drugs, crime and prostitution.

It had seen happier times thanks in part to the Manningham Mills, which kept the area in reasonably good economic health for nearly three quarters of the twentieth century, helped by orders for uniforms during the First and Second World War. Large Edwardian houses lined the streets giving them a grand appearance.

However, by the 1970s the mills were employing far fewer people. Money in the area was drying up and the grand family houses were turned into bedsits, flats, care homes or offices.

Despite considerable efforts in the 1980s to rejuvenate the business, Manningham's lifeblood was ebbing away and by 1990 the mills employed a few hundred instead of many thousands.

The mills closed in the early 1990s and, as a result, the area reached its numbing nadir in the last decade of the millennium, marked by deprivation and social unrest, not to mention drug problems and prostitution.

However, in the mid-1990s, Manningham achieved another type of fame with the screening of television drama series *Band of Gold*, featuring a group of women who lived and worked the city's red-light district.

It was written by Kay Mellor who, a few years earlier, had been driving through Bradford one night when she and her husband took a short cut up Lumb Lane. As they slowed down at a junction, a sex worker approached the car and bent her face down to the driver's window.

The face haunted Kay. 'We saw her for only a moment then drove on,' said the screen and stage writer, who was originally from Leeds. 'What shocked me was that she was all of about 15, and her face still had that early teen chubbiness. She was somebody's daughter, somebody's sister probably...and there she was on the street, putting herself in all sorts of danger.' Mellor went back later to find the girl and offer her some kind of help, only to be told her name was Tracey and she'd moved to Birmingham because of 'pimp problems'.

She went searching for the girl in Birmingham, and was told she'd moved to Sheffield. Enquiries there proved fruitless. 'She could now be in the abyss,' said Kay. 'Who knows what might have happened to her because some of these girls and women just disappear.'

This brief encounter with the unknown Tracey prompted Kay to write about sex workers and their lives in three series of *Band of Gold*, which attracted huge audiences between 1995 and 1997. Unsurprisingly, it was criticized locally at the time for encouraging an influx of prostitutes and punters and harming police efforts to clamp down on such activities.

In more recent years, the red-light district has shifted away from the residential streets of Manningham to the more discreet corners of the industrial Sunbridge Road area. Despite this, many residents still complain about sex workers conducting their business outside their homes and leaving used condoms and needles strewn around.

To their credit, West Yorkshire Police have carried out many operations in the past ten years to try to solve the problems. One crackdown saw kerb-crawlers sent letters warning them they had been spotted trawling the streets; another saw them banned from loitering in the area bounded by City Road, St Michael's Road and White Abbey Road. But sadly, prostitution and its associated problems is as much an issue now as it was during the Yorkshire Ripper's killing spree.

Manningham remains poor and run down, with a mixture of commercial and residential properties, many of which are abandoned. One such property is Oak Avenue, a stone's throw from Lumb Lane.

This dilapidated 1960s purpose-built block of flats, two storeys high at the front and three at the back and comprised of many cheap, self-contained bedsits, is ready for demolition. Most of the windows are smashed or boarded up, large sections of the roof are gone and graffiti and evidence of late-night fires are all around.

To the right-hand side of the property, in the middle of the ground floor, is the boarded remains of Flat 3: once home to 32-year-old Patricia Atkinson.

Patricia, or Tina as she was known, moved into the bedsit in April 1977 and it would be here that she would be brutally murdered by the Yorkshire Ripper.

She had grown up in the Thorpe Edge district of Bradford. In 1960, when she was 16, she met her husband, Ramen Mitra, a Pakistani, at a dance hall in the town. By then she was working as a burler, removing loose threads, knots, and other imperfections from cloth, at a mill in Greengates, Bradford. By early April 1961 the pair were married and they lived for a short time with Tina's parents before moving to their own home at Girlington, an area of Bradford next to Manningham where they had three daughters.

Unfortunately, the marriage was not to last. Tina grew bored of her life and perhaps having married so young, she felt she had not done any real living. She was good looking and enjoyed attention from men. This put an eventual strain on the marriage and ended with Tina leaving the family home. Her husband was awarded custody of the children.

The next few years saw Tina's lifestyle deteriorate. She advanced from casual promiscuity to full-time prostitution and alcoholism.

On 12 April 1977, just ten days before she was murdered, Tina rented the small bedsit at 9 Oak Avenue. This put her one step ahead of most of the girls working the red-light district who served clients in dark corners, up against walls, on patches of waste ground or in the backs of cars.

Flat 3 could only be reached via the main front entrance of the apartment block. Upon entering, you walked down the staircase directly opposite the entrance to the ground floor and from there you took a left along a wide corridor into the side wing of the property. Turning left once more, Number 3 was on the right-hand side.

In the flat, there was a small bathroom straight ahead and an equally small kitchen. Next to that was a door to the joint living room and bedroom.

The room was fairly basic. A double wooden bed was on the right and a small dining table covered with a white tablecloth was on the left of the bed, against the chimney breast. In the left-hand corner, next to the window, was a three-bar electric fire. An oak dressing table with mirror was in front of the large, rectangular window, along with two dining room chairs. There was also a two-seater sofa and a small electric heater plugged into the wall next to the door.

In the far corner, there was a small fire escape door, which led directly outside the block. This would have proved a much easier entrance to use but access was blocked by a large oak wardrobe, which had been pushed directly in front of it.

She probably did this to add a bit more security and to give her peace of mind when sleeping at night. As the fire escape was blocked, the only access to the room was through several locked doors in the communal apartment block. On Saturday night, 23 April 1977, Tina went out determined to have a good time. She visited her regular drinking haunts, which included the rough-and-ready boozer, Perseverance, located at 161 Lumb Lane. The building exists to this day but having lost its licence following a drugs raid, it is now, ironically, a pharmacy.

After leaving there, Tina made her way up to the Carlisle Hotel – a rather squalid drinking den, that doubled as a strip club on weekends – located at 86 Carlisle Road and only a ten-minute walk from Oak Avenue. It is still a pub after all these years and has kept the same name.

Tina had now been drinking for most of the day and was in the mood for a party. As the evening rolled on it became apparent that the stripper who had been booked by the Carlisle wasn't going to turn up and Tina clambered on to the stage. No doubt she caught the eye of a few male admirers, after all she was attractive, slim and dressed in tight blue jeans, a largely unbuttoned blue shirt and a short leather jacket. But she was in no condition to entertain the Saturday night crowd and was taken off stage.

The manager of the Carlisle decided she had had enough to drink, and between 10.15pm and 10.30pm the staff remembered her announcing that she was leaving and watched her stagger towards the exit. She set off in the direction of what appeared to be her next destination, the International Club in Lumb Lane.

She was last seen by another street girl at about 11.10pm, weaving and staggering her way down Church Street towards St Mary's Road, completely drunk, having imbibed the equivalent of twenty measures of spirits.

At this point, the women working in Bradford's red-light district had been unaffected by the fear that plagued the 'sisterhood' in neighbouring Leeds, where the murders meant prostitutes walked the streets in teams conspicuously noting punters' number plates. In Bradford, they still felt safe enough to come out on their own from 4.30pm, looking for trade among workers leaving factories.

This was about to change.

Sutcliffe had been driving through the streets of Manningham when he spotted Tina on the corner of St Paul's Road. It would appear she had not gone directly to the International Club, but had opted to join the other ladies of the night on the pavement instead. However, she was staggering round in circles and banged on the roof of a parked Mini, shouting obscenities.

Sutcliffe would later say: 'It was obvious why I picked her up. No decent woman would have used that language.'

He drew his car alongside her and quick as a flash, she jumped in. She told him she had a flat not far away where they could go so they made the short trip to Oak Avenue and parked up outside the block of flats. Tina staggered out of the car and led the way.

Sutcliffe quickly followed, but as he was leaving his car he retrieved a claw hammer from under his seat and hid it in his coat.

Together they walked through the main door, down the stairs and entered her bedsit. Once inside, Tina went to the other side of the living room to draw the curtains while Sutcliffe hung his coat on the back of the door and quietly retrieved the hammer.

Tina took off her coat and sat down on the side of the bed. Sensing his opportunity, Sutcliffe walked over and hit her on the back of the head. She fell off the bed and onto the floor motionless and, according to Sutcliffe, made a 'horrible gurgling sound'. He hit her with the hammer again and she lay there for a short period of time as her dripping blood stained the carpet. He then picked her up under her arms and hoisted her back onto the bed.

In doing this, he left a boot print on the bedsheet between the wall and the body. The size 7 Dunlop Warwick wellington boot print would later be matched to the one found close to the body of Emily Jackson just over a year earlier in Leeds.

Once he had positioned her lying on her back in the centre of the bed, Sutcliffe pulled her blue bell-bottomed jeans and white knickers down below the knee, exposing her genitals and legs.

He pushed up her T-shirt and black bra to expose her abdomen and breasts.

He hit her body repeatedly with one end of the hammer and violently clawed at her flesh with the other end. According to Professor Mike Green, assistant pathologist to Professor David Gee, this resulted in 'oblong marks, cuts and abrasions to the chest, abdomen and pubic region...severe puncture marks on the vagina [and] several lacerations to the left-hand side of her body.' Horrifically, the poor woman was still alive during the attack and continuing to make 'gurgling sounds'.

At some point he turned her over onto her front, with her face on the pillow turned to the left facing the wall and her arms spread out by her side. Her body was smeared with blood as she was manoeuvred by Sutcliffe's bloody hands. He unfastened her bra strap and repeatedly attacked her back with the claw end of the hammer. The blood distribution on the bed indicated that he inflicted two more blows to the back of her head while she lay on the bed. There were four major depressed fractures to the skull caused by the hammer blows, which left crescent-shaped wounds on her skull.

The killing was different from the others. This had been committed indoors in a lit room as opposed to on the dark waste lands of Leeds.

Sutcliffe quickly cleaned himself up and prepared to leave, but before doing so he lifted Tina's bedsheets up and pulled them over her broken body, before covering her with a thick, flowery, patterned duvet. All that could be seen was a bloody arm, one side of her blood-soaked face and matted dark hair on the striped pillowcase.

As he opened the door to leave, he could hear Tina continuing to make strange noises, but he knew she would be in no state to tell anyone anything, so he left the dying woman on the bed and closed the door behind him.

It would be a further eighteen hours before her body would be discovered by long-time friend, Robert Henderson, at 6.30pm the following evening. He knocked on the door and when she didn't answer he tried the door handle and discovered it wasn't locked. He pushed open the door and moved slowly into the flat and into the joint living area and bedroom. He noticed a pool of blood on the floor and saw a lumpy bundle on the bed covered in bed linen. Her face was beaten to a pulp and unrecognizable.

He rushed to caretaker Jack Robinson's flat shouting that there had been a murder.

At first Robinson didn't believe him and shouted: 'Rubbish! Don't be so hysterical!' But Henderson was insistent so the caretaker phoned the police, and then went to see for himself. Later, he would tell the police: 'All I could see was her head, an arm and blood on the pillow, but I knew she was dead.'

News of a new 'Ripper' attack now made headlines in the national newspapers and on radio and television. Sunday newspapers dispatched feature writers to Leeds and Bradford to prepare in-depth stories. London Weekend Television sent its *Weekend World* team to the north to report on what it saw as a compelling story.

DCS John Domaille of the western crime area led the investigation into the crime and established an incident room at the area headquarters at Bradford.

Very little evidence was forthcoming in the case apart from the footprint on a bedsheet apparently made by a wellington boot and similar to a print left on the thigh of the earlier victim, Emily Jackson.

Due to the fact Tina travelled mainly by taxi, a decision was made to interview all taxi drivers working in the Bradford area. Approximately 1,200 were seen but no useful information was obtained. Her murder was linked with other crimes in the series in 'special notices' issued on 9 and 30 May 1977.

It was a professional nightmare for detectives. A sadistic maniac was randomly choosing vulnerable women and then slaughtering them. There was no motive as such, only the inner compulsions of a sick and twisted mind wielding a murder weapon. The only connection between the victims was that they were all women down on their luck and they had absolutely no relationship with the murderer.

It was clear that the Ripper had expanded his territory to include Bradford and, for what would be the only time, he had committed the murder indoors. By now the police were well aware that they were facing a brutal assassin who would not respect geographic bounds. The Leeds Ripper was now the Yorkshire Ripper.

Patricia Atkinson was buried at 11am on 27 June 1977 in section T of Scholemoor Cemetery in Bradford. She is buried in grave number 803 and it bears her married name of Mitra.

Today nothing remains of the contents and decor of the bedsit, in which Patricia Atkinson was brutally murdered. It's just a ghostly, burnt-out shell. It has been badly scorched by fire over the years and has been used as a dumping ground for all sorts of broken sink units, blankets and plastic bin bags. The layout of the room, however, is exactly the same as it was in 1977 – the large rectangular window, the chimney breast, the plug sockets and the small fire escape door are all there and can easily be compared to photographs taken at the time.

Of all the murder sites examined in this book, I found this the most disturbing to visit. It's certainly not one I would encourage anyone to visit by themselves and nor would I wish to return anytime soon. A dark atmosphere lingers around its walls, reminding you of the terrible events that occurred here more than forty years ago.

CHAPTER 8

Jayne MacDonald

'This man has got to be caught. He has got to be stopped for the public good and the good of himself. There is no doubt in my mind that he will strike again. The big questions are when, where, and who is going to be his next victim?'

Assistant Chief Constable George Oldfield

The murder of Jayne MacDonald would make the Yorkshire Ripper international news and the focus of an intense local hatred, which had not existed during the previous four murders. It would appear public attitude had been clouded towards the idea of prostitution. People had convinced themselves that as long as *decent, respectful* women were not conducting the seedy hazardous occupation and it was only prostitutes getting murdered, there was nothing to fear.

The fact that prostitutes were always at risk from unbalanced men who could assault, or even kill them, when faced with their sexual inadequacies didn't seem to matter to most people reading the news, and they felt the women were working the streets out of choice. Sympathy and understanding was sadly lacking in many households across the district.

However, Jayne MacDonald would be the first non-prostitute, or 'innocent victim', as she was described, to die by the hands of the Yorkshire Ripper. The small, 16 year old had only left school six months earlier and had been walking home alone from a night out in Leeds when she was killed. Everyone agreed that her murder was appalling, pointless and undeserved. Where once he'd brought fear to the streets, the Ripper now took that fear into the homes and minds of all who lived in Yorkshire.

Just two months after the murder of Patricia Atkinson in Bradford, Sutcliffe had returned to his old haunts in the Chapeltown area of Leeds.

So much writing on the Yorkshire Ripper describes the whole of Chapeltown as the red-light district, but it actually refers to just a couple of streets. The majority of Chapeltown was once an ordinary, respectable, Victorian suburb, which has certainly gone downhill since its heavy-grit stoned houses were populated by Jews on their way up from the inner-city ghetto. The former chapels, from which the area got its name, soon became synagogues and today have become mosques as a mixed Asian and Indian population has moved in.

In the 1970s, one area popular for prostitution was the junction of Chapeltown Road and Harehills Avenue, perhaps largely to do with the Hayfield Hotel, a stunning Victorian building which was opposite the junction at 241 Chapeltown Road. Originally built in 1869 by a hay merchant as Hayfield House, it had been converted to the Hayfield Hotel in the 1970s and from there descended into a notorious drop-out centre for prostitutes and all sorts of villains.

In a single year, it bore witness to thirty-one serious crimes including one murder, three rapes, five attempted murders, four woundings with intent, an indecent assault, four assaults including an assault on a woman police officer, two burglaries, three drug offences and four of criminal damage.

So it's not surprising that, in July 2002, its licence was finally refused following recommendations by police after a catalogue of shootings. Unsurprisingly, once it closed its doors a police report showed that the crime rate in Leeds had fallen dramatically. Unfortunately, in the same year this once stunning building was demolished.

In 1977, despite countless warnings by the police, the surrounding area was frequented by prostitutes looking to make money to feed an alcohol or drug habit or simply in order to survive. Even with the threat of attack ever present, they continued as normal.

At the time of the original Jack the Ripper murders in 1888, the police found that women responded fatalistically to warnings that they should keep off the streets. They preferred running the risk of being murdered to the certainty of going hungry. It seemed little had changed in the near 100 years since.

At the back of the Hayfield Hotel, there was a stretch of nineteen Edwardian and semi-detached houses, which ran up between the centre of two streets, Reginald Street and Reginald Terrace. At the far end of this row was a derelict building which, between 1948 and 1973, served as the Psalms of David synagogue. This building would later become the Chapeltown Community Centre before being demolished in the 1980s.

In between the row of houses and the synagogue was a patch of waste ground, which was used by the local children as a makeshift play area.

In the pre-health and safety era of the 1970s, this was a rough-and-ready place for the kids to play. It was put together by old timbered railway sleepers, telegraph poles and any other odds and ends you could throw in to make the place adventurous for young children. Next to the playground and attached to the boundary wall of the synagogue, was a single-storey, white-painted club house with a flat pitch roof. This was covered in graffiti and surrounded by high timber fencing, which at one time would have formed a secure perimeter to the club house, but by 1977 most of the fence had been destroyed or broken up. In between the fencing and the right-hand side of the club house, and just in front of the boundary wall, was a patch of waste ground strewn with abandoned carpets, tin cans, bottles and general household rubbish.

It was here at 9.45am on Sunday, 26 June 1977, that two young children playing in the adventure playground nearby, decided to cross over into the fenced area and noticed the body of a woman lying among the discarded rubbish by the old synagogue wall. One child recalled in a statement to the police:

'I saw a body on the ground so I told the others. There was a brown bag about four strides away and I did not touch her. I told a man in Reginald Street about the lady. I told him the lady was dead. We went up to the shop and told a man there what we had seen.'

The body of Jayne MacDonald lay face down with her head pointing towards the wall and the right side of her body lying next to the fence. Her legs were straight out but her feet were crossed, the left over the right; her left arm was bent up with the hand beneath her head and her right arm stretched out.

She had been wearing a grey jacket, which was now pushed up to the shoulders to expose her bare back. Her blue and white checked skirt was also pushed up exposing the upper part of her thighs. She was still wearing one of her high-heeled yellow shoes and the other lay nearby. Her black tights had been ripped but were still in place.

Lying nearby was her handbag and from the contents police were able to identify her as Jayne Michelle Macdonald of 77 Scott Hall Avenue. This was the same street that Wilma McCann had lived on, at Number 65, just six doors away from Jayne who lived with her parents, Wilfred and Irene MacDonald. It was Jayne and her friend, Irene Bransberg, who had witnessed Wilma McCann leaving her house the night she was killed and the rear of the Macdonald house looked out onto Prince Philip Playing Fields where Wilma's mutilated body had been found nineteen months earlier.

Since leaving Allerton High School on Kings Lane in Leeds, six months earlier, Jayne had gained employment in the shoe department of Grandways supermarket on the nearby Roundhay Road. An attractive young girl with shoulder-length light brown hair, a bright smile and sunny personality, she was soon popular in the shop and on Saturday nights she liked to go roller skating or visit the local disco.

Saturday, 25 June 1977 was a warm summer night and, as Jayne left to go to the town centre, the streets surrounding her home were buzzing with people. She kissed her parents goodbye and made her way into town where she intended to meet up with some friends at the Hofbräuhaus, a large Bavarian-style tavern in the Merrion Centre. One of Jayne's favourite places, it was a replica of the Munich Bierkeller and was full of chatter and singing. Young people sat at long wooden tables, drinking steins of beer and singing *The Happy Wanderer* as it was thumped out by a 'German' band, which basically consisted of a Liverpudlian, a Geordie and some local Leeds lads, wearing lederhosen and feathered Tyrolean hats.

It was there, during the course of the evening, that she met 18-year-old Mark Jones and they danced together. At 10.30 pm, they set off as part of a crowd in the direction of Briggate, the main shopping street. They were hungry and Jayne had suggested going for fish and chips. Mark, of Rigton Approach, Leeds, would later say:

> 'We danced at the Hofbräuhaus, and about 10.30pm we walked into the city centre with a number of friends. As we were walking she said she would like some chips in the centre, so we had some chips and then she said she had missed her last bus, so we sat on a bench by C&A. It got to about 12 o'clock and we went towards York Road by the Woodpecker. I told her I lived near there and my sister would drive her home, but she didn't seem bothered either way. We got near the house and I saw that my sister's car wasn't parked there, so we walked up towards St James's Hospital. We went into a field and lay there for about three-quarters of an hour. I didn't try to have sex with her. Then we walked towards Beckett Street. I told her it was getting late and I would have to go home. I told her which way she could get home and the last time I saw her was by the main gates at St James's. We arranged to meet the following Wednesday.'

The two parted company outside the main gates of the hospital at around 1.30am. Jayne decided to take a short cut home through the vice area of Chapeltown. She continued walking and came out of the maze of streets near the Grandways supermarket, where she worked. She continued past the Gaiety on Roundhay Road, where Emily Jackson was last seen, and walked along Chapeltown Road in the direction of the Hayfield pub, Reginald Street and her home.

Unbeknown to her, Sutcliffe had been prowling the red-light area in his car. He had spent that night in the company of Ronnie and David Barker, who lived on the same street as Peter and Sonia lived with her parents. After a night of drinking in the pubs of Bradford, Sutcliffe dropped them at the end of Tanton Crescent, Clayton, Bradford, but instead of going home, he turned the car around and headed to Leeds.

By 1.30am, he had already driven up Roundhay Road and into Roundhay Park – where he murdered Irene Richardson in February 1977 and just further along, off the Roundhay Road, he dumped the body of Emily Jackson in Manor Street in January 1976. It was almost 2am when Sutcliffe caught site of Jayne walking alone along the Chapeltown Road.

He parked and watched her for a few minutes and, despite his later claim that he thought she was a prostitute, it is this author's opinion that he knew full well she wasn't. This is why he made no attempt to bring the car alongside his victim, as was his practice when picking up a prostitute. Instead he waited until she had crossed the junction of Harehills Avenue and had walked up Reginald Street beside the Hayfield Hotel. The street lights where Jayne was now walking had been switched off at 11.30pm, so the opportunity to catch the girl off-guard in the dark presented itself. Quick as a flash he drove up and into the hotel car park and, before getting out of the car, removed a hammer and a kitchen knife from under his seat and put them in his pocket. Crossing through the car park, he made his way out onto Reginald Street and proceeded to follow Jayne. She was three quarters of the way up the street and was now parallel with the adventure playground on her left-hand side. A few more steps and she would be back into the residential side of Reginald Street, and perhaps this is why Sutcliffe struck when he did. He smashed his hammer into the back of her head and she crumpled to the floor, blood staining the ground where she lay.

He hit her again with the hammer and then dragged her, face down, about 20 yards through the top entrance of the playground and into the corner behind the wooden fence and up against the boundary wall. He said later that her shoes made 'a horrible scraping noise' along the ground as he dragged her.

He hit her once more with the hammer, pulled her clothes up and stabbed her in the abdomen. He stabbed her in the same wound as many as twenty times, causing it to become much more enlarged. He then flipped her over and onto her face and thrust the knife in and out of the same wound in her back, penetrating the heart, kidneys and lungs. When she was found, a broken top of a bottle with a screw top had been inserted deeply into the gash in her stomach. This had either been done deliberately by the killer or it had lodged there when the body was flipped over.

Satisfied that he'd finished, the Yorkshire Ripper then wiped his knife clean on her back, returned to his vehicle and made his escape from the car park, leaving the body of Jayne Macdonald face down in the rubbish and dirt where she would be discovered eight hours later by children.

The killer had once again appeared and disappeared like a phantom, and this in itself added to the gossip-driven mythology surrounding both his identity and the supposed ritual slaying of his victims.

The world's focus and immense pressure was now on West Yorkshire Police to deliver decisive action. They would have to double their efforts. The Ripper must be caught.

West Yorkshire's Chief Constable Ronald Gregory decided to put his senior, most experienced detective in charge of the Ripper investigation. Assistant Chief Constable (ACC) George Oldfield would become the most famous and visible police officer in the Ripper inquiry. He had succeeded Donald Craig as head of West Yorkshire CID in 1973. Donald Craig had solved all of the seventy-three murder inquiries he had led in the three years he was head of the department. Now the focus was firmly on George Oldfield to live up to the reputation of his predecessor. Oldfield was a tireless workhorse and demanded the same from his officers. He arrived on the scene and was greeted by Professor David Gee, the pathologist who would examine all the Yorkshire Ripper victims, and whose expert opinion on every Ripper killing would be vital. Oldfield got to work immediately.

A mobile police post with towering radio mast and humming generator was set up in Reginald Street. The street was cordoned off and detectives with clipboards knocked on every door.

These door-to-door enquiries saw 172 police officers interview 679 houses in twenty-one streets. A total of 3,780 statements were taken from 13,000 people interviewed. But where could they store this information? Computers were in their infancy and there were certainly no criminal databases outside of a filing cabinet and paper. So, George Oldfield introduced the idea of index cards for all officers gathering statements and information. Anything which an officer felt was relevant to the case, including details of a person of interest, would be written down on one of these cards and placed in the files alphabetically.

The tyre tracks left behind at the Irene Richardson murder were the subject of intense investigation. Their rear track width of between 4ins 1½cm and 4ins 2½cm, applied to twenty-six different vehicles, which seemed to narrow it down to the quite positive delight of DCS Jim Hobson who was leading the tyre investigation.

But when the statistics came back, it highlighted the monumental task that lay ahead. A staggering 100,000 vehicles in West Yorkshire would have to be checked, and hopefully before the killer changed any of his tyres. Today that process could be done at the touch of a button, but in the 1970s, before modern computer data, the investigators had to arrange with all the local taxation offices to compile a list of the cars that belonged in the relevant category. Once this was done, teams of officers would physically go out at night and check the tyres of all the cars. This included a check on cars parked in side streets and pub car parks in the red-light district.

Measurements would have to be precise as a simple quarter of an inch more or less would add a dozen more cars to the list. If the owner changed just one tyre, it would render the exercise pointless. It became apparent other methods would have to be adopted.

While all this was going on, Leeds police decided to clamp down on prostitutes in the Chapeltown area. Over the next few weeks, 152 women were arrested and reported for prostitution and a further sixty-eight were cautioned. Knowing very well that this tactic could only work for so long, they advised the street workers to let a friend know if they decided to go off with a stranger, or at the very least take the registration of the vehicle.

Policewomen volunteers, posing as prostitutes, were deployed to the street corners of the red-light district in an attempt to lure the killer. It was a dangerous and risky tactic but they were monitored at all times by other police officers close by and instructed to never get into a car. They were equipped with shortwave radios so officers were able to take down descriptions of kerb-crawling punters, as well as the make and model of their cars.

A system of flagging was also introduced. Police would go undercover and make notes of car registration numbers of anyone seen cruising the area. If a car appeared more than once, the owner became a suspect; three times and they would be brought in for questioning.

It was a similar method used by the Metropolitan Police fourteen years earlier when a serial killer began stalking the Hammersmith area of London. Between 1963 and 1965, up to seven prostitutes may have fallen prey to the killer dubbed 'Jack the Stripper' by the media, on account of all the victims being stripped of clothing before being dumped in the River Thames or surrounding side streets. All the women had been strangled. In the course of the investigation over 7,000 suspects were interviewed using the flagging method and, when the suspect list had been whittled down to just ten possibilities, one of those suspects committed suicide. Despite not being able to prove who the killer was, the police were content that there would be no more murders, and they were right. The case of 'Jack the Stripper' remains open to this day.

For West Yorkshire Police, the day-to-day costs were stacking up. So far over 175,000 people had been interviewed with a further 12,500 statements taken down not to mention the 100,000 vehicles that now needed checking. At one point, 250 officers were working full time on the case and a total of 343,000 hours in wages had been paid out.

The check on all the possible car owners with the right tyres was three quarters complete when George Oldfield made a disastrous decision and decided to abandon that particular line of inquiry. This outraged Hobson, who had spent so much time and energy on it. He argued that most of the vehicle owners had already been questioned and there was only a small number left.

Despite his protests, he was overruled and it was made clear that there simply wasn't the manpower to run several murder investigations, plus the tyre inquiry, which had yet to yield any results. The workload would have to be shifted elsewhere.

This would prove to be a fateful decision. The Ripper's car was on the uncompleted list.

Jayne MacDonald was laid to rest in Harehills Cemetery in Leeds and just over two years later she was joined by her father Wilfred, who died in October 1979. Those that knew him said he never recovered from the sight of his murdered daughter and developed breathing complications soon after her death. It's probably more accurate to say the poor man died of a broken heart. For the next two years, a small wooden cross, made by Wilfred using the wood from her bed, marked the gravesite, until it was destroyed in a cruel act of vandalism. Someone had come into the graveyard and had smashed the cross then defaced the letters 'RIP' on the cross to spell out 'RIPPER'. Jayne's mother, Irene, couldn't afford a headstone but, in a wonderful act of generosity, a headstone was donated by the Leeds Co-operative Society on 19 June 1981. It is still there today.

The housing area and waste ground, which made up the adventure playground where Jayne was murdered, is now part of Reginald Park. The Edwardian houses that once occupied the land were demolished in the mid-1980s, along with the Chapeltown Community Centre, formally the Psalms of David synagogue.

The original layout of the street can still be found using maps and photographs, and when put together it is easy enough to locate the murder site. The area where Jayne's body was found is now a grassy bank of the park, and a small picnic table sits on the spot that her body was found over forty years ago. There is no indicator or sign to reveal its dark history.

Jayne MacDonald's murder was immediately linked to the deaths of Wilma McCann, Emily Jackson, Irene Richardson and Patricia Atkinson in a West Yorkshire Police circular issued to all police forces on 27 June 1977. The investigation ran from Millgarth Police Station in Leeds, where incident rooms dealing with the Jackson and Richardson murders were already operating.

A description was obtained of a man seen talking to Jayne shortly before the time of her death. This had much in common with the description of the man thought to be responsible for attacking Maureen Long almost two weeks later.

CHAPTER 9

Maureen Long

'It sounded like a baby crying, but when we went over to look, we found this poor woman lying face down in the dirt.'

Resident of Mary Street Caravan Park, Bradford

Of all the women who survived an attack by the Yorkshire Ripper, Maureen Long is perhaps the most well-known; mainly due to her miraculous ability to survive a full Ripper attack and be left for dead by the killer.

It was two weeks after Jayne MacDonald's murder and the victim was a 42-year-old mother-of-three grown up children, who lived in Farsley, a district of Pudsey which lies 4 miles to the east of Bradford and 6 miles to the west of Leeds.

At the time, Maureen Long's address was 22 Donald Street, Farsley, where she had lived for three years with a man named Ken Smith. But she was also known to reside with her estranged husband Ronnie at 1 Rendel Street, Laisterdyke, a neighbourhood on the outskirts of Bradford.

Maureen was a hardened woman who had been brought up on a rough Bradford estate but she was full of life and enjoyed an evening's drinking in and around Bradford. To all who knew her she was a friendly sort and loved to dance in many of the clubs the city centre had to offer.

At 7.30pm on Saturday, 9 July 1977, Maureen was out on the town when she bumped into her estranged husband Ronnie and she agreed to spend the night with him after she had finished partying. By midnight she had made her way across the city to 101 Manningham Lane, home to the famous Tiffany's nightclub, once known as the Mecca Ballroom. There she danced with many men and several dozen witnesses claimed she was very drunk by the time she left around 2am.

Sutcliffe had also been in town that night, drinking in several pubs with his mates, Ronnie and David Barker. Just as he did on the night of Jayne MacDonald's murder, he dropped the Barkers home at the end of Tanton Crescent, Clayton and drove off alone but this time to the Manningham area of Bradford.

As he passed the crowds who had spilled out onto the street at closing time, he spotted the small 5ft 1in frame of Maureen Long staggering along the road, dressed in a long, black evening dress, wearing black, patent leather wedge shoes and carrying a large brown imitation leather handbag.

He stopped the car and asked her: 'Are you going far?' 'Are you giving me a lift?' she queried. 'If you want one,' he said. She got in. As they drove on, Maureen told him she had been to the Mecca. She told him where she lived, and that she lived with a man who was an ex-boxer and that he was a spoilsport and would not take her to the Mecca.

She directed Sutcliffe to 1 Rendell Street, just off Leeds Road, which was where Ronnie lived. She pointed to a row of terraced houses and said that was where she was going but asked him not to stop outside but to drive past and wait on the corner.

Maureen asked whether he 'fancied her' and when Sutcliffe said he did, she said they could go inside if no one was at home. She got out and knocked at the door of the house, banging at it for a minute or two before giving up and returning to the car. She said she knew a quiet spot where they could go, and directed him to nearby Bowling Back Lane, a run-down industrialized area of Bradford, which even today houses disused gasworks, engineering works, scrap yards, factories, railway yards, the remnants of Bradford Metropolitan District Council's unwanted housing stock and traveller camps.

Birkshall Lane is a side street that connects to Bowling Back Lane. It was, and still is, a cobbled stone street leading downhill to what was once waste ground but today is a council landfill site. It's pretty much the same as it was in the 1970s and, as you drive by, you still see high stone walls on the right-hand side, beyond which still lies the Mary Street caravan site for travellers, located next to G.M. Windows wholesalers. To the left used to be a raised patch of waste ground littered with rubble, old tyres and discarded items of household junk. In 1977, this was open and could easily be accessed, but today it is fenced off and occupied by the Matthew Kitson truck repair yard at 25 Mount Street, Bradford. About 200 yards down the cobbled lane and directly between the caravan site and the waste ground was a small lay-by, hidden from view of Bowling Back Lane and a perfect spot for courting couples seeking privacy. This was the quiet spot Maureen Long was talking about.

As the couple parked up, Maureen announced that she 'needed a piss'. She got out, walked across the lane, climbed half way up the slight bank that led to the waste ground and crouched down to urinate. Sutcliffe followed her to the bank and delivered a crushing blow to the back of her head with a hammer.

After she slumped to the ground, he took hold of her wrists and pulled her up the bank onto the waste ground. He hit her on the head again, ripped her dress off her shoulders and down to her waist, pushed up her bra to expose her breasts and with her knickers already pulled down to her knees and her dress hitched up to her waist, produced a thin knife he had taken from the kitchen in Clayton and began the usual Ripper stabbing signature. He stabbed her nine times, once on her left shoulder, four times in the side and front of her torso, with one slashing stab wound tracking down from her breast to below her navel. He flipped her over and stabbed her another four times in the back. During the attack, he looked up and noticed one of the caravans at the Mary Street camp had its lights on but this didn't scare him off, and he continued to stab at his victim.

When he was sure he had killed her, he dragged a discarded mattress that had been abandoned on the waste ground and threw it over her. In doing so, he stumbled in the rubble and lost his balance and fell. He put out his right arm to cushion his fall, but this left a bloodstained partial palm print on a discarded hand basin.

At this point he heard a dog barking, so he made a hasty getaway back to his car and, probably sensing, correctly, that the street was a dead end, reversed it back up Birkshall Lane and onto Bowling Back Lane. As he pulled out onto the road he may have noticed that the barking dog had alerted the attention of Frank Whitaker, a nightwatchman from the nearby ironworks unit (today it's K.T. Motors of Bowling Back Lane), who came out to see what his Alsatian was barking at. Sutcliffe took off at speed, past the watchman and in the direction of Bradford city centre.

Whitaker would later report what he had seen to the investigating officers but his recollection wasn't entirely accurate. He said he saw a car, which he believed was a white Ford Cortina Mark II with a dark roof (it was really a Ford Corsair), and due to the fact he was looking up the hill towards Birkshall Lane, he thought the car had pulled out of Mount Street (the street next to Birkshall Lane) – an understandable mistake from where he was standing. He did note the time correctly as 3:27am.

By all accounts Maureen Long should have been dead, and it is testament to her tough nature that she remained alive, despite suffering such horrific wounds. The cold air would slow down the blood flow and she managed to regain consciousness five hours later, but as she was suffering from blood loss and hypothermia all she could do was cry and whimper.

At 8.45am, two traveller women were roused from their nearby caravan which overlooked the waste ground where Maureen lay.

At first they took her whimpers for a baby crying. The women decided to investigate and followed the noise until they came to the discarded mattress and found a shivering and petrified Maureen Long lying underneath.

An ambulance arrived and rushed her to Bradford Royal Infirmary, where they saved her life. She was then taken to a neurosurgical unit at Leeds General Infirmary for the more complex task of saving her brain from permanent damage. She was hospitalized for nine weeks.

The police fingertip search of the scene uncovered the partial bloody palm print on a piece of ceramic sink and although convinced it belonged to the attacker, the print wasn't good enough to be used for any detection. But the investigators, led by George Oldfield, must have felt an immense sense of relief to know that a woman had survived a guaranteed Ripper attack. They could now gain an accurate description of their nemesis. Unknowingly, they already had the best description of the Ripper from survivor Tracy Browne but her case was never linked.

Their joy would be matched by a sense of fear for Sutcliffe. Reading through the newspapers he received a nasty shock when he discovered that Maureen had survived. He would later claim that he thought it was 'end of the line' for him, as she would certainly be able to identify him. But to the dismay of the police and the delight of Sutcliffe, Maureen Long was suffering from amnesia.

She had remembered going to the cloakroom at the club and walking towards the city centre. She also remembered his white Ford with the black roof. But the description of her attacker – a white, well-built man, aged 36 or 37, about 6ft 1in tall, puffy cheeks, thickish eyebrows, collar-length wiry blond hair, noticeably large hands – relieved Sutcliffe of some of his worries about being caught. Nevertheless, he disposed of the hammer just in case.

His only real concern was the description of his car by the nightwatchman. A month later, in August 1977, he sold the white Ford Corsair to Ronnie Barker. When it broke down, Sutcliffe reluctantly took it back, stripped the car down and redistributed the spare parts around the replacement car he had bought in September 1977 – a red Ford Corsair.

Later on, after Sutcliffe's arrest, he claimed to have come face-to-face with Maureen Long in the Kirkgate shopping centre in Bradford. He was sure she would recognize him but to his relief she didn't. However, the encounter must have shaken him up and it must have occurred to him that, at some point, she may regain her memory. I will return to this point later.

CHAPTER 10

Jean Jordan

*'I drove my wheelbarrow over this girl five times without noticing.
On the sixth time I looked down and thought it was a tailor's
dummy…but there she was, faced smashed in and disembowelled.'*

Actor Bruce Jones who played Les Battersby
in *Coronation Street*

Manchester is a vibrant city with a population of 20 million. Positioned in the north west of the country, some 200 miles from London, Manchester spreads itself over 60 square miles. With local government reorganization in 1974, it became Greater Manchester, absorbing a number of local towns such as Salford, home of the artist L. S. Lowry and actor Albert Finney. Many of its grimy back-to-back houses were originally built to house the millworkers who provided the backbone to this industrial city.

Manchester dwarfed the Leeds and Bradford conurbation, and was the hub of many industries. It was the northern headquarters of the national newspapers, who all had offices and printing plants there.

Sadly, Bradford and Manchester in the 1970s had similar tales to tell as far as poverty was concerned. From the early nineteenth century to the 1940s, both cities had flourished due largely to the manufacturing of textiles. Yet both suffered a decline by the late 1950s and, today, Manchester has some of the most deprived areas in Britain. One such area is Moss Side or 'The Moss', which recently scored first on the government's index of urban deprivation. The area has had high levels of unemployment, poverty and social exclusion for years. Sixty per cent of households receive benefits and a third of local people are long-term unemployed. Ethnic minorities form a third of the population and lone parent households abound.

In the 1970s, Moss Side was to Manchester what Chapeltown was to Leeds. A tumbledown, vice-ridden ghetto, where police patrolled in pairs and the only decent people seen on the streets at night were residents hurrying home through the cesspit into which their neighbourhood had been transformed by pimps, street gangs and drug pushers.

Just like Chapeltown in Leeds, and Bradford's Manningham, Moss Side's red-light district was a once prosperous area that had fallen on hard times and its large, terraced houses had long been converted into flats, offices and bedsits. Depravity was rampant. It was known for its 'shebeens' – unlicensed, late-night drinking dens that proved a dangerous allure to outsiders wanting to 'slum it' in a break from the norm.

Like any poverty-clad area with a large ethnic community, racism was widespread, especially in the local newspapers. Any misdemeanours committed by black immigrants were magnified, with particular attention paid to prostitution.

For instance, the *Manchester Evening Chronicle* dubbed Moss Side 'Little Harlem', describing it as 'A hot bed of vice and corruption [where] God-fearing people have to live next door to blackguards, pimps, prostitutes and thieves.'

In an area dominated by barely habitable concrete council flats, Lingbeck Crescent and its neighbour, Gretney Walk, were the worst of all. Two rows of low-rise, deck-access flats off Princess Road infested with mice and rats. The lifts never worked and dustbins were never emptied. The flats had bubbles of mould on the walls and the warped wood was soaking wet. These Dystopian conditions were emphasized by the graffiti on one wall, which read, 'Join the housebreakers' association – cost: one TV.'

Originally these blocks were thought to represent the best of modern social housing and the aim of their open layout was to honour and foster community. But from the very start it was a disaster. The blocks were erected too quickly, and their construction inadequately supervised. Reinforcing bolts and ties were missing and there were problems with condensation due to poor insulation and ventilation. Vermin spread rapidly through the estate's ducting. The buildings were a death trap and this came to a head when a child fell to her death from a balcony in 1974. The following year, 643 residents signed a petition to be moved and the local council had to admit that no family should live above the ground floor in any of the deck-access homes. However, it would be a further twenty years before these horrendous dwellings would be demolished to make way for red-brick terraces and functional low-rise flats.

Scottish Jean Jordan was one of the many poverty-stricken residents at Lingbeck Crescent during the 1970s. There, she scraped a living alongside her common-law husband, Alan Royle, and their two children.

Pretty, with a shy smile, long auburn hair and a slim, leggy 5ft 6in frame, many men found the 20 year old appealing. She had arrived in Manchester at the age of 16, having run away from Motherwell. As she wandered, lost and lonely, around Manchester station hoping the police wouldn't swoop on her and send her back home, she met 26-year-old Alan Royle, an unemployed chef, who offered her a cup of tea and a cigarette. The two of them struck up a conversation and, possibly finding common ground, developed a relationship and were very soon living together in Alan's council house in Wythenshawe. Here they would stay for the next four-and-a-half years, during which two children, Alan and James, were born.

By 1977 the young couple were starting to grow apart. The pressure of extra mouths to feed and growing economic hardship had taken its toll. They continued to live together in their new council house in Lingbeck Crescent but led separate lives. Alan tended to disappear for two or three days at a time, and Jean would often take unexpected trips back to her native Scotland and stay with relatives in Glasgow.

Unbeknown to Alan, Jean had also got friendly with a group of women who earned their living on Manchester's streets. These prostitutes introduced the slim and pretty Jean to the relatively easy money to be made on the kerbs of Moss Side and Cheetham Hill. To them, she was known as 'Scotch Jean' and they described her as 'quiet, shy and timid'.

On 1 October 1977, Alan went out with his friends, and when he returned the children were still asleep, but Jean was not there. He assumed she had gone out with her friends and when she didn't return the next day he assumed she had gone on one of her unannounced trips to Scotland to visit her relatives. But she hadn't. She had gone out to ply her trade and in doing so had met her demise at the hands of the Yorkshire Ripper.

It was shortly after 9pm on 1 October when Jean Jordan was standing at her usual beat on Princess Road in Manchester's Moss Side, and a car pulled up alongside her. She walked over to the passenger-side window to ask if the driver wanted business but as she did, a second car pulled up behind it. Perhaps it was the driver's dark, youthful looks and soft voice which attracted Jean, or maybe there was something about the punter in the first car that was off-putting, but whatever it was, Jean decided to go with the young, well-dressed man with the dark beard. It would be a fatal mistake.

Sutcliffe had familiarized himself with the geography of Manchester, in particular the red-light district, during earlier visits with his friends, Ronnie and David Barker. Four days earlier he had moved in to his new £16,000 house at 6 Garden Lane Bradford, with his wife Sonia and he had also bought another second-hand car. This red Ford Corsair replaced the white Ford Corsair, which had been involved in many of his attacks and murders, and which he'd sold to Ronnie. He had decided to test out his new car and, as he was aware of the intense police presence around Leeds and Bradford, he decided to head towards Manchester.

He'd recently read an article in a church magazine, in which a priest wrote about the dangers of prostitution in the Moss Side area. Grateful for the tip, he thought it would be a good place to visit while the police were concentrated elsewhere.

He set off from his new home and drove the 40 miles to Manchester, crossing over the Pennine Hills, and south along the M606, arriving into Manchester city centre just under an hour later. He would later recall the moments leading up to the murder:

> 'I went through Manchester town centre – Princess Street I think it was – followed it all the way down past the university, which eventually came out near the Moss Side area. It was a run-down area and almost immediately on arriving there I saw several girls plying for trade. I pulled up at the kerbside and asked a girl if she wanted business. She was very slim with light coloured hair, not bad looking. She told me if I waited further along the road she would meet me there. I drove on 200 yards and made a right turn, then a three-point turn to face the main road once again.
>
> 'After a couple of minutes, the girl drew level. She saw my car just as she was going to get into another car which had stopped for her. I think this was an 1100, a light-coloured one, either grey or fawn. She didn't get in but came over to me, which I suppose was the biggest mistake she ever made. She came up and got into my car. She told me she was going to go with the man in the other car until she saw me.'

In the car, Jean explained it would be five pounds and that she knew a secluded spot further up the road. Normally in the cold or rainy weather she could use a small bedsit on Claremont Road, that was shared by a fellow prostitute, Anna Holt, for the purposes of sex. But when conditions were fine and dry, as they were that night, it was easier to take the quick 1-mile drive to a dark patch of waste ground adjacent to the allotments next to Southern Cemetery.

Within a few minutes, they turned left off Princess Road and along a narrow track that ran through iron gates and into the cemetery. Once through the gates, a sharp right, a drive of 30 or 40 yards and a left turn would bring them to a small, square patch of overgrown waste land. Not turning left would have brought them to the allotments.

Visiting the site today, it's easy to see how people have been confused about the exact location of the crime scene. A 7ft metal border fence has since been put up around the allotments but in 1977 there was only a 3ft high wooden picket fence that divided the allotments from the adjacent waste ground.

When the metal fence was added it took up 8ft of the waste ground, including the murder site. Some think the murder occurred inside the allotments that stand there today but the crime scene was at the boundary line between the waste ground and the new allotments.

When I originally requested the crime scene location through the Freedom of Information Act, I was told this information would not be made available to the public, or the man hours couldn't be justified to search through the files. This is infuriating when you consider the fact it's such a high-profile case and we know what happened and to whom.

I, and fellow Yorkshire Ripper researcher Darren Field, spent many hours looking through reports and watching old TV news footage and we eventually lined up the crime scene as accurately as possible to the sheds that still line the route.

The area was, and still is to this day, shielded from the traffic by high hawthorn hedges. It was easy to see why this was a favourite haunt of the Moss Side prostitutes and their clients, and I wouldn't be surprised if it remains so today.

Sutcliffe parked the car on the grass next to the allotments and produced a five pound note. Jean took it and placed it in a disguised compartment of her handbag. Sutcliffe glanced over towards the boundary of the allotments and spotted a small blue shed, which lay just 30 yards in front.

He suggested leaving the car and going over to the shed, claiming his uncle owned it and there would be plenty of room and some heating in there. As the couple started to get out of the car, he retrieved a hammer he had concealed down the side of his seat and hid it inside his coat. He followed Jean into the darkness of the waste land.

It soon became apparent that this was the rear of the shed, by the boundary fence and the entrance was located inside the allotments. There was no access from where the couple were standing. Jean went to climb over the fence and as she did so, Sutcliffe brought his hammer down onto the back of her head. She fell to the ground moaning loudly and he continued to smash down the hammer eleven times onto her head causing massive depressed fractures to the skull which left her face unrecognizable. He also battered her shoulders, neck and upper trunk and continued to do so until the moaning had stopped.

At that moment, another car which had been standing idle further into the allotments, switched on its headlights and revved up its engine, preparing to pull out. It would appear the murderer and his victim were not the only ones using the seclusion of the area. In a quick, desperate act, Sutcliffe dragged Jean's body into the undergrowth, out of sight and threw away her handbag, making sure nothing could be seen as the car drove out of the allotments.

He stood with his back to the hedge as he watched the car drive down past him and out onto the road. He then went back to deal with the body of Jean Jordan.

Before he could settle into his usual mutilations, he spotted another car through the trees. It had come down Princess Road and was now signalling to come into the waste ground where Sutcliffe was standing. He ducked down behind his car as it came past him and entered the allotments, where it turned round and parked in the exact place as the one that had just left. Jean Jordan's 'quiet' place was far too busy for him to continue and he had to abandon the body and retreat to his car and back to Yorkshire.

Before leaving, he managed to place a large wooden door that had been discarded in the field, on top of the body to conceal it further.

He set off in the direction of Bradford, but as he drove along it crossed his mind that he had left a valuable clue behind – a clue that could ultimately lead investigators to his door. The money he had paid Jean was a brand new five pound note, which had come from his wage packet and could, with a bit of detective work, be traced back to his workplace and ultimately himself.

He now had two alternatives: he could go back to try and get it, with the likely risk of being spotted, or he could continue on to Bradford and sit it out. He needed to be back in Yorkshire in reasonable time so it didn't look as though he'd travelled so far away, and he didn't want anyone else seeing his car next to the spot where Jean Jordan would no doubt be found. He decided to sit it out.

He was surprised to see nothing in Monday's paper about the Yorkshire Ripper having struck for the first time in Manchester. Every day after that he looked but found no news of the murder. The explanations were simple; he had hidden the body too well to be discovered, the area was only busy after dark and Jean Jordan had not been reported missing. Alan Royle had assumed Jean had simply made one of her unplanned trips to Scotland and he got quietly on with looking after the children himself.

When, after a week, there was still no news, Sutcliffe took this as confirmation that her body was still where he had hidden it and had not been discovered.

Over the next couple of days, he must have contemplated what would happen if – and surely when – Jean's body was discovered. It's here that he demonstrated a criminal cunning in order to confuse investigators from linking the murder to crimes committed by himself in Yorkshire. He knew the biggest tell-tale sign would be the signature hammer blows to the head. It was time to take a risk.

Peter and Sonia had recently purchased their first proper home at 6 Garden Lane, Heaton, Bradford. The three-storey, detached house would remain their home right up until his arrest in 1981. To this day Sonia still lives there. But it was the housewarming party he held on Sunday, 9 October 1977 that would give him the ideal opportunity to go back to Manchester and provide himself with an alibi should he need it.

Considerate as ever, he offered to take his parents, John and Kathleen, sister Jane and brother-in-law Ian home to Bingley after the party ended around midnight.

After making the final stop to drop his mum and dad off at Cornwall Road, he headed for Manchester, accompanied with a hacksaw he had taken earlier from his garage.

Since it was a Sunday and traffic was light, he made the outskirts of Manchester within three-quarters of an hour. Fifteen minutes later he was parked by the Princess Road allotments and was heading into the waste land to find Jean's body.

Not surprisingly, the dead woman was exactly where he had left her, concealed from view in the undergrowth. He pulled the decomposing body further out from where it was hidden and frantically searched around to locate the handbag in which she had placed the £5 note he had given her. He could not find it. He began stripping off all her clothing, removing her boots, bra, coat, underwear, cardigan and jumper, searching every item one by one for any trace of the money. He was not successful.

Either in frustration, anger at being thwarted in his mission to find the note, or by a clever desire to disguise the killing as the work of another, he attacked the corpse in a frenzy of slashes and deep cuts. He added immense sweeping gashes, 8-inches deep, to the decomposing flesh, from the shoulder to the left knee and thigh. He stabbed and sliced at her breasts, chest, stomach and area round her vagina eighteen times.

The savage cuts ripped the stomach wide open and extended deep into the abdomen and into the front of the backbone. These exposed the intestines and because of the decomposition, the stench that erupted when her stomach opened up caused him to vomit, but he continued to attack the body.

Just as his predecessor, Jack the Ripper, had done almost 100 years before in London, he reached in, pulled out her intestines and left them wrapped around her waist.

With her already flattened head, this made Jean Jordan the worst mutilated body he would ever leave. But he wasn't done yet.

Picking up the hacksaw, he attempted to cut through the dead woman's neck. However the hacksaw was blunt and, try as he might, even by using a broken piece of glass which lay nearby, he could not get through the bone. Enraged at his failures that night, and thinking his capture was almost assured, Sutcliffe kicked and stamped on the body a few times. Frustrated, and figuring he had been at the scene long enough and was pushing his luck by staying any longer, he gave up, got in his car and headed for Bradford. When Sutcliffe got home, he was surprised to find he did not have much blood on his clothing. He put his trousers into the garage and later disposed of them by burning them with some garden rubbish.

At noon that day, two allotment holders, a Mr Morrissey and 23-year-old Bruce Jones (who would later play Les Battersby in the long-running soap opera, *Coronation Street*), were helping a friend in the adjoining new allotments and went to get some discarded house bricks from the disused land. They had not initially noticed the body lying in the grass but on one of the return trips, Bruce Jones' wheelbarrow ran over a part of the corpse and he noticed the naked woman lying on her back, her arms spread apart and in an advanced stage of decomposition. It was a sight that he later admitted would stay with him for the rest of his life.

It was revealed at the inquest that when Chief Inspector Tony Fletcher arrived to take fingerprints, his first thought was that 'someone had dug up a body from the nearby cemetery and cut it to bits.'

A brief story about the murder appeared in that night's *Manchester Evening News*. It prompted Alan Royle to telephone the police to say he suspected it might be his common-law wife Jean Jordan, and he was able to identify her clothing. Anna Holt, prostitute and friend of Jean's, had also read the reports and gone to the police and said it might be her. Confirmation that it was Jean Jordan came when, after an extensive search of her flat where they had not found her fingerprints as Alan did most of the cooking and cleaning, her left thumbprint was found on a lemonade bottle.

Within five days, police had what Sutcliffe had been so desperate to obtain – Jean Jordan's green, imitation leather handbag. Despite a fingertip search of the disued land, the team of uniformed officers halted their search at the wire fence that separated the allotments from the waste ground. This wire fence has since been replaced with a 10ft metal fence, which surrounds the entire perimeter of the allotments. It is padlocked and closed to the public.

A man called Mr Cox had found the handbag on the morning of Saturday, 15 October, on the other side of the wire fence, inside the allotments. It lay just 150 yards away from her body, hidden in the undergrowth. In one of the two external pockets, police found a concealed compartment. Inside was a folded-up, brand-new five pound note.

DCS Jack Ridgeway was head of the Manchester CID during the Ripper inquiry and would deal with two of the Yorkshire Ripper murders, Jean Jordan and the later killing of Vera Millward. He knew right away that the best clue to the identity of the killer was this five pound note.

The note was passed to the Bank of England, which was asked to trace where it was issued. Detectives learnt it had been sent from its printing works to the Leeds branch of the Bank of England, just a few days before the murder. The trail then led to a parcel of notes, which had been dispatched to Midland Bank and then dispersed to several branches in Leeds and Bradford. The suspicion was that the fiver had been distributed as part of a firm's payroll. The serial number of the note, AW51 121565, was released to the press and people were asked to check notes they had received in their pay as it was one of sixty-nine consecutively numbered notes.

Delays with trying to trace other notes from the same batch – by starting the inquiry too late and not immediately informing the public about it – resulted in a lost opportunity to restrict the number of people who could have received the note.

Manchester Police were drafted into West Yorkshire and the Shipley branch of Midland Bank became the focus of their attention. Staff at the branch were asked to help identify which batch of notes the fiver had come from.

Thirty-four firms in West Yorkshire, which could have issued the fiver in a pay packet, were scrutinized by police. They included an engineering company in Bradford, which had received money for the payroll at the relevant time. A list was obtained of every single employee so they could be seen individually by police.

Sutcliffe, employed by T. & W.H. Clark (Holdings) Limited in Shipley, one of the firms that could have received the note, was visited at home by detective constables Edwin Howard and Leslie Smith at 7.45pm on 2 November. He and his wife were both at home and Sutcliffe appeared relaxed, casual and not at all perturbed by the visit. He said he had been at home the night of the murder, a month earlier, and had gone to bed around 11.30pm. Sonia confirmed his story. When questioned about the second date, when the killer had returned to the body, Sutcliffe had an apparently solid alibi – he and his wife had been having a housewarming party. He could not produce any five pound notes that he had received in his pay packet a month earlier on 29 September.

Six days after the first interview, Sutcliffe was questioned again about the five pound note by two different policemen. He and Sonia gave the same stories as they had given the previous police visitors. They also allowed their house to be searched and nothing incriminating was found.

Sutcliffe's mother signed a statement saying she saw him at the party. It seems incredible now that detectives did not probe his alibis harder. Had they done, they would have discovered that the excuses did not account for all his movements on the days in question. But police were overwhelmed with information in an increasingly desperate, sprawling investigation. There was no CCTV, and forensic technology was not what it is now.

Having found nothing to arouse their suspicions, the detective constables filed a five-paragraph report stating Sutcliffe had denied being a punter of prostitutes and that his wife had given a general alibi for the night of the murder. 'Not connected' was the conclusion drawn in regard to the Jean Jordan murder.

The five pound note investigation ended up being wound down and Peter Sutcliffe became just another of the 250,000 names on file.

CHAPTER 11

Marilyn Moore

'I had been taken over completely by this urge to kill and I couldn't fight it. I went to Leeds one evening in December 1977 to try again.'

Peter Sutcliffe

On 14 December 1977, 25-year-old prostitute Marilyn Moore survived a vicious attack by Sutcliffe and managed to provide one of the best photofits of the suspect from a known Ripper victim. As well as this, a clue found at the scene linked this attack to the Irene Richardson murder.

Marilyn Moore had been conducting business on the small side street of Gipton Avenue, which lies just of the main Roundhay Road in the red-light district of Leeds. It was an area synonymous with the early Yorkshire Ripper murders. In the next street was the Gaiety pub where Emily Jackson had been picked up in 1976; two streets in the opposite direction was Cowper Street, where Irene Richardson was picked up and young Jayne MacDonald had walked past here five months earlier before being murdered close by in Reginald Street.

As Marilyn walked along onto Spence Place around 8pm, a car passed by her slowly. In anticipation that the car would turn around and come back, she crossed Spence Place and turned right into Leopold Street at the junction with Frankland Place. Today it's located next to Chapeltown Health Centre.

She saw the car parked at the kerb but the driver was now outside the car, standing by the driver's door. He appeared to be waving. She would later say he looked like the dark, moustachioed Jason King, secret agent hero of the eponymous TV series, which was popular at the time.

Unknown to Marilyn, her movements earlier in the night had been monitored by Sutcliffe. He had sat in his car, across the street from where she was working, and watched as she refused to get into a punter's car on Leopold Street. He knew she was the cautious kind and no doubt wary due to the recent murders.

Showing a sly and cunning intelligence, he had purposefully cruised past her to gain her attention then, as he turned the corner he parked, jumped out and pretended to be waving someone off to their house. He even shouted, 'Bye now. See you later. Take care!'

As Marilyn walked past him, he asked whether she was doing business and after agreeing on a price of five pounds, they were on their way to a quiet place she knew behind Brown's Mill on Buslingthorpe Lane in the Scott Hall area of Leeds.

It was an area known to Sutcliffe as well. Two years earlier he had brutally murdered Wilma McCann less than 400 yards away on the playing pitches off Scott Hall Avenue.

In the car, Sutcliffe said that his name was Dave and when asked what he had been doing back on Leopold Street he replied that he had been saying goodbye to a sick girlfriend. He mentioned two prostitutes, Hilary and Gloria, and said that Hilary had a Jamaican boyfriend. Marilyn knew two prostitutes by the same names and knowing her punter was familiar with the area put her more at ease.

Sutcliffe drove up Scott Hall Road and turned left into Buslingthorpe Lane and Marilyn directed him to turn left again, into a narrow dirt track called Stonegate Lane, which ran down behind the back of the old mill. It was a notorious spot for prostitutes and their clients. Today Brown's Mill lies abandoned and derelict; one end of the laneway has been closed to the public and the other is now part of a car repair yard, closed off with a large, red iron gate.

When they parked, Sutcliffe suggested they get in the back seat and Marilyn agreed. But after climbing out of the front passenger door she found the back passenger door locked. 'It's OK, I'll get it,' said Sutcliffe. He got out of the car, but had already reached down to pull out a hammer that had been hidden down the side of his seat. As he came round to open the passenger door, he tried to hit her on the head with the hammer, but as he swung it, he slipped in the mud and lost his balance, causing his hammer blow to only graze Marilyn's head.

She screamed but Sutcliffe managed to regain balance and hit her harder with a second blow, which felled her. Still conscious, she covered her head as hammer blows rained down, hitting her hands and wrists. She grabbed his legs and continued to scream as all the while Sutcliffe hit her, shouting 'Dirty prostitute bitch!' She felt more blows before slipping into unconsciousness.

Luckily, her screams had caused a dog to start barking at nearby Scott Hall Farm, and when Sutcliffe noticed two people walking down the lane, he realized it was time to leave. He jumped back in his car and revved up the engine, spinning his wheels, but they slipped in the mud and for a moment the car wouldn't go anywhere. However, after a few moments he managed to get it back onto rough ground and turned the car sharply to the right. With much wheel spinning, he managed to get away and back to his home in Bradford, leaving his victim still alive.

When Marilyn Moore regained consciousness, she staggered towards the road to get to a telephone and call for help. When she reached the road, a teenage couple saw her and one of them ran to phone for an ambulance. Marilyn was taken to Leeds General Infirmary for emergency surgery, which included relieving pressure on her brain from a depressed fracture of her skull. She had eight lacerations on her head caused by hammer blows, severe bruising and several cuts on her hands from where she had tried to protect her head. Her injuries required fifty-six stitches.

She described her assailant as a white man about 28 years of age, 5ft 7 to 5ft 8ins tall, of stocky build with dark wavy hair, a medium-length, neatly trimmed beard and a 'Jason King' moustache. After giving police his name, over a thousand men called Dave or David were identified in the nominal index, which police had built up for the Ripper crimes. All were interviewed but none could be implicated. Due to the severity of her injuries, police thought her description of her suspect might not be reliable and it was later revealed by Chief Constable Ronald Gregory that she had been taken to St James's Hospital in Leeds to be questioned under deep hypnosis.

She said the car was a dark coloured or maroon vehicle, about the size of a Morris Oxford. Sutcliffe was, in fact, driving his red Ford Corsair. The police found an important clue in the tyre tracks – the front wheels had the same India Autoway crossply tyres that were on the car used in the murder of Irene Richardson. There was no doubt that the Yorkshire Ripper had been the one who had attacked Marilyn Moore.

Unfortunately, although Marilyn's description of the car was accepted, the police placed less reliance on her description of the assailant. In retrospect, her identification of the car was wrong while her description of her attacker matched Sutcliffe fairly accurately.

Once the photofit she produced was released to the public, a 1975 survivor of the Ripper, Tracy Browne, instantly recognized the similarity to the man who had attacked her. She went straight to Keighley Police, only to be ignored.

CHAPTER 12

Yvonne Pearson

'You can get a nutter in London just the same as you can in Bradford.'

Yvonne Pearson, shortly before her murder

Yvonne Pearson was more upmarket than the usual run-of-the-mill Yorkshire street girl. She dressed carefully, with style, and evidence of regular trips to the hairdressers could be seen in her expensively bleached blonde hair. The 22 year old made sure her makeup was always perfect, and although she was based in Bradford, she was in the habit of travelling to big cities across the country where she gained clientele from the wealthy business community.

With her lissom figure and page-boy style haircut, she had a passing resemblance to Joanna Lumley's character Purdey in *The New Avengers* TV series and plenty of interest and custom came her way. Back in Bradford she even boasted that she had cracked the Arab market.

She was well-liked and well-known; most of the women on the game in Bradford in 1978 knew Yvonne Pearson. Several had paired up with her from time to time and worked the Lumb Lane district as a patrolling couple. She was also well known in the local pubs where she would go drinking with her friend Patricia 'Tina' Atkinson, the Ripper victim who had worked from her bedsit on Oak Avenue.

Yvonne also operated out of a small flat in Bradford, or if plying her trade in the bigger cities such as Birmingham, Manchester or London, she would use a hotel room, rented by herself or a wealthy client.

But things would soon change with the arrival of the Yorkshire Ripper.

Death had brushed past her in April 1977 when the Ripper killed her friend Tina Atkinson, and again, in November of the same year, when close friend and call girl Jane McIntosh was murdered in London. Jane had moved south from Bradford because of the man with the hammer, but according to an associate who later spoke to the papers, Yvonne's attitude was: 'You can get a nutter in London just the same as you can in Bradford.'

This would prove horribly prescient when Jane McIntosh was stabbed to death in a Bayswater hotel over a diamond studded bracelet and some money.

After Tina and Jane were murdered, Yvonne was particularly careful. She let all and sundry know she carried a lethal-looking pair of scissors in her handbag, and that she was prepared to use them, should the man they called the Ripper come calling. She also took a decision on where she would ply her trade. Her two friends had been murdered in their rooms, so Yvonne decided to give up working in flats and began taking punters to pieces of waste land. The open-air trade may have been cheaper and nastier but it did, at least, give her a chance to run away.

However, the Ripper murders had also increased the number of police patrols in the area so it was no surprise when, in early January 1978, she was arrested for soliciting. She was due at Bradford Magistrate's Court to answer that charge on 26 January. One of the conditions of her bail was a curfew between the hours of 7pm and 7am. She had already been fined twice for soliciting and as this was her third arrest, a custodial sentence looked likely, so likely in fact that she had already arranged for a friend to look after her kids should she be sent to prison.

On Saturday 21 January, she spent most of her cash shopping – probably in Morrisons in Westgate – and although she was short of money she fancied a night out.

Having made tea for her 2-year-old daughter Lorraine, and fed 5-month-old Colette, she started to get ready before leaving the children in the care of her 16-year-old neighbour, Selma Turley.

She dressed in a black polo neck jumper, black trousers, green and black wavy striped woollen jacket with wide sleeves and black shoes, said goodbye to the babysitter and left her small terraced house at 4 Woodbury Road, Heaton. She took with her a black, leather, strapless handbag which she carried under one arm. Its contents included an address book with twenty-six names, addresses and telephone numbers, a pair of scissors (her defence against the Ripper) and a near empty purse.

There was just enough for a couple of drinks at the Queens or the Flying Dutchman – two of her favourite pubs on Lumb Lane.

Within fifteen minutes, Yvonne had walked down to the Flying Dutchman; she loved its friendly, noisy atmosphere and lively reggae music. She sipped pineapple juice and played a game of pool with a prostitute friend.

At 9.30pm she told her companion that she was 'off to earn some money' and she wandered out of the pub and into the darkness of Lumb Lane.

Meanwhile, that night Sutcliffe had been helping move his parents to a new home near to the centre of Bingley. When he left before having a drink, his brother, Mick, and his father, John, assumed he wanted to get home to Sonia. However, Sutcliffe bypassed his home when he drove from Bingley to Bradford and was soon cruising down Lumb Lane in his red Corsair.

As he drove along, he narrowly avoided getting into an accident when a light grey Mark II Cortina backed out of a side street, known as Southfield Square, in front of him – the driver obviously not looking where he was going. Sutcliffe braked hard and screeched to a halt to avoid a collision.

Just then, there was a tap on the window and he was surprised to see a blonde-haired woman dressed in a black sweater and black trousers by the front passenger side. She opened the door and climbed in. He asked where she had sprung from, and she said, 'Just good timing. You can put it down to fate.' She then suggested a place they could do the business.

He swung the car round and proceeded back down Lumb Lane, turning right onto Gracechurch Street and right again onto White Abbey Road. Within a few hundred yards he had taken a left into Arthington Street, a derelict area with a tract of waste land used as a rubbish dump and an unauthorized children's playground, and flanked by a bakery and a motor mechanics garage.

It was one of several short dead-end roads that ran at right angles to the main B6144 road, Whetley Hill. On either side was rough waste ground, created by the demolition of a row of terraced houses several years before. Towards the far end was a large open space covered in long grass. To the back was a steep bank and, closer to Arthington Street, there were piles of burned rubbish and discarded household items, including a broken sofa. Being just off the main White Abbey Road and away from public eyes, the dark waste ground was a favoured spot for prostitutes.

Sutcliffe drove his car to the far end of Arthington Street and turned right, onto the patch of ground that lay between Jack Andrews' auto repairs garage and a long brick wall, which marked the boundary of the derelict ground.

He asked her how much she wanted. She said, 'It depends how much you can afford. A good time five pounds, more than a good time ten pounds.' She unbuttoned her jeans and Sutcliffe suggested they move to the back seat. They both got out, and in the process Sutcliffe retrieved a thick walling hammer lying down by his feet and went around behind her. Yvonne tried the handle of the door but it wouldn't open. Sutcliffe reached in through the passenger window and opened the back door from the inside and stood back.

As she opened the door, he hit her on the head with the hammer. She crumpled to the ground and started to moan loudly. He hit her once more and then grabbed her ankles and dragged her along the rough ground on her back about 20 yards to where the old sofa was lying in the grass.

She was still moaning loudly.

Almost immediately, another car appeared and pulled in alongside his. Sutcliffe pulled her beside the sofa and hid from view.

Yvonne was still moaning and to stop her making a noise, he grabbed handfuls of horsehair from the discarded sofa and began stuffing it into her mouth and down her throat, holding her nose at the same time. After a while, he released her nose to see if she was still making a noise. She was so he grabbed it and held it again.

Eventually, the car drove away. Later Sutcliffe said it 'seemed like hours' before it finally left.

Now he was alone with his victim, he pulled her trousers and knickers down, pushed up her top and bra and started kicking and beating her around the head. He used such force that it smashed her skull into seventeen pieces on one side and four on the other. He kicked and jumped down on her bare chest with the weight of both feet, fracturing her ribs and damaging the internal organs. Such was the violence shown to the body that the pathologist, who would later carry out the autopsy, initially thought Yvonne had been involved in a road collision.

No knife was used in the attack, because he hadn't intended to kill this particular night and didn't have a knife with him. He would later claim he was actually going home when Yvonne knocked on his car window and the opportunity arose.

When he had finished, he tore up tufts of grass and clumps of soil and dumped them onto her battered corpse before covering the makeshift grave with the old sofa.

Back at Yvonne's flat in Woodbury Road, the babysitter anxiously watched the clock on the mantelpiece ticking away the hours. Television had long since closed down for the night and there was still no sign of Yvonne. The young girl put the latch on the door and settled down to stay the night. When she hadn't arrived by the morning, Selma phoned Yvonne's friends and told them she was missing. The friends were the people who were to take in the children if Yvonne was imprisoned the following week.

Yvonne Pearson was reported missing the following Monday but, while there was concern for her welfare, there was also the suspicion that she had 'gone to ground' to avoid her impending court appearance. The police checked derelict areas, and enquired about her whereabouts with other police forces, but no information was forthcoming.

Because of her London links, it was thought she might be in the capital. Despite her friends and relations assuring police that it was unthinkable that Yvonne would desert her children, the investigating officers considered it a possibility. Many people jumped bail before a court appearance that may land them in prison.

Nevertheless, police did consider that Yvonne could be another Ripper victim and so the press was alerted to her disappearance. The national media dismissed it and gave it virtually no coverage. To their credit the local press, television and radio did cover it at length.

'Definite' sightings of Yvonne in London, Wolverhampton and Bradford transpired to be false. As the days crept into weeks, the council decided her rented house had been abandoned and bricked it up. It didn't help the investigation that Roy Saunders, Yvonne's ex-partner and father to her kids, had removed all the furniture and told neighbours that Yvonne had gone to live in London.

It would be a further two months before Yvonne's decomposing corpse would be found by a young man taking a short cut across the Arthington Street waste ground, and by that time the Yorkshire Ripper would have already claimed another victim.

Arthington Street has been redeveloped over the last four decades and is now lined with Indian textile companies such as Ramis Crown and Atique Fashion Wear. Jack Andrews' auto repairs garage, next to where Yvonne was murdered, is now Suits Me clothes wholesalers. This building, and the one currently occupied by the Bradford Gym at the far end of Arthington Street, are the only original buildings left from the time of the Ripper.

The waste ground where Yvonne's body lay undiscovered for several months has been tarmacked over and is now the forecourt of Luqmans Autos.

The police were left with several puzzles. To begin with, they found it inconceivable that her body would not have been discovered earlier as her arm was sticking out from underneath the sofa. Their only conclusion was that it may have been moved by a dog. Secondly, a copy of the *Daily Mirror* dated 21 February – exactly one month after the murder – was found under one of her arms. This looked as though it had been placed there deliberately to make the date of the attack look a month later than it was. Perhaps Sutcliffe knew he had been seen on 21 January. He would later deny that he had returned to the body, even though this has to be the case.

The third, and most important puzzle, was whether or not it was a Yorkshire Ripper killing. There were the massive head wounds, but Professor David Gee's examination led him to believe they had been caused by a boulder and not a hammer. There weren't any stab wounds, but her clothing had been arranged in typical Ripper fashion, with her bra and sweater above the breasts and her other clothing pulled down. At first, the police discounted it as a Ripper killing, but later it was included in his catalogue of murders and attacks.

The murder was investigated by DCS Laptish of the western crime area and another incident room was established in Bradford. Little evidence was forthcoming in connection with this crime, largely because of the lengthy time lapse between the murder and the discovery of the body. In May 1978, a West Yorkshire Police circular linked it with other crimes in the Ripper series.

The pieces could only be put together when Sutcliffe himself admitted it. This is an extract from his arrest interviews in 1981:

'The one I did after Moore was Yvonne Pearson at Bradford. I was driving along Lumb Lane, in my red Corsair, from the city centre. A light grey or fawn Mark II Cortina started backing out of Southfield Square on my left as I approached, so I slowed down to let it out. That's when I saw Yvonne Pearson, she was blonde and was wearing dark trousers. On reflection it was a very fateful moment for her, me just slowing down as she came along.

'She stepped straight up to the car as I stopped and tapped on the window. She asked me if I wanted business. This was one time when I was genuinely going home as it happened, but I still had a hammer in the car on the floor, under my seat. I told her to get in. She suggested that I turn the car round and she told me where to drive.

'Oh, I've just remembered it might have been a walling hammer that I used on Yvonne; there was [sic] two walling hammers in the garage of the house when I moved in. I remember I put one in the car when I threw the other one away at Sharps. It might still be in the garage somewhere.'

In 1978, the 'Prostitute Murder Squad' was formed of the growing number of investigators drafted in to solve these heinous crimes.

However, the press dubbed it the 'Ripper Squad' and it stuck. The Ripper Squad was Detective Superintendent Dick Holland (Bradford Area), Detective Chief Superintendent Peter Gilrain (Bradford Area), Detective Chief Superintendent Jim Hobson (Leeds Area), Assistant Chief Constable George Oldfield (West Yorkshire), and Detective Superintendent Alf Finlay (Leeds).

CHAPTER 13

Elena Rytka

'People throughout West Yorkshire are incensed at these Ripper killings. We believe somebody, somewhere knows something – they must know the identity of this mad killer.'

Conservative Councillor Rita Verity

It had been ten days since Sutcliffe had last killed. Yvonne Pearson still lay undetected under a broken sofa on the waste ground off Arthington Street. This time he set his sights on Huddersfield.

So far Huddersfield had escaped the shadow of the Ripper although the name was spoken about in pubs, clubs and red-light districts all across the country. The prostitutes in Huddersfield no doubt sought solace in the fact the killer had not ventured into their neck of the woods. But it would be a false sense of security.

Less than a thirty-minute drive from Bradford city centre, Huddersfield's red-light district wasn't as well known to Sutcliffe as Leeds and Bradford. However, the area around Great Northern Street where the prostitutes plied their trade was on Sutcliffe's delivery route for work. It was during one of these deliveries that he first noticed the women doing business there and within three days he had decided to pay them a visit.

Great Northern Street was, and still is, concentrated in a heavily industrialized area just a few hundred yards from the shopping and business centre. In the 1970s this was very much a depressed, desolate section of the town which once held a premier position in the wool trade. It housed an abattoir, cattle market and wood yard. A dirty canal still runs nearby, although the pottery kilns and gasworks that once stood beside it are now gone.

A refuse dump once stood at one end of the street and at the other was a derelict school house, with smashed out and boarded-up windows. In the middle were the run-down public toilets, a well-known pick up point for prostitutes as well as homosexual men who took part in 'cottaging', which involved arranging sexual encounters with other men in lavatories. These toilets once stood on the left-hand corner of Great Northern Street by the junction of Hillhouse Lane.

By 1978 many of the houses that stood on one side of the road were empty and vandalised, awaiting demolition as the industrial estate expanded. The surrounding roads were unadopted and scarred with potholes, parts of which were still cobblestoned.

Today the industrial estate is well-lit and security fencing protects the modern business units that have replaced the brick and wood warehouses. The public toilets have long since been demolished and the roads have been tarmacked. The only remnant from the 1970s is Garrards Timber on the corner of Great Northern Street. Although its back yard no longer boasts the open, sprawling maze of wood from the 1970s, when prostitutes and their clients could hide between the rows of sawn timber stacked 8–10ft tall.

However, if you take a detour today into one of the side streets, such as Myrtle Street or Ray Street, and into Lower Viaduct Street which runs directly alongside the old viaduct, parallel to Great Northern Street, you are thrust back into the grotty world of the 1970s red-light district.

Here you are met with dark and mostly deserted railway arches, badly lit with leaking drainpipes and dark corners in every direction. It's easy to see how these 80ft railway arches, under the Leeds to Manchester railway line, once formed makeshift brothels for street walkers and their clients looking for a quick knee trembler up against its wet walls. I would hazard a guess that they are still used for such activity, because the world's oldest profession is still alive and well in exactly the same area.

At the time of writing, prostitutes still ply their trade along the entire length of Great Northern Street and junction of Lower Fitzwilliam Street in Hillhouse and, for the general public, the street is a no-go area after working hours.

In early January 1978, two new faces appeared on the Huddersfield prostitution circuit – 18-year-old twin sisters, Rita and Elena Rytka (who was known as Helen). Originally from Leopold Street in Chapeltown, Leeds, these daughters of a Polish mother and a West Indian father, had not had a pleasant upbringing. In fact, most of their lives had been spent in a succession of children's homes.

They were born on 3 March 1959 but by the age of 3, their parents had split up. Their mother had walked out of the family home and their father was unable to cope by himself. The split left four children of Jamaican and Polish parentage in local authority care – Helen and Rita, and their 1-year-old twin brother and sister.

As Roman Catholics, they were placed with the Leeds Diocesan Rescue, Protection and Child Welfare Society and eventually moved to St Theresa's home, Thistle Hill, Knaresborough, which was a home for about fifteen children run by the sisters of the Holy Family of Bordeaux.

At the age of 15, Helen read a series on fostering in *The Yorkshire Post* and it encouraged her to write a poem called *Lonely and Unloved*. Included with it was a touching letter saying what it would mean to them to be fostered. The letter was printed in the paper on 6 May 1964.

The letter read:

Dear Sir/Madam

I am writing to you, sending my views on fostering and adoption. I have read two of your articles on fostering in the Yorkshire Post, April 22nd and April 23rd, and I think it is a marvellous idea. I am a child in care and have been for 12 years. If my twin sister and I got fostered out together it would be like winning £1000 on the football pools. But money is not involved, LOVE is.

I have enclosed a poem called Lonely and Unloved just to give you a good idea of what it is like to be lonely and unloved. I did not sit down for hours on end to compose this poem, but I just wrote it down, changing only a few words to make it rhyme.

I wrote it not from my head, but from my heart, because only from the heart can the feelings of loneliness be expressed and only from the heart can the feelings of being unloved lie deep within.

To get fostered out together means to us a place of love and care and it is then that you feel wanted, because someone realises what love really is and to get fostered out is part of love itself.

We can only wait, hope and pray that we will be fostered out together, but someday I hope we will.

The poem read:

LONELY AND UNLOVED
Loneliness is to live in a world
Where people do not care.
Loneliness is to go outside,
To find no one is there, and
You fall down in despair,
Falling on your knees in prayer.
Asking God to rescue you,

From this cruel snare,
But no one comes
No voice is heard…
Unloved is to miss the love
That all parents should give.
Yet they cast you aside
Put you out of their minds.
They put you in care.
There is no love there.
Yet the staff really care
Or they wouldn't be there.
Yet I know I shall die,
As my years drag by,
Oh, why was it me, Lord?
Why?
I have trusted you so.
Clung to you close.
Each day I have prayed above,
Yet I wait for the day
When I am treated with love.
For a child's greatest joy is to
Know that they are loved.

The printed letter and poem gained the attention of a civil servant and his family, who volunteered to foster the twins at their large home in Dewsbury. But it was not to be a permanent home. A local nun who knew the girls said the arrangement broke down and the sisters were returned to care in West Yorkshire.

In September 1975, St Theresa's closed down. It is now boarding kennels. The sisters of the Holy Family of Bordeaux moved to Bradford. Sister Margaret, who was in charge of the home, recalled that the girls did not return to the nuns' care but were frequent visitors to the new home.

Certainly, Rita lived for a few months at the West Haven Hostel for Catholic girls in Huddersfield Road, Dewsbury and Helen was a regular visitor.

In March 1978, the girls turned 18, at which point local authority responsibility for them ceased. However, the social services department in Leeds continued to support Rita until the autumn because she had been awarded a place at Batley Art College; Helen had gone to work as a £20-a-week packer at a confectionery factory at Heckmondwike. The deputy director of Leeds social services Derek James told the *Telegraph & Argus*: 'I gather they had a flat after that which the society helped them find.' This flat was at 48 Granville Road, Frizinghall, Bradford about five minutes from the red-light district of Manningham Lane. It's been reported that around this time, Helen began working as a prostitute and had been warned several times by police.

For reasons that remain unknown, Rita dropped out of art school, moved out of the house she shared with her family and disappeared. After searching, Helen found her in a squalid bedsit in an Edwardian house in the northern fringes of Huddersfield close to the M62. Flat 3, 12 Elmwood Avenue, Birkby, was small and grotty, and the house's equally grotty rooms were occupied by drop outs, alcoholics and drug users. Rita had become desperately short of cash and had also started selling herself, but on the streets of Huddersfield. My suggestion is both Helen and Rita had worked the streets in Manningham, but with the mounting Ripper investigation and the ever-increasing police presence, it was becoming more and more difficult. Rita opted to go to Huddersfield in November and Helen followed in December.

Over the next few weeks, the Rytka sisters worked the Great Northern Street area, earning them the money to buy decent, fashionable clothing. Helen dreamed of becoming a soul singer.

Although he had never struck in Huddersfield, the Ripper was a constant threat. Helen and Rita developed a way of working, which although hardly foolproof, was designed to deter would-be attackers. They would accept clients at roughly the same time, give them a precise twenty minutes and afterwards they would attempt to rendezvous in the same place – the notorious block of public lavatories at the market end of Great Northern Street. As one twin got into a car, the other would take down the registration number in view of the driver, and then destroy the details once they had been returned safely.

It was a good plan. The chances of the Yorkshire Ripper attacking them would be very slim if he knew that his licence plate was recorded by a witness and would be given straight to the police if any harm should befall the woman in his car.

Tuesday, 31 January 1978 was bitterly cold; snow lay on the streets and those that worked them stamped their feet to keep their circulation going. With collars turned up and hands in pockets, the working girls shivered while waiting for their next client.

Helen and Rita Rytka left their flat at around 8.30pm to patrol their beat in the concentrated red-light area in Great Northern Street with the railway viaduct arches and timber yard. At approximately 9.10pm, Rita saw her sister safely into a dark-coloured car on the other side of the street. At the same time, Rita was picked up by a man in a Datsun.

Helen arrived back five minutes early, and it was here that she was spotted by Sutcliffe. He pulled his red Corsair up and beckoned her over. Perhaps it was his soft voice or his well-groomed appearance that made him look harmless but, for reasons unknown, he managed to persuade her to abandon her careful routine of waiting for her sister to return and convinced her that there was time to earn a quick few quid in the nearby timber yard before her sister got back. Helen accepted the offer.

She climbed into the passenger seat and the pair drove the short distance to the rear of Garrards Timber on Lower Viaduct Street. Sutcliffe planned to use his tried-and-tested method of attack – suggesting they have sex in the back seat and then attacking her from behind as she opened the backseat door. However, probably conscious of getting back to her sister quickly, she undid her trousers as soon as he turned off the engine and indicated that she was ready to begin. Unexpectedly and despite himself, Sutcliffe became aroused, and using the excuse he had to urinate, got out of the car. When he came back, she agreed to get out so they could have sex in the back of the car.

Helen got out of the passenger side and went round to the rear nearside door. Sutcliffe picked up a hammer from under his seat and walked round the front. By the time he got to her she had opened the rear door and was getting in when he swung the hammer at her head, but it caught the edge of the top of the door and diminished the impact with her skull to a mere tap.

Helen assumed he had hit her with his hand. Terrified, she jumped back and shouted, 'There is no need for that, you don't even have to pay.' Sutcliffe was surprised: he had expected her to shout for help. Instead she asked, 'What was that?' He replied, 'Just a small sample of one of these' and swung the hammer again. This time it hit her hard on the head and pushed her forward. She stumbled backwards and fell down by the front tyre moaning loudly.

He suddenly realized that what he was doing was in full view of two taxi drivers who were only 35 yards away up the right-hand side of the wood yard. Their cars were parked one behind the other facing him and the drivers were stood talking to each other.

Sutcliffe grabbed Helen by the hair and dragged her into the darkness at the rear end of the wood yard. He began stripping off her clothes and throwing them away over the wall and fence. She had stopped moaning but she wasn't dead: her eyes were open and her hands were up to ward off further blows. He got on top of her and covered her mouth with his hand. She started to struggle and he told her to keep quiet and that she would be all right.

As he was aroused he decided to have sex with her 'as the only means to keep her quiet', he would say later. She was the only one of his victims he had intercourse with.

After the taxi drivers left, Sutcliffe went back and retrieved the hammer he'd dropped by the car. Amazingly, as he did this, Helen clambered to her feet, and as Sutcliffe was turning back towards her, she tried to run past him. He hit her on the back of her head and she crumpled to the floor. He hit her a further four times. In all she suffered six lacerated wounds to the head; one in the centre of the forehead, three to the right side and two to the back.

After producing an 8-inch knife that he had taken from his kitchen, he stabbed her in the chest. Although initially there appeared to be three stab wounds in the chest area, it was apparent at the autopsy that he had thrust his knife through the same two wounds at least thirteen times, piercing the heart, lungs, aorta, liver and stomach.

Helen Rytka now lay dead in the dark timber yard, just thirty-one days shy of her nineteenth birthday.

Meanwhile, Rita had returned to the designated meeting spot by the toilets. She stayed for a while in the cold waiting for her sister, but when it became obvious she wasn't coming, she headed back to their flat in Highfields, thinking she may have taken a client back there.

By the time the morning came, Rita knew all was not well. Neither of them had ever stayed out all night with a client and Helen certainly would never have gone out so late without letting Rita know. The dilemma she faced was, should she go to the police to report Helen missing? This would be admitting to soliciting and if she did, and Helen turned up, it would be a very awkward situation.

Workmen arriving at Garrards Timber the morning after the murder noticed a bloodstained patch in the mud, and a pair of black lace knickers on the ground. These were later nailed to the door of the workmen's shed as a joke and crude reminder of the sorts of things that went on after dark in the yard.

It would be a further three days before Rita overcame her fear of the police and reported her sister missing. At 3pm on Friday, 3 February a police dog handler arrived at Garrards Timber and was greeted by foreman Melvyn Clelland who informed the officer about the blood on the ground and the underwear found by the workmen. Until the police arrived, Clelland hadn't really given it much thought as similar items, including used condoms, were discovered there all the time. He would later tell the *Telegraph & Argus*: 'It is a regular haunt for prostitutes and homosexuals. It is ideal for prostitutes because it is dark and lonely and it's unlikely they would be disturbed.'

Within ten minutes, the dog had picked up the scent and discovered the body of Helen Rytka. She had been wedged into a narrow 18-inch gap behind a pile of timber and a disused garage, next to the steep railway embankment. She had been covered with a sheet of asbestos. Her bra and black polo neck jumper had been pushed up above her breasts, but apart from her socks, all her other clothing had been removed. It was scattered over a wide area; one of her shoes was found 20 yards away.

Her blood had splattered the door of the foreman's shed and a bloodstain on the ground proved that the body must have been left lying there at some point. From here the body had been dragged into the corner and hidden from view. Curiously, the autopsy would suggest the body had lain for a considerable time before being moved – maybe overnight according to one investigator. It's a part of the murder that has so far remained a mystery.

Within a couple of hours of the body being discovered, a large piece of polythene sheeting had been hung between the wall and the stack of timber to form a makeshift tent, protecting the murder scene from rain which felt like it might turn to snow. A truckload of equipment arrived which included more sheets, privacy barriers and flood lighting. The whole yard was lit up as police, on hands and knees here and on the grassy embankments of the viaduct, set to work gathering any evidence they could.

A mobile command room was wheeled into position in the adjacent street and dozens of officers knocked on doors as the hunt for eye witnesses commenced. The area where Helen was last seen was a relatively crowded place and ACC George Oldfield was convinced that someone must have seen the killer. With this in mind he gave an optimistic interview to the press claiming he was closer than ever to finally nailing the Yorkshire Ripper.

However, the appeal for witnesses proved disappointingly unsuccessful.

Due to its location and reputation as both a red-light district and a homosexual hangout, most men who might have seen something in the Great Northern Street area were not forthcoming for obvious reasons. Eventually Oldfield was forced to make a desperate plea to the public:

'I can appreciate the reason for the reluctance of many persons who have been in that area to come forward, but it could be in their best interests for them to do so to avoid embarrassment in the future, especially if we have to make enquiries to trace them which we will be obliged to do.'

Investigators managed to track down the owner of a brown van that had been seen cruising around the area on the night of the murder. It transpired that the driver's kink in life was to follow and watch the prostitutes with their clients. He did indeed see the two sisters working the street, but to the dismay of the police, the man had decided to follow the wrong sister. Had he decided to follow Helen, he would have witnessed the murder.

In the week following the murder, snow fell on Huddersfield, muffling traffic noise and thinning out the people on the street. Each evening, as darkness fell, a small army of police officers, men and women working in pairs, descended on the red-light district. Most were in plain clothes and all kept a low profile. They kept an eye as a handful of working girls hung around in bars, cafes, and on street corners – though always under bright street lights.

Helen's face was on police posters all over the area, staring down from grimy windows and sooty brick walls.

On the morning of 9 February, ACC George Oldfield appeared on the popular *Jimmy Young* Radio 2 show. In an appeal to housewives listening in, he pointed out that someone – perhaps a wife, mother or girlfriend of the man – probably knew the Ripper's identity. He begged them to come forward if they knew anything at all, or suspected anything, in order to help prevent another murder.

In the eyes of the public, however, the time was right to take action and offer a reward for finding the killer. If someone did know who he was, or had suspicions, perhaps an offer of hard cash would produce results.

This was certainly the view of *The Yorkshire Post*, the county's influential and highly respected morning paper. However, the idea of a reward ran counter to official Home Office policy. The Home Office announced that it 'did not regard rewards as effective measures', largely because they set a precedent. There was always a danger that, in future, the public would hang back and not pass on information until the reward was large. *The Yorkshire Post* and its sister paper *The Yorkshire Evening Post* disagreed, and offered £5,000. Hard on the heels of their announcement, a public fund was established to raise extra money.

A high level committee of Yorkshire-based solicitors, doctors, businessmen, Leeds city councillors as well as a vicar and bank manager launched the 'Catch the Ripper' fund and over the next few days, collection boxes started appearing in pubs, clubs, shops and factories.

Conservative councillor Rita Verity, who was in charge of the fund with her colleague Mary Sexton, told *The Yorkshire Post*:

> 'We have formed this committee because people throughout West Yorkshire are incensed at these ripper killings. We believe somebody, somewhere knows something. They must know the identity of this mad killer and we are hoping a bit of bribery will make someone talk and reveal the Ripper's identity. Within the next few days we intend going around shops, pubs, clubs, factories and other business premises, asking the owners or managers if they will put a collection box on their counters.'

At 11am on Thursday, 9 March, Helen Rytka's funeral was held at St Thomas's Church, Huddersfield, with her sister Rita, family, friends and staff from social services in attendance. After the service, she was laid to rest in section MU of Scholemoor Cemetery, Bradford. Her grave is number fifty-one.

Today the rear of the wood yard where Helen was murdered is the yard for A.K. Spares garage. The wood piles of timber and the garages are no longer there and while the steep banks of the viaduct remain, the trees have grown to cover it from view. The small wooden fence has been replaced with metal fencing, high walls and a metal gate entry system. The days of prostitutes frequenting the yard for the purposes of business appear to be over, yet on any given night the dark archways of the viaduct and the adjacent Great Northern Street still play witness to the oldest profession in the world.

Above: 57 Cornwall Road, Bingley, where John and Kathleen Sutcliffe (top and middle) raised their family of six children including son Peter (bottom).

Right: Sutcliffe's first police mugshot in 1969, having been charged for going equipped for burglary.

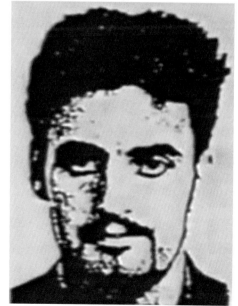

Left: Wilma McCann whose body was found on the sloping grass of Prince Philip Playing Fields in Leeds (top) and (below) the crime scene location today.

Below: Crime scene location map of the Emily Jackson murder.

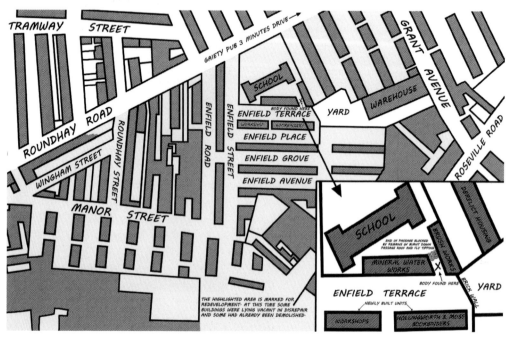

The Emily Jackson murder site in Leeds, then and now.

Peter and Sonia at home.

Photofit reconstructions of the man who attacked A) Anna Rogulskyj, B) Tracy Browne, C) Marcella Claxton D) Marilyn Moore.

O - Marks the location of the initial hammer attack, Irene was then dragged out of sight behind the sports pavilion to point - X

(Top) Irene Richardson lies lifeless on the grass in Roundhay Park, Leeds; (A) a photofit reconstruction of the clothes she was wearing on the night she died; (bottom) the murder site.

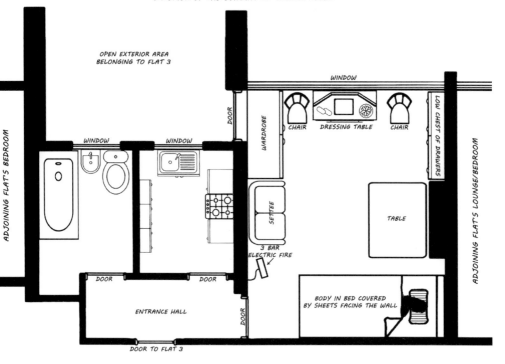

EXTERIOR OF THE BUILDING AT GROUND LEVEL

OPEN EXTERIOR AREA
BELONGING TO FLAT 3

WINDOW

DOOR

WARDROBE

CHAIR   DRESSING TABLE   CHAIR

LOW CHEST OF DRAWERS

ADJOINING FLAT'S BEDROOM

WINDOW   WINDOW

ADJOINING FLAT'S LOUNGE/BEDROOM

SETTEE

TABLE

3 BAR
ELECTRIC FIRE

DOOR   DOOR

ENTRANCE HALL

DOOR

BODY IN BED COVERED
BY SHEETS FACING THE WALL

DOOR TO FLAT 3

CORRIDOR INSIDE THE BUILDING

Above: Crime scene map of the bedsit where Patricia Atkinson was murdered.

Right: Patricia Atkinson's bedsit where she was murdered, then and the burnt-out shell it is now

Above left: The boarded-up remains of Flat 3, 9 Oak Avenue where Patricia Atkinson (inset) lived and died.

Above right: Assistant Chief Constable George Oldfield.

Below: Jayne MacDonald; (inset) the corner of the adventure playground where the 16-year-old's body was found and (right) a picnic bench marks the murder site today.

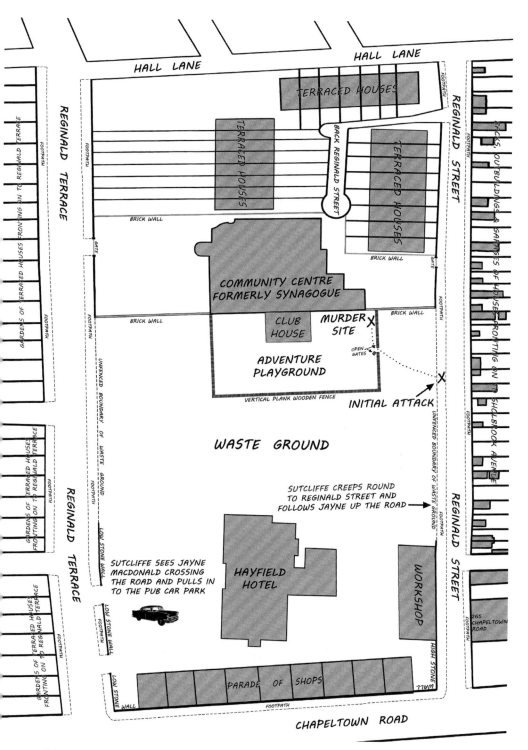

Crime scene diagram of Jayne MacDonald's murder in Leeds.

Birkshall Lane, Bradford.

Left: (a) Maureen Long; (b) the layby where Sutcliffe parked his car; (c) the Mary Street caravan site and (d) where her body was found under a discarded mattress.

Below: A crime scene examination of Jean Jordan's murder, outlining where the body was found, where it had originally been hidden and how her clothes were scattered around her.

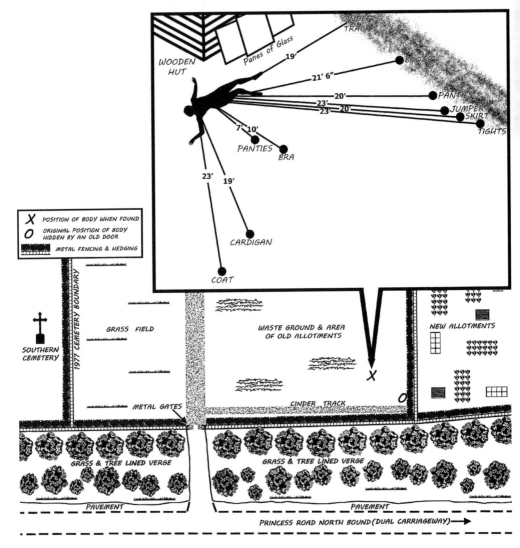

The forecourt of Luqmans Auto Repairs, Arthington Street, Bradford

Above: (a) Yvonne Pearson; (b) the building that was once Jack Andrews' garage; (c) police investigate waste ground where Yvonne's body was found hidden under a discarded sofa; X marks the location today.

Right: The body of Elena Rytka was found wedged into an 18-inch gap between a timber yard and garage wall in Huddersfield. Today it's the forecourt of A.K. Spares.

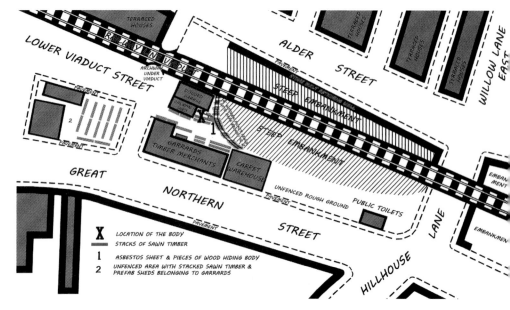

The crime scene map outlining where Elena Rytka's body was found.

When hauliers T. & W. H. Clark (Holdings) Limited hired lorry driver Peter Sutcliffe, they asked him to pose in his cab for the company's promotional calendar.

X marks the location of the Vera Millward (inset) murder site today in the heavily redeveloped Manchester Royal Infirmary. The circle indicates where the original car park compound was located.

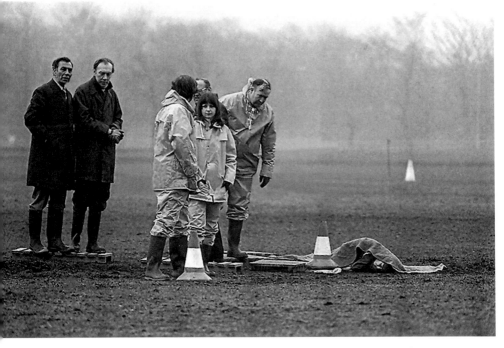

The body of Josephine Whitaker lies under a blanket in Savile Park Halifax.

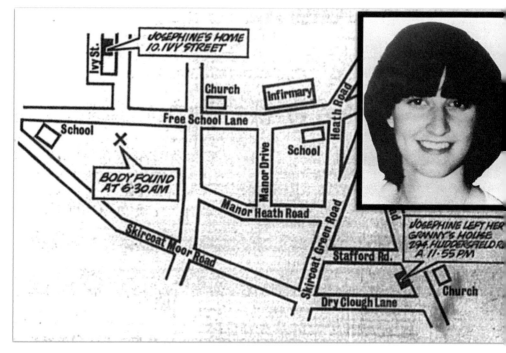

Crime scene map of where Josephine Whitaker was discovered in Savile Park Halifax.

(L-R) Dick Holland, George Oldfield and Jack Ridgeway playing the 'I'm Jack' tape at a press conference.

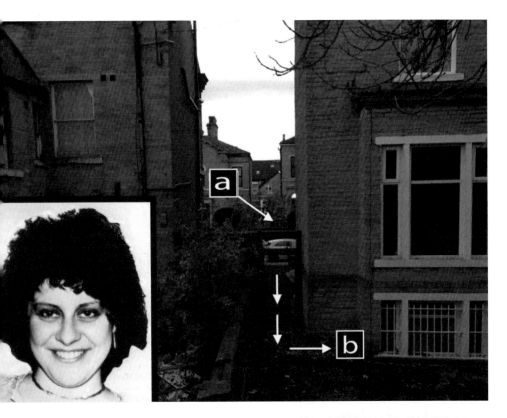

Above: Barbara Leach (inset) was attacked as she walked along Ash Grove (a), dragged to the rear of number 13 Back Ash Grove, murdered then wedged into a bin recess area (b).

Right: The dustbin recess area at the rear of 13 Ash Grove, where Barbara Leach's body was discovered hidden under a piece of carpet.

IMPORTANT NOTICE TO STUDENTS AND STAFF

The recent tragic death of a Bradford student by the notorious 'Ripper' murderer has caused alarm to many students and their families and the warnings issued by the Chief Constable Mr. Ronald Gregory on telelvision and in the press should be taken more seriously.

We feel that our students are both sensible and responsible people and that they will observe certain simple precautions to ensure the safety of women students on the Campus.

1) Women students are strongly advised **not to go out alone during the hours of darkness.**
   Remember the saying 'There is safety in numbers'. It is worth the time and trouble to accompany your friend.

2) After late-night disco's walk home with a group of friends.

3) Don't take lifts from strangers.

Above all—
DON'T PUT YOURSELF AT RISK!

Issued by Bradford College Students' Union and Bradford College

In the wake of Barbara Leach's murder, Bradford University distributed warning notices to all students living on campus or in surrounding areas.

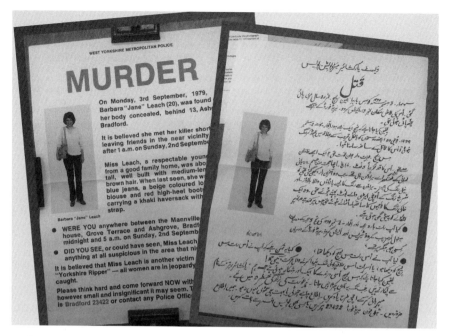

WEST YORKSHIRE METROPOLITAN POLICE

MURDER

On Monday, 3rd September, 1979, Barbara "Jane" Leach (20), was found her body concealed, behind 13, Ash Bradford.

It is believed she met her killer shor leaving friends in the near vicinity after 1 a.m. on Sunday, 2nd Septemb

Miss Leach, a respectable youn from a good family home, was abo tall, well built with medium-len brown hair. When last seen, she w blue jeans, a beige coloured lo blouse and red high-heel boot carrying a khaki haversack with strap.

Barbara "Jane" Leach

● WERE YOU anywhere between the Mannville house, Grove Terrace and Ashgrove, Bradf midnight and 5 a.m. on Sunday, 2nd Septemb

● DID YOU SEE, or could have seen, Miss Leach anything at all suspicious in the area that ni

It is believed that Miss Leach is another victim "Yorkshire Ripper" — all women are in jeopardy caught.

Please think hard and come forward NOW with however small and insignificant it may seem. T is Bradford 23422 or contact any Police Offic

Following Barbara Leach's murder, thousands of posters were distributed asking for help from the public. Appeal notices were also printed in Urdu to appeal to Bradford's large Asian community.

The redeveloped Grounds of Claremont Gardens, Farsley, Leeds

The body of Marguerite Walls was discovered stripped and partially covered with grass cuttings just off New Street, Farsley, in the grounds of Claremont House.

Above: Jacqueline Hill who was discovered on waste ground at the back of the Arndale Centre in Leeds. Today the area is a fenced-off staff car park.

Below: Jim Hobson (left) and Ronald Gregory (right) roll out the massive publicity campaign aimed at catching the Ripper. However, their focus on the hoax letters and tape would allow the Ripper to remain free.

HELP US STOP THE RIPPER FROM KILLING AGAIN.

LOOK AT HIS HANDWRITING.

I have already written concerning the recent
Ripper murders. I told him and
I am telling you to warn them I'll strike
again and soon when heat cools off.

LISTEN TO HIS VOICE.

PHONE LEEDS (0532) 464111.

IF YOU RECOGNISE EITHER REPORT IT TO YOUR LOCAL POLICE.

One of the posters that appeared on billboards nationwide as part of the huge publicity campaign to apprehend the Ripper.

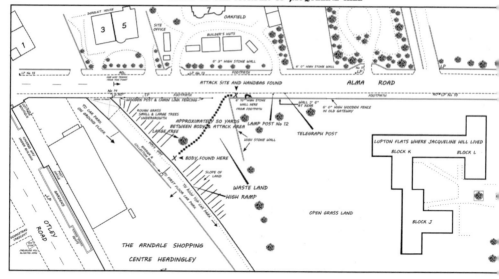

Detailed crime scene map of the Jacqueline Hill murder, showing the initial attack on the street and how her body was dragged into the undergrowth behind the Arndale Centre in Leeds.

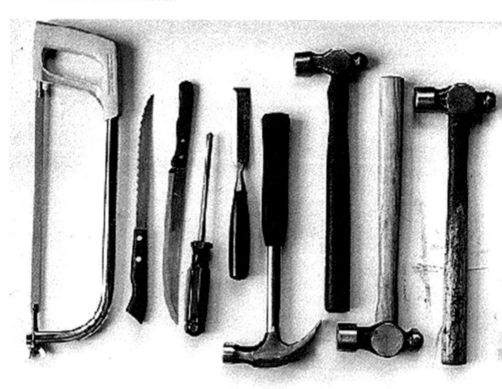

A gruesome display of tools used in the Yorkshire Ripper's reign of terror.

The driveway of Light Trades House at 3 Melbourne Avenue, Sheffield. Sutcliffe was discovered here with his next intended victim, Olivia Reivers (inset).

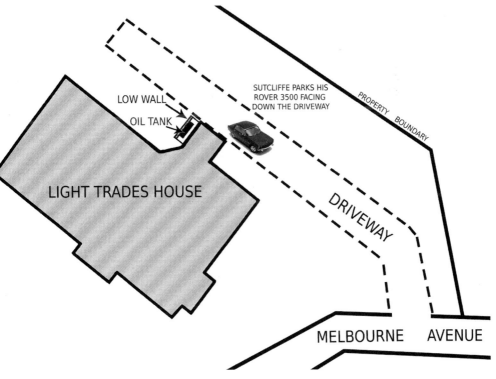

Crime scene diagram showing where Sutcliffe's car was parked when he was finally arrested in Sheffield. Officers would later discover a hammer and a knife behind the oil tank at the rear of Light Trades house.

Above: The brown Rover 3500 V8 Sutcliffe was driving when he was arrested in Sheffield.

Left: Peter Sutcliffe arriving at Dewsbury Court, having finally been arrested in 1981.

Above: Police Sergeant Robert Ring (left) and Probationary Constable Robert Hydes (right) were commended for bringing the Yorkshire Ripper to justice.

Below: A jubilant George Oldfield, Ronald Gregory and Jim Hobson following Sutcliffe's arrest.

Left: Sutcliffe arriving at the Old Bailey in London.

Below: Sutcliffe explaining his 'mission from God' to a packed courtroom at the Old Bailey.

15 Halstead Square on Sunderland's Hylton Lane Estate. It was here that 23-year-old John Humble recorded the infamous 'I'm Jack' tape.

Police standing guard outside Sutcliffe's home, 6 Garden Lane, Heaton, Bradford.

The known murder victims and survivors of the Yorkshire Ripper's five-year reign of terror.

CHAPTER 14

Vera Millward

'There were three screams – each just the one word: "Help!"
Then silence.'

Witness in the grounds of Manchester Royal Infirmary

On 8.15am, Wednesday, 17 May 1978, two yellow work vans belonging to a Rochdale landscaping firm, arrived in the grounds of Manchester Royal Infirmary. A team of six gardeners, hired to maintain the grass and flowerbeds, parked in the corner of a bricked compound near the junction of April Street and Livingstone Street close to the private wing of the infirmary.

As he exited the van, one of the gardeners, Jim McGuigan, noticed what looked like a discarded doll or mannequin lying against a wire fence, which was a temporary barrier where part of the wall had collapsed. As he drew closer, he recoiled with horror. The 'doll' was a slightly built woman, whose head had been smashed in and whose body had been mutilated by stab wounds. A passing nurse, who saw the men huddled round the body, came to investigate. She saw the woman's corpse and a doctor was immediately summoned from the nearby infirmary. He confirmed that she was dead.

Three-and-a-half months after the murder of Helen Rytka, the Yorkshire Ripper killed his last prostitute. Her name was Vera Millward.

Born in Madrid during the Spanish Civil War and brought up during the lean years of the Second World War, Vera Evelyn Millward arrived in Britain during the 1950s as a domestic servant. She married soon after and had five children. But by the 1960s, when the youngest child was 15, her husband died and the children under 18 were taken into care. In desperation, Vera turned to prostitution – gravitating to the seedier areas of Hulme and Moss Side in Manchester's notorious red-light district.

The 40 year old went under the aliases of Anne Brown and Mary Barton. Despite this, she did not avoid the long arm of the law and by the time of her death, had racked up several convictions for soliciting.

By 1978 she was living with her common-law husband, a 49-year-old Jamaican called Cy Burkett, in a ground-floor flat in Grenham Avenue, Hulme – not far from the home of Ripper victim Jean Jordan. The couple had two children, a boy aged 6 and a girl aged 8.

In constant pain from a stomach ailment and weighing less than eight-and-a-half stone, Vera's face was prematurely lined with suffering. She had only one lung and had undergone three operations in 1976, 1977 and May 1978. A desperately ill woman, she ignored police warnings and, for the sake of her children, regularly joined the 400 prostitutes who made their living on the streets in Manchester, loathing every minute of what she was forced to do for money.

It was common knowledge that the women who worked the back streets and alleyways around Moss Lane and Denmark Road in Moss Side, would take their clients to one of two discreet places. It was either a patch of ground next to the Southern Cemetery and allotments, where Scotch Jean Jordan was murdered, or a section of waste ground near the grass and flowerbeds of the car park at Manchester's Royal infirmary. Both afforded the women and their clients privacy from public eyes.

On Tuesday, 16 May, Vera left her home at around 10pm, telling her boyfriend that she was going out to buy some cigarettes and pop to the chemist to buy some drugs for her stomach pains. Knowing what she really meant, he did not expect to see her for a few hours.

The truth was on Tuesdays and Thursdays she had a regular client who would park outside her flat and flash his headlights. This one was well-to-do and drove a 1963 maroon Mercedes. For about five years he had been meeting Vera every week – 'Just for a chat', he would later tell police – and would give her small gifts of food and money.

Popping into the local shop, she bought two packets of Benson and Hedges and went to wait on the corner of the street for her regular. That particular Tuesday, however, he didn't turn up. Vera decided to hang around for other business.

Unfortunately, that night the Yorkshire Ripper had decided to try his luck once again in Manchester.

Leeds was considered too hot with the ongoing car checks carried out by investigators and Bradford was far too heavily policed, especially since Yvonne Pearson's broken body had been discovered on waste ground in Bradford two months ago.

It had been seven months since Sutcliffe had last struck in Manchester and he felt it was safe to pay it another visit. Later he would recall his movements when he arrived in the area in his red Corsair:

> 'When I got there, there was no sign of any girls, so after reaching a nightclub on a corner in a small labyrinth of terraced houses about three-quarter-mile square, I took the third left after the nightclub, which was a long street running from one end to the other of this area. I drove down to the bottom end and there I saw a woman obviously waiting to be picked up… . I stopped and asked her if she was doing business. She said yes, but it would have to be in the car. The price was five pounds. She got in and I drove off.'

They made their way along Upper Brook Street, took a right onto Hathersage Road and another right which took them into Livingstone Street and the grounds of the Royal Infirmary. It was a familiar route used by many of the prostitutes. As they approached the junction of April Street, there was an opening in the wire mesh fence which formed the perimeter of a section of waste ground that was used as a car park, just behind the private patients' wing. He drove through the gap, took a sharp right then reversed the car until his bonnet was pointing towards the exit, ready for a quick getaway.

What took place in the car is unknown, but at some point Sutcliffe suggested they move into the back seat; a now familiar method of catching his victim unawares.

What is known is Vera left the car and went to the back door. Sutcliffe retrieved a hammer from under his seat, walked round the back of the car and positioned himself behind the unsuspecting woman. As she was opening the rear door he struck her on the back of the head, and she fell backwards. She scrambled on her hands and knees, moaning loudly, when he hit her again at least once.

She may have let out a series of screams during the attack. A man who was taking his young son to the Royal Infirmary heard what he would later assume were Vera Millward's dying screams. 'There were three screams – each just the one word: "Help!" Then silence,' he would tell police. Apparently, no one else heard them.

Sadly, this lone witness decided they were probably from a patient having a nightmare in the nearby hospital, ignored it and carried on his business. One of the investigating detectives would later remark: 'The trouble with this whole area is that screaming in the night is not unusual.'

Vera was flat on her face and unconscious. Sutcliffe dragged her by her wrists about 12ft to the fence and in the darkness began mutilating her. After he was done, he left her on top of a pile of rubbish by the fence in the corner of the car park.

When Vera was found the next morning, she was lying on her right side, face down, arms folded beneath her, and her legs were straight. Her face was covered by a large paper sheet.

Like the murder of Irene Richardson, her blue and brown reversible checked coat had been draped over her body and now covered her from knees to neck. Her blue canvas wedge-heeled shoes had been placed neatly on her body. The heavy hammer blows to the skull created three savage wounds and caused many fractures, including a laceration of the brain.

Vera's blue cardigan, floral-patterned, yellow, sleeveless dress and underskirt had been raised to expose the abdomen and she had been slashed so viciously across the stomach several times that her intestines had spilled out of the wounds and onto the ground.

Her white bra was still in place, and she been stabbed in the chest repeatedly, cutting through to her ribs and penetrating the left lung, liver and stomach. The weapon had been thrust into the wound three times in different directions without being withdrawn completely. A similar multiple wound was located on her back; her right eyelid had been punctured and the eye bruised.

Taking charge of the investigation on the ground was DCS Jack Ridgeway, head of the Greater Manchester Central Crime Area. At first, he was determined to keep an open mind about the killing, but within a few hours investigators had confirmed that they were dealing with another Yorkshire Ripper murder.

What stunned investigators was that the killer had taken greater risks than ever before. The site of the murder was very public, with 800 patients and staff in the surrounding hospital buildings. The whole area was floodlit and the car parks nearby were in constant use by hospital visitors, as well as prostitutes and their clients.

Police were fortunate to find and cast the impressions made by all four tyres of the suspect vehicle. From these casts and the measurements obtained, scientists at the North Western Forensic Science Laboratory were able to assemble a list of only eleven vehicles within the suspect range. One of these was the Ford Corsair that the murderer was eventually known to be using at the time of the attack.

The tyre tracks, with their common denominators of India Autoway crossply tyres with a track width of 4ins 2cm, were consistent with those found at the Irene Richardson murder scene and the Marilyn Moore attack scene. This, coupled with the injuries the victim received, was convincing evidence that the Yorkshire Ripper had crossed the Pennines again and killed in Manchester for the second time.

Once more ACC George Oldfield was frustrated about the lack of public cooperation, suggesting that resentment of a prostitute's way of life could well be the reason. He summed up the public attitude as thus: 'Why should we be concerned? They chose to lead this kind of life, so they must face up to the risks that go with it.'

The murder of Vera Millward would be not only the last known attack by Sutcliffe in 1978 but also the last murder or attack on a prostitute. The known attacks would not resume until April 1979. I suspect there was a lull because he didn't feel safe in his usual stomping grounds. Activity in Chapeltown in Leeds was heavily monitored. However, the number of unmarked cars containing plain clothes policemen and women pretending to be preoccupied with each other didn't fool the streetwalkers, so it's unlikely the kerb crawlers missed their presence either.

Lumb Lane in Bradford also became the focus of a heavy police presence. Helen Rytka had been killed in Huddersfield but that is a relatively small and easily policed town, so Vera Millward was struck in Manchester. And now the police were monitoring that city too.

Additionally, police were collecting car registration plates, and these had been fed back to the national vehicle registration computer so repeat visitors to the red-light areas in Leeds, Bradford, Huddersfield and Manchester could be checked out

Sutcliffe's red Ford Corsair had been seen in these places repeatedly and he now received a visit at home from a detective. Luckily, he had an acceptable excuse for driving through these areas – his work took him to various places and Chapeltown and Lumb Lane were both on his route home. Nevertheless, the questioning seemed to scare him.

Another reason for the hiatus was due to his mother becoming gravely ill. He was close to her bedside during the final six months of her life and Sutcliffe was torn up with grief for five months following her death.

When his grief had passed and he eventually returned to the streets, his killings would take on an even more sinister pattern (and be similar to his earliest attacks). The victims would not be prostitutes, or even women who were in or near red-light areas. He would not try to pick them up in his car, nor – other than the first in this new series – would he engage them in conversation. No woman was safe.

On 13 August 1978, police knocked for a third time on Sutcliffe's door. Officers had been staking out the red-light districts noting down car numbers and Sutcliffe's red Ford Corsair had been spotted seven times in Bradford. The interviewing officer was Detective Constable (DC) Peter Smith. DC Smith found Sutcliffe in overalls decorating the kitchen and he did not seem to mind the interruption. Without revealing that the police were conducting the secret monitoring of vehicles in the red-light districts, DC Smith enquired generally about Sutcliffe's movements. Sutcliffe would later say: 'I told him I couldn't say exactly what I'd been doing, but that I had to drive that way to work and back.' Asked whether he used prostitutes, Sutcliffe said he didn't.

Sonia, who was also there, backed up her husband and said he rarely went out at night and when he did she was usually with him. She also said that they had been at Rockerfellers, a discotheque in Leeds on the night of one of the murders. Both Sutcliffe and his wife had difficulty remembering what they did on the weekend of 16 and 17 May when Vera Millward was murdered, but Sonia believed her husband would have been home all evening.

DC Smith did not check the tyres on Sutcliffe's red Ford Corsair, nor was he aware that Sutcliffe had recently purchased a black Sunbeam Rapier, which had already been spotted nine times in the Manningham red-light district.

Three months later on 23 November 1978, DC Smith made a return visit to give Sutcliffe his fourth police interview, this time enquiring about Sutcliffe's banking arrangements and about his vehicles. Unfortunately, Sutcliffe's purchase of the black Sunbeam Rapier had eventually resulted in the sale of the red Ford Corsair. Smith would later visit the new owner of the car to check the tyres, but by then the tyres had been replaced.

Today the site of Vera Millward's murder has been lost with the changes that have taken place to Manchester Royal Infirmary in the last forty years. April Street and Livingstone Street no longer exist, but the footprint of the waste ground that was used as a car park where her body was discovered can still be made out by using old maps and layouts of the area. With help from fellow researchers, Chris Routh and Dean Garth, it was possible for me to pinpoint as close as possible where the crime took place.

The waste ground has been built on and the children's unit is now there. Behind it you can see the recently built Harrington Buildings which have replaced the private infirmary block that once overlooked the murder site. The spot where Vera Millward met her death is now a private recreational area where children play, blissfully ignorant of the terrible events of the past.

CHAPTER 15

Josephine Whitaker

'You don't know who you can trust these days.'

Peter Sutcliffe

On the night of 4 April 1979, Sutcliffe ventured out to the streets once more. It had been forty-six weeks since his last kill. The pervasive police presence in the well-known red-light areas of Bradford, Leeds and even Manchester, had caused him to go further afield in search of his next victim. These new tactics were to cause near-panic throughout West Yorkshire as people realized that any woman, not just prostitutes, was at considerable risk every time they went out at night.

Sutcliffe had spent the earlier part of the night drinking with Trevor Birdsall in the bars around Bradford and shortly after closing time, he dropped Trevor off at his home. However, instead of heading to his own home, Sutcliffe went in the opposite direction, towards the neighbouring town of Halifax.

A place of steep, cobbled streets, mills and carpet factories, Halifax had no red-light district and no reputation for prostitution, thus police presence was low and allowed him plenty of freedom to cruise the streets unnoticed.

By 11.30pm, Sutcliffe had made the thirty-minute journey over the hills in his sporty Sunbeam Rapier and arrived into the town centre, down past the Bull's Head pub and up past the main office building of the Halifax Building Society. He drove slowly around the district of Bell Hall and gravitated towards the playing fields of Savile Park. This was a public park, which had been converted from farmland in the 1870s. It was lined on all sides by substantial Victorian residences in yellow sandstone, blackened by years of pollution. It was the 'posh' end of town, a place of sturdy stone villas and cottages standing in neat rows around the elegant, tree-lined roads that crisscross the open park and its series of playing fields.

Although not the usual place for a serial killer to be lurking around, Sutcliffe wouldn't be the first to visit. In 1913, 14-year-old

Halifax-born John Reginald Halliday Christie would be having his personality shaped by the events and circumstances of his childhood in and around Savile Park.

As an awkward teenager, he had attempted to seduce a girl in the park but, although they kissed and cuddled, she told friends he was 'slow'. They laughed at him and called him nicknames such as 'Reggie-No-Dick' and 'Can't-Do-It-Christie'. These taunts would haunt him throughout his life and Christie, a regular visitor of prostitutes, would go on to murder eight women, including a number of prostitutes and his wife, Ethel, at his London home, 10 Rillington Place.

It was grimly ironic that Sutcliffe was now in Christie's teenage stomping ground and waiting to claim his tenth victim.

For 19-year-old Josephine 'Jo' Whitaker, fate would play a cruel hand in the events of that night. The Halifax Building Society clerk had left her home at 10 Ivy Street, only 250 yards from Savile Park, where she lived with her mother, Avril Hiley, stepfather Hayden Hiley and two younger brothers, David and Michael. She took a fifteen-minute walk to visit her grandparents, Tom and Mary Priestley, at their home at 294 Huddersfield Road. She was eager to show them a new silver cocktail watch for which she had just paid £60 from a mail order firm. When she arrived, she found her grandfather watching TV but her grandmother was out at a church function. Jo waited patiently with her grandfather and after her grandmother returned home and she showed her the watch she said she'd walk back home.

Her grandparents were reluctant to let her walk back in the dark and offered her a bed for the night, but the pretty teenager refused. She had to get home, she said, because she was wearing her contact lenses and wanted to clean them before putting them away in their special case. The case in question was sitting on her bedside table at home.

Tom Priestley had been suffering from a chest complaint, so when he offered to walk Jo home she declined the offer, knowing that his condition would be aggravated by the walk. Besides, she was a healthy girl, 5ft 8in tall and was not afraid of the dark. And this was Halifax, which was not part of the Ripper territory.

She left around 11.40 pm and started on the route that would take her across Savile Park. Although her parents had always advised her to stick to the longer route along well-lit Main Street, she opted for the short cut, walking across the park's dark sports' pitches towards Free School Lane and the suburb of Bell Hall, Halifax, and then onto Ivy Street. It was a route she was familiar with and it would slice a few minutes off her journey.

Meanwhile Sutcliffe, who was circling the park in his car, caught a glimpse of Jo making her way home. She was wearing a skirt, with a multi-coloured pattern on a black background and white lace trimming, a pink jumper, a light brown checked hacking jacket and brown heeled shoes. He knew she wasn't a prostitute but he had made up his mind. Parking up, he retrieved a ball-pein hammer from under his seat and a large Philips screwdriver, specially adapted and sharpened so it resembled a bradawl. During Sutcliffe's eventual trial, the prosecution would describe it as 'done in a way to make it what you may think is one of the most fiendish weapons you have ever seen.'

He quickened his pace and within a few minutes had caught up with the unsuspecting girl. Unlike Jayne MacDonald, he didn't strike her right away but started a conversation. He asked her if she had far to go and she said, 'It's quite a walk.'

The pair continued along the road and all the while Sutcliffe waited for his moment to strike. His short height and high, weedy voice had probably reassured Jo and she started to converse with him. She told him she'd just left her grandparents' house and that she had considered staying there but had decided to walk home. As they talked, she and Sutcliffe made their way along the street that bordered the park where they were spotted by a man out walking his dog. It was here Jo mentioned that she normally took a short cut across the field. Sutcliffe replied saying: 'You don't know who you can trust these days.'

They left the well-lit street and journeyed into the darkness of Savile Park. They continued their conversation as they cut diagonally across the grass.

Around 30 to 40 yards away from the main road and with Ivy Street in sight, Sutcliffe made his move. He asked her what time it was on the clock tower located to their right. She looked over at the clock and when she relayed it back, he said, 'You must have good eyesight.' He lagged behind her, pretending to look closer at the clock but pulled out the hammer that had been concealed in his jacket and stepping forward quickly, struck her on the head. She stumbled, and he struck her again, fracturing her skull from ear to ear and causing her to crumple to the ground, where she lay groaning loudly. He looked round and spotted a figure in the near distance walking along the main road. The man, who had been walking home, would later claim to have 'heard a strange noise, a wail, the sort that makes your hair stand on end.' Sadly, despite hearing this noise more than once, he continued on his way, oblivious to the fact the Yorkshire Ripper was committing another murder less than 30 yards away.

Sutcliffe took hold of Jo by the ankles and dragged her face down away from the road and further into the park. When he thought it was a safe distance from the road, he stopped. Then he heard voices from somewhere behind him to his left. At least two people were walking along the path across the park towards Huddersfield Road.

Jo was still moaning loudly. To shut her up, Sutcliffe pulled out the sharpened screwdriver, pulled some of her clothing off and, in a frenzy, stabbed her repeatedly in the chest and stomach. She would have twenty-one stab wounds to the trunk, with further multiple stab wounds to the back and six wounds to the right leg. He also stabbed her several times in the vagina, with some of the thrusts showing signs of reinsertion through the same wound. This had been carefully and methodically done, in the dark, with almost no injury to the external parts of the vagina

When he'd finished, he left her face down in the wet grass and double backed the way he had come, back to his car and made a quick getaway to Bradford.

It would be a further five hours before anyone in the Bell Hall suburb would learn about the murder on their doorstep. At 5.30am, the first bus of the day arrived on Free School Lane, driven by Ronald Marwood. As he passed Savile Park, he saw what he thought was a curious bundle of rags lying on the grass. Having no time to get off the bus and investigate, he waited until he was back at the depot before reporting it to his supervisor, but it wasn't considered important enough to contact the police. It wouldn't be until 7.20am that the police would phone the depot and tell them to move the bus stop at Savile Park Road away from the crime scene. Only then did they realize that Ronald Marwood's report about the bundle of rags was, in fact, the body of Josephine Whitaker.

At 6.30am, Jean Markham made her way to work along Savile Park Road. She arrived at the bus stop and waited patiently. However, as she stood there, her eyes became fixed on a mound directly opposite her, about 50 to 60 yards further into the park. Out of curiosity she crossed the road and, as she got closer, noticed a woman's shoe lying on the grass. She then realized a young woman was lying on the ground. She went up to her and after seeing she was dead, ran back to her home to alert the authorities.

The woman's near-hysterical 999 call brought the wailing of police sirens from the town centre to the once peaceful Savile Park. When the first officers arrived on the scene, they didn't think for a minute that Jo had been a victim of the Yorkshire Ripper. It was suggested that she had been a victim of a hit-and-run accident out on the road, and had crawled to where she was found.

However, it wasn't long before ACC George Oldfield arrived on the scene. Not far behind was Detective Superintendent (DSI) Dick Holland and, arriving later from Manchester was DCS Jack Ridgeway, by now a familiar face to his West Yorkshire colleagues.

Together they looked down with anger and sadness at the body at their feet. They knew right away that this was no car accident, and they didn't need to wait for confirmation from the post mortem. As her clothes were moved to reveal the front of her body, the frenzy of stab wounds and battered skull made it very clear indeed that after a forty-six-week lull, the Yorkshire Ripper had returned. He had now gained himself the grisly distinction of doubling the 'score' of his Whitechapel namesake of 1888.

Some 250 yards away in the Whitaker family home, nobody had noticed that Jo had not returned from her grandparents the previous night. Her 13-year-old brother David had been the first up that morning and had nipped over to the shop for his newspaper run. He was returning across the playing fields when he saw the police activity and saw the shoe that he recognized as belonging to his sister. He ran home to tell his mother and stepfather. After checking her room, finding it empty, and distraught with fear and grief, they called the police.

The Yorkshire Ripper story was now international news. The fact that the killer was no longer selecting his victims from the red-light districts sent shockwaves through Britain, in particular West Yorkshire. A tired and sullen-looking George Oldfield went before the cameras to confirm what they all feared, that no woman was safe. He said:

> 'We have a homicidal maniac at large and I believe he lives in the West Yorkshire area. This man will continue to kill until he is caught. We cannot stress how careful every woman must be. Unless we catch him, he will go on, and on... . The man is obviously mentally deranged, but has now changed his pattern. The girl was perfectly respectable, in an open space and legitimately going about her business. We always felt he would strike again, but we are now faced with a new situation.'

'The dead girl', he announced 'was badly beaten about the head and suffered injuries to the body.' Pressed for further details, he remained tight-lipped. West Yorkshire Police had, from the start, pursued a policy of secrecy about the extent and nature of the

Ripper's mutilations, fearful of carbon-copy attacks and the time-wasting business of checking out false confessions

Jo Whitaker was the first 'non-prostitute' murdered since Jayne Macdonald and she was described by George Oldfield as an 'innocent victim' (a clumsy choice of words: weren't the prostitutes also innocent victims?). The parents of Jayne MacDonald broke their two-year silence to comment on this new and most ghastly murder.

At their home in Leeds, a broken Irene and Wilfred MacDonald pleaded: 'If anyone has any suspicions, please come forward. How many more must die before people wake up and realize it could happen to someone they love?'

Wilfred went on to say that he would always remember his daughter Jayne kissing him on the head and leaving the family home the night she died. He also revealed the horror of having to identify her body. He said:

> 'It was her hair, I can't get it out of my mind. It had looked so blonde and soft a few hours before, and now it was hard and caked with blood. I have been suffering from asthma ever since. I beg anyone who might be able to offer any shred of help which might lead to the Ripper's capture to remember the way I felt when I looked down upon my darling that morning. Let them try to imagine my hell and for God's sake let them not remain silent a second longer.'

Jayne's mother, Irene, spoke of the torture the family had been put through:

> 'No one can ever know what it is like when your child is murdered. I wept when I heard about Josephine Whitaker. For those they left behind there will never be peace again. A murder doesn't just end with the victim. It spreads hideous ripples throughout a family. In a way it kills them all.'

Wilfred MacDonald died six months later.

Today Savile Park remains very much the same as it did in 1979. The Edwardian houses still line the perimeter of the playing fields, making it relatively easy to locate the crime scene. The bus stop at the junction of Savile Park Street and Free School Lane, where Jean Markham was standing when she first noticed the body, is in the same place as it was almost forty years ago. There is no marker or memorial to Josephine Whitaker. There is, however, a small metal bench, directly across from the bus stop, which looks out to where her body would have been. It wouldn't be too much trouble for the council to replace it with a more fitting memorial to this murdered woman.

It would be over a month before Jo was finally laid to rest in the grounds of All Saints Church Yard in Halifax. Her grave is number 112a of section five, the same plot as her great grandparents, Henry and Susey Priestley. Both died in the late 1940s and never met her.

Further down Free School Lane, at the junction off Savile Park Road is St Jude's Church. This is where Jo was christened and where her memorial service would be held, attended by over 600 people. The chairman of Halifax Building Society read the lesson, while detectives mingled with the mourners. The service was conducted by the Reverend Michael Walker. He said: 'This tragedy has made many conscious of the devotion to duty of our police. This service would be inadequate without my expressing the town's appreciation of the police and the town's prayers that their efforts might soon affect the murderer's arrest.'

He asked the congregation to remember Josephine in their prayers as well as her family, neighbours and colleagues at work, and the police who bore such a burden of responsibility.

Surprisingly, he also asked for prayers for the murderer too: 'He needs help. He is someone's child, husband or father. Pray not only for Josephine and her family but for the Ripper and his family, they may be unwittingly protecting him.'

A sense of shock stayed with the community as many struggled to come to terms with such a terrible deed happening in their neighbourhood. They mourned not just for Josephine but for themselves. Their quiet area of Halifax, like so many others across West Yorkshire, would now be haunted by the dark shadow of the Ripper.

Fortunately, the latest murder, as gruesome as it was, did offer police three important clues that, if put together with all the other evidence, could lead the investigators in the right direction.

Boot prints had been found beside Jo's body that were consistent with those found at the Emily Jackson and Tina Atkinson murders. The prints looked like they were from moulded rubber or composition soles, found most often in industrial protective or Army-type boots. The sole impressions indicated a size 7, but the police established that anyone with a shoe size of up to 8½ could comfortably wear the boots. The right sole showed some wear and twisting in the centre, possibly from the wearer regularly pressing some sort of pedal with his right foot. This suggested that the killer could be a lorry driver.

Josephine Whitaker's wounds also contained traces of milling oil and metal particles. The oil was commonly used in engineering shops and, with the metal particles and the boot prints, this made the police think the killer might be a skilled machine tool-fitter, an electrical or maintenance engineer, or a skilled or semi-skilled worker with engineering or mechanical connections.

There were also curious marks on Jo's left breast. Detectives kept an open mind about what caused them. They could have been scratched by the killer's fingernails as he carried out his customary act of pulling his victim's bra upwards, or by the V-shaped wedge of a claw hammer, as seen in the killing of Tina Atkinson. Another suggestion was that they were bite marks that showed the perpetrator had a gap between his two upper front teeth. Sutcliffe had such a gap in his front teeth.

The public responded instantaneously to Oldfield's appeals for help. When the victim had been a prostitute, it was difficult to get people to talk or admit they were in the area, but now that a 'respectable' and 'innocent' woman had been butchered, the public were more forthcoming. Details were circulated of a number of cars seen in the area around the time of the attack, along with the photofit of a man reported kerb-crawling in Halifax that night. He was described as being 'of scruffy appearance, with a Jason King-style moustache and square-shaped face and jaw'. After being shown the photofit, surviving Ripper victim Marilyn Moore claimed to recognize the 'Dave' whom she had also described as having a Jason King-style moustache when he attacked her in Chapeltown just before Christmas 1977.

Surely once the police had cross-referenced all those men who worked in the lorry-driving business with those who had a size 7 to 8 shoe, then cross-referenced them with the computer checks on kerb-crawling cars and the recipients of notes from the batch of new five pound notes, which included the one that ended up in murdered Jean Jordan's handbag, Sutcliffe's name would have stood out among the 8,000 investigated. Closer enquiries would have revealed not only his likeness to the photofits but also his previous car with the give-away India Autoway crossply tyres on the front wheels, the impressions of which were found in tracks left by the murderer at more than one crime scene.

Sutcliffe would have become the number one suspect and perhaps the case could have been wrapped up pretty quickly following Jo Whitaker's murder. But, unbelievably, the case was about to take an unexpected turn, leaving Sutcliffe off the hook for another two years.

CHAPTER 16

I'm Jack

'I have the greatest respect for you George, but Lord, you are no nearer to catching me now than four years ago when I started.'

Wearside Jack

Perhaps the most well-known story in the Yorkshire Ripper case involves the hunt for the character known as Wearside Jack, the man behind the infamous 'I'm Jack' hoax tape. His involvement in the case, and the media sensation it created, would divert the entire police investigation away from West Yorkshire and indirectly lead to Sutcliffe remaining free to kill three more women. It would tarnish the reputation of all the leading officers involved and would change the way murder investigations were handled in the UK.

Early in 1978, and unknown to the public, West Yorkshire Police had started receiving mocking letters claiming to be from the killer himself. Each letter had been sent from Sunderland, near Newcastle upon Tyne, about 90 miles north east of the Ripper's hunting ground. Each one had been signed Jack the Ripper.

Five weeks after Helen Rytka's death, ACC George Oldfield received the first of these letters. It was posted from Sunderland on 8 March 1978. Here is the letter as it was written:

Dear Sir,

I am sorry I cannot give my name for obvious reasons I am the ripper. Ive been dubbed a maniac by the press but not by you You call me clever and I am. You and your mates haven't a clue that photo in the paper gave me fits and that bit about killing myself no chance Ive got things to do, My purpose to rid the streets of them sluts. my one regret his that young lassie Macdonald did not know cause changed routine that nite, Up to number 8 now you say 7 but remember Preston 75, Get about you know, you were right I travel a bit You probably look for me in Sunderland don't bother I am not daft just posted letter there on one of my trips. Not a bad place compared with Chapeltown and Manningham and other places

Warn whores to keep of streets cause I feel it coming on again. Sorry about young lassie.

Yours respectfully
Jack the Ripper

Might write again later I not sure last one really deserved it. Whores getting younger each time. Old slut next time I hope, Huddersfield never again too small close call last one.

Within a week, a second letter arrived, this time addressed to the editor of the *Daily Mirror*'s northern editions in Manchester. Here is the letter as it was written:

Dear Sir,

I have already written Chief Constable Oldfield 'a man I respect' concerning the recent Ripper murders. I told him and I am telling you to warn them whores I'll strike again and soon when heat cools off. About the Macdonald lassie, I didnt know that she was decent and I am sorry I changed my routine that night, Up to murder 8 now You say 7 but remember Preston 75. Easy picking them up don't even have to try, you think theyre learn but they don't Most are young lassies, next time try older one I hope. Police haven't a clue yet and I don't leave any I am very clever and don't think of looking for any fingerprints cause there arent any and don't look for me up in Sunderland cause I not stupid just passed through the place not bad place compared with Chapeltown and Manningham can't walk the streets for them whore, Don't forget warn them I feel it coming on again if I get the chance. Sorry about lassie I didn't know.

Yours respectfully
Jack the Ripper

Might write again after another week gone. Maybe Liverpool or even Manchester again, to hot here in Yorkshire, Bye.

I have given advance warning so its yours and their's fault.

At first the Ripper Squad, and George Oldfield in particular, viewed the letters as the work of a crank. But as time went on and they thought more about the contents of the letters, not everyone was convinced it was the work of a hoaxer after all.

In the letter sent to the *Daily Mirror*, the writer had urged Oldfield to 'remember Preston 75'. This was almost certainly a reference to the unsolved murder of Joan Harrison, a 26-year-old prostitute addicted to the morphine in cough mixtures, whose body had been found in a lock-up garage in Preston, Lancashire, on Sunday, 23 November 1975. Her murder came less than a month after the body of the Ripper's first murdered victim, Wilma McCann, had been found in Leeds.

Joan Harrison's body was discovered by Mildred Atkinson as she walked along Berwick Road at the rear of 3 Frenchwood Street. Mrs Atkinson noticed that the door of a derelict garage on the property was flapping and banging in the wind. When the door blew open she saw a body lying face down on the concrete floor, a coat over its head and blood on the ground beside it. Her first thoughts were that it might have been a drunken man who had banged his head. In reality, she had discovered the body of the murdered Joan Harrison.

Her trousers had been pulled down, her bra pushed up, one of her legs was out of her tights and underwear and one of her boots had been removed. The other boot was placed on top of her leg and her coat was laid neatly on top of her body.

The post mortem was unable to determine the exact cause of death or pinpoint the time of death. The death certificate said she had died from 'haemorrhage and shock caused by multiple injuries, murder by person or persons unknown.'

Joan Harrison had one U-shaped laceration on the back of her head. Lancashire Police concluded that she had been hit with the heel of a woman's shoe, though none was found and she had been wearing boots. Later it was thought the injury could be consistent with an attempt to hit her with a hammer. There were also extensive injuries to her head, face, body and legs which, it was concluded, had been caused by violent kicking and stamping. There were no stab wounds.

There were bite marks on her left breast, which had been put there a short time before death. These indicated a clear gap in the front upper teeth. A semen test on Joan's body indicated that the man who killed her had a blood group B, which was in common with only six per cent of the population. Semen deposits were taken from her vagina and anus as both showed signs of intercourse at around the time of death.

Although there were marked similarities to a Ripper attack, her murder hadn't previously been regarded as his work. Detectives from West Yorkshire Police were concerned that the letter-writer was drawing attention to the Harrison murder but they were still not ready to bite.

It wouldn't be until two months later, on 16 May 1978, when the body of Vera Millward was discovered in the grounds of Manchester Royal Infirmary that detectives sat up and took notice of the letters.

The writer had claimed: 'Old slut next time I hope' and 'Maybe Liverpool or even Manchester again'. At the age of 40, Vera Millward was the oldest victim so far and her murder was committed in Manchester. Could it just be a coincidence?

Ten months later and eleven days before the murder of Josephine Whitaker, another letter arrived at George Oldfield's office in Wakefield bearing a Sunderland postmark. It was the same postmark as the others, and the envelope was written in the same hand as the two previous letters exactly a year before. Posted on 23 March 1979, the letter as it was written, was as follows:

> Dear Officer,
>
> Sorry I havn't written, about a year to be exact but I havn't been up North for quite a while. I was'nt kidding last time I wrote saying the whore would be older this time and maybe I'd strike in Manchester for a change. You should have took heed. That bit about her being in hospital, funny the lady mentioned something about being in the same hospital before I stopped her whoring ways. The lady won't worry about hospitals now will she I bet you are wondering how come I hav'nt been to work for ages, well I would have been if it hadnt been for your curserred coppers I had the lady just where I wanted her and was about to strike when one of your cursen police cars stopped right outside the land, he must have been a dumb copper cause he didn't say anything, he didnt know how close he was to catching me. Tell you the truth I thought I was collared, the lady said dont worry about coppers, little did she know that bloody copper saved her neck. That was last month, so I don't know when I will get back on the job but I know it wont be Chapeltown too bloody hot there maybe Bradfords Manningham. Might write again if up North.
>   Jack the Ripper
>   PS Did you get letter I sent to Daily Mirror in Manchester.

With the third letter came apparent confirmation that the writer knew more about the murders than anyone else. The fact that Vera Millward had been a patient at the Royal Infirmary, Manchester was not considered to be in the public domain. The only person who could know that was the killer himself.

An examination of the gummed flap of the envelope, which the writer had licked, revealed he belonged to the rare blood group B, the same blood group as the man who'd had sexual intercourse with Joan Harrison shortly before her death. There were also traces of metal filings and machine oil, the same substances that would later be found in Josephine Whitaker's wounds. It was around this time that George Oldfield must have felt he was on to something.

At a press conference called two weeks after Josephine Whitaker's murder, Oldfield made the first public reference to what was to become known as 'the Geordie connection'. He appealed to engineering firms in the North East to contact the police if any of their workers regularly visited West Yorkshire, and vice versa. Squads of detectives were dispatched to process whatever information could be gleaned from the many thousands of potential sources in both regions.

The attitude was, if it wasn't the Ripper who had written the letters, the writer knew something about the murders and he had to be found. But although the letters had come from Sunderland, there was nothing in them to prove he came from there.

His next correspondence, however, would leave no doubt.

At 2pm on Tuesday, 26 June 1979, George Oldfield walked into a lecture theatre at the West Yorkshire Police training academy in Bishopgarth to a crowded press conference that he had called. Dozens of news reporters and journalists had amassed for what would prove to be one of the most sensational moments in British criminal history. On the table in front of Oldfield was a portable tape recorder and, as silence fell upon the room, DSI Dick Holland leaned over Oldfield's shoulder and pressed the play button. There was a hiss as the first few inches of blank tape rolled through the machine, and then an unmistakable Geordie voice filled the room:

'I'm Jack. I see you are still having no luck catching me. I have the greatest respect for you, George, but Lord, you are no nearer catching me now than four years ago when I started. I reckon your boys are letting you down, George. Yer can't be much good, can yer?

'The only time they came near catching me was a few months back in Chapeltown when I was disturbed. Even then it was a uniform copper, not a detective.

'I warned you in March that I'd strike again. Sorry it wasn't Bradford. I did promise you that but I couldn't get there. I'm not sure when I will strike again but it will be definitely some time this year, maybe September or October, even soon if I get the chance. I'm not sure where. Maybe Manchester; I like it there, there's plenty of them knocking about.

'They never learn, do they, George? I bet you've warned them, but they never listen. At the rate I'm going I should be in the book of records, I think it's eleven up to now, isn't it? Well, I'll keep on going for quite a while yet. I can't see myself being nicked just yet. Even if you do get near, I'll probably top myself first.

'Well, it's been nice chatting to you, George.

'Yours, Jack the Ripper.

'No good looking for fingerprints. You should know by now it's clean as a whistle. See you soon. Bye. Hope you like the catchy tune at the end. Ha ha!'

The recording was followed by twenty-two seconds of the song *Thank You for Being a Friend* by Andrew Gold.

The tape had been posted from Sunderland and arrived on 19 June 1979. The envelope, in which the cassette was sent, was taken to Wetherby Forensic Science Service Laboratories, Audby Lane, Wetherby. Every cassette tape has batch numbers but the sender had filed these off, which showed his attention to detail, or criminal cunning. The adhesive gum on the envelope contained traces of saliva and it was deduced from this that the person who licked the envelope, and therefore very possibly the writer, and therefore very possibly the Yorkshire Ripper, was blood group B secretor (Sutcliffe was a non-secretor). Handwriting experts concluded that the person who had sent the tape was also responsible for the three previous letters.

The press conference came about following a high level secret meeting held in Halifax with representatives from Manchester, Lancashire and Sunderland police forces. The question was, what should they do with this new information? Oldfield consulted all the senior detectives on the case and talked about going public with the letters and tape. He felt that playing the voice to the public would be a positive move and fairly easy to deal with. This was also the common consensus of the constabulary, in the expectation of a quick arrest.

It would prove to be a fatal decision.

The contents of the tape filled every newspaper and television and radio news bulletins across the country for a week. In one night alone, the taped message was heard 15 million times. There was an overwhelming feeling that this was the best lead detectives had. Somebody somewhere must know this voice. A special 'Dial the Ripper' hotline was set up for callers to listen to the tape in the hope that someone would recognize the voice. Despite the number of lines being doubled, the phone number was almost permanently engaged over the coming weeks and months. As far as the public was aware, this was the Yorkshire Ripper. Far from being the easy-to-manage public inquiry George Oldfield had envisaged, so many people thought they knew who the Ripper was that police received 2,500 calls in the first two days.

Linguistic experts were called in to identify the accent. Professor Stanley Ellis and Jack Windsor Lewis from Leeds University were able to confirm that not only was it a Sunderland accent, they pinned it down to the village of Castletown. They believed the person on the tape had been born there and picked up the accent from his friends and neighbours as he grew up. Castletown was a former mining village on the north banks of the River Wear and by the end of three months, a staggering 200,000 people from around that area had been questioned or interviewed. Police had also visited 25,000 homes. Stanley Ellis was also tasked with going to all the pubs and clubs in Sunderland with a small tape recorder and playing it to everyone in the bars. He also had the mammoth job of listening to every single voice recording taken by the police during their enquiries.

As the investigation intensified and no positive results were forthcoming, doubts started to creep in to the minds of several officers. Even the voice experts questioned why the sender of the tape hadn't been found. After a few weeks they came to the conclusion that there was no way the person on the tape could have got through the net. So he must have been questioned and had a cast-iron alibi for not being the Ripper. Meaning he was most likely not the Ripper.

Then a Bradford councillor spotted similarities in the letters reportedly coming from the Yorkshire Ripper with letters sent 100 years before, during the Jack the Ripper murders of 1888. Councillor Anthony Emmott was familiar with the Jack the Ripper murders and was aware that hundreds of hoax letters had been sent in that case as well. When the letters from both cases were put together it was quite obvious that the author of the Yorkshire Ripper letters had simply copied the style of the Jack the Ripper letters.

Phrases such as 'gave me fits' and 'ha ha' appeared in both letters. It was almost theatrical. It was as though the modern writer was donning a top hat, putting on a cloak and carrying a Gladstone bag to recreate the image of the original Ripper stalking the streets of Whitechapel in 1888. When faced with the similarities, other officers began to lose confidence in the authenticity of the letters and tape.

Soon the linguistic experts voiced their own concerns to the Ripper Squad. They had also reached the conclusion that the letters and tape must be a hoax. They felt that the accent on the tape was so distinctive that the sender must be living among people who speak the same way. If the person whose voice was on the tape lived in Bradford or Leeds, he would have already come to the attention of the police. Likewise, if he lived in Sunderland or Castletown he must have been questioned and dismissed. Meaning he probably wasn't the Ripper.

They weren't the only people with serious doubts about the Geordie connection. In the Ripper files was a top-secret report, sent soon after the tape was received, by senior officers of Northumbria Police, the force that had spent eighteen months trying to trace that elusive, mocking voice. This detailed dossier ended with the warning that the tape, and therefore the letters, were nothing more than a sick hoax. The report used the same argument that the linguistic experts had put forward and went on to suggest other reasons why the Ripper messages were thought to be fakes.

Firstly, the style and choice of words were an imitation of the gloating letters Jack the Ripper was thought to have sent to Scotland Yard in 1888. There were several paperbacks on sale about these Victorian murders, all of them containing the text of Jack's letters. The letter-writer had probably done no more than buy one of the books and loosely copied the style.

One of the main reasons the letters had been accepted as the Yorkshire Ripper's handiwork was because they contained details that could be known only to the killer. Or so they thought. But having done a massive trawl of newspaper files, Northumbrian detectives had come up with a disturbing fact – almost every detail that made the letters seem genuine had, at some time or other, been published in the press. For example, the idea that Joan Harrison's murder might be linked to the Ripper murders had already appeared in the *Daily Mirror* on Tuesday, 12 April 1977. The main headline was 'Murder Hunt for Jack the Ripper' but in a smaller subsection of the page was an article titled 'The Preston Connection', which detailed everything that was known about the Harrison murder.

The same was found regarding Vera Millward being a patient at the Royal Manchester Infirmary. When re-examining the tape, it was noted that the opening line says, 'I'm Jack. I see you are still having no luck catching me.' Why use the word 'see'? If the speaker really had been the Ripper, he would have known the police were no closer to finding him. The word 'see', said the report, implied that the man was someone whose only knowledge of the case was coming from watching television and reading newspapers.

However, the most obvious error that nobody seemed to have picked up on at the very start was in the contents of the first letter that was sent to George Oldfield on 8 March 1978. The writer complains that he hasn't been given full credit for his murder total. He writes, 'Up to number 8 now, you say 7 but remember Preston 75?' The letter arrived soon after the killing of Helen Rytka in Huddersfield who, indeed, was the eighth victim if Joan Harrison was included in the tally.

However, the real killer would have known there was another victim, Yvonne Pearson, whose rotting corpse was lying undiscovered on waste ground in Bradford. She had been killed seven weeks before the letter was posted. Her body was discovered after the letter had been written. If the writer really was the Ripper, he had the ultimate ace card to play. He could have easily written: 'You haven't even found a victim I killed in January. Look in Arthington Street.' This would have left no doubt as to the authenticity of the letters.

What should have been apparent to every police officer from the very start was the fact he didn't mention that murder, because he didn't know about it.

This really should have been the end of the intense Wearside Jack inquiry that had taken valuable police focus away from Bradford and Leeds, but George Oldfield and other senior detectives could not be deterred from chasing their phantom hoaxer. In a desperate attempt to prove that the tape was genuine, Oldfield called on the assistance of FBI special agents John Douglas and Robert Ressler to construct a psychological profile of the Yorkshire Ripper. After listening to the tape, Ressler said to Oldfield: 'You do realize, of course, that the man on the tape is not the killer, don't you?' Oldfield chose to ignore this observation. The assistant chief constable then approached Tracy Browne, the schoolgirl who had been attacked by Sutcliffe in August 1975. She was adamant the voice on the tape was not the same as her attacker. She had spent thirty minutes in his company and she knew he had a soft-spoken Yorkshire accent.

Despite this, the whole investigation maintained its focus on the North East and any hope of catching the Yorkshire Ripper evaporated when West Yorkshire Police circulated a confidential report to other forces titled: *Murders and Assaults Upon Women in the North of England.*

The eighteen-page special notice outlined all the known attacks, detailing as much information known to police. It contained details of the injuries and guidance on related issues such as the tyre marks and combinations from three of the attacks, samples of handwriting, eyewitness descriptions of the attacker, such as the gap in his front teeth, and details of the taped message.

It also gave five reasons why a suspect could be eliminated from the inquiry.

1. Not born between 1924 and 1959
2. If he is an obvious coloured person
3. If his shoe size is size 9 or above
4. If his blood group is other than B
5. If his accent is dissimilar to a North Eastern (Geordie) accent.

If the edict was followed, it would be impossible to catch either the Ripper or the hoaxer. The Ripper would be dismissed because he didn't have a Geordie accent and the hoaxer would be dismissed because he didn't have a gap in his front teeth and probably had an alibi for the night of any of the murders.

Sutcliffe was an almost immediate beneficiary of this directive: his high, flat, but undeniably Yorkshire vowels would help him survive his next police interview by the skin of his teeth.

Following the overloading of information and lack of manpower needed to investigate all the cars spotted in the red-light areas of Leeds, Bradford and Manchester, it was decided that the main focus should be only on the cars that had been flagged up as being in all three areas. Sutcliffe's black Sunbeam Rapier had been flagged up a total of thirty-six times between 26 June 1978 and 22 November 1978.

However, it would be a further seven months before officers got round to chasing up this lead. On 29 July 1979, DC Andrew Laptew and DC Graham Greenwood visited Sutcliffe at home. Of the nine times Sutcliffe was interviewed by police, this would be the most crucial. For the first and only time his answers and demeanour did not allow him to avoid the suspicion of the officers and Laptew said there was 'something not quite right about this man'.

When the two detective constables arrived at Sutcliffe's door, they weren't aware that he had already been questioned about the five pound note found in Jean Jordan's handbag, or about the number of times his previous red Corsair had been spotted in red-light areas. It was also unfortunate that by the time they got round to interviewing him, he had already sold his black Sunbeam Rapier and replaced it with a Rover 3.5 Saloon. The new owner had already changed the tyres. However, once the two detectives came face to face with Sutcliffe, the first thing that stood out to DC Andrew Laptew was the likeness Sutcliffe had to the description given by Marilyn Moore. He would later recall: 'He had a striking resemblance to the photofit of the woman who was attacked in Buslingthorpe Lane in Leeds. He had a gap in his teeth, which again was indicative of the attacker of two of the women who were killed.'

Sutcliffe was the same height and build as the man described by two survivors; he had a beard, a Jason King-style moustache, collar-length black hair, dark complexion and smallish feet. He was also a lorry driver, one of the suspected occupations of the Ripper. Laptew said: 'He stuck in my mind. I was not ninety-nine per cent certain, but he was the best I had seen so far and I had seen hundreds. The gap in his teeth struck me as significant. He fitted the frame and could not really be taken out of it.'

Laptew would recall the coldness he felt from both Peter and Sonia when he used his tried-and-tested method of breaking the ice with couples he interviewed:

> 'I remember Sutcliffe and his wife seemed to have no sense of humour. I looked at his wife and said now was a good time to get rid of her husband if she wanted to. Normally this would cause a laugh or a reaction from those I spoke to, but with them there was nothing. Just straight faced and cold.'

When questioned about his car being seen in the Ripper hotspots, Sutcliffe claimed, again, that the Bradford red-light sightings were on his route to and from work, the Leeds sightings were when he visited a nightclub with his wife, and he totally denied being in Manchester when his car was sighted. The Leeds sighting was later loosely alibied by Sonia, although her recollections were hazy. At one point in the questioning Sonia agreed to leave the room, giving the officers an opportunity to probe him further about his possible use of prostitutes. Sutcliffe continued to deny he used prostitutes, saying that he had no need of such women since he hadn't been married very long.

The interview lasted for a full two hours and, recalling events in later years, DC Laptew said that he'd asked a colleague: 'Why don't we bring him in?' and his colleague replied: 'No. We have been told specifically do not bring anybody in.' The orders were that no one was to be arrested without the approval and permission of ACC Oldfield and submission of a full report.

Instead, the detectives opted to collect a sample of Sutcliffe's handwriting and search his car and garage. Finding nothing to connect him to the murders, they left empty handed but were far from happy.

Both DC Laptew and DC Greenwood felt there was something not quite right about Sutcliffe and when they arrived back at the station Laptew began to dig around for more information. He soon discovered that Sutcliffe could have been one of the employees to receive the five pound note in his pay packet and he also discovered, through the Regional Criminal Records Office, that Sutcliffe had been convicted for 'going equipped to steal' in 1969. Unfortunately, Laptew did not check with the Criminal Records Office at Scotland Yard, where there were two important and vital details – the burglary tool had been a hammer and Sutcliffe had also been arrested in the red-light district of Manningham Lane.

Laptew compiled a two-page report, detailing his and DC Greenwood's suspicions and noting the key points of interest:

A: The loose alibi

B: Sutcliffe's denial of having been to Manchester after a positive sighting of his vehicle

C: Sutcliffe's strong resemblance to the Marilyn Moore photofit (which they had previously been told to disregard since Moore was as an 'unreliable witness')

D: That he took size 8½ shoes (which was close to the size of prints found at the scene of the murder of Josephine Whitaker)

E: That Sutcliffe had a pronounced gap between his top front teeth

F: That for a man who was being interviewed in connection to a series of murders, Sutcliffe's attitude was almost too casual

Laptew made sure he took the report personally to his superior officer, Dick Holland the superintendent in charge of the inquiry. What happened next beggar's belief! His report was dismissed instantly as the inquiry was now focused on the killer being from the North East. A quick check of Sutcliffe's handwriting showed it didn't match the letters sent from Sunderland and Dick Holland then asked: 'Has he got a Geordie accent?'

'No, he's local,' replied Laptew. 'He's from Bradford, and he's a dead ringer for the photofit.'

Holland exploded into a rage. 'Photofits! If anybody mentions photofits to me again they will be doing traffic for the rest of their service.'

Andrew Laptew was left feeling humiliated in front of all his colleagues and said later: 'I could have crawled under the crack in the door.'

Laptew's report was routinely marked 'to file' where it would languish with thousands of others in the massive backlog of reports not yet filed in the system, thus allowing Sutcliffe to escape yet again from further and more probing investigation.

The belief in the tape and the public perception of the Ripper also hampered the actions of those who were close to the real killer and had begun to get suspicious. Trevor Birdsall had suspected for some time that his friend may have been the elusive Ripper. He knew about Sutcliffe's obsession with prostitutes and he was even present during three of the non-fatal attacks on women in 1969 and 1975. He was getting close to voicing his concerns to the police when he, like everyone else in the country, was told the killer was from the North East. It eased his mind and, for the time being, he dismissed the notion that his mate Peter could be the killer.

The police investigation in Wearside was a thorough and massive trawl. Besides interviewing Castletown men living in the North East, an attempt was made to track down, through school and birth records and Department of Health and Social Security (DHSS) computer records, every male born there, and those who may have left the immediate area. Early in 1980, Sunderland Police stated that they had completed 60,000 interviews, 16,000 vehicle checks, added 11,000 companies to the police index records, taken 7,000 handwriting specimens and logged 5,500 telephone tips.

The hunt for Wearside Jack continued into 1980 without any success. No one had been 'fit into the frame' of the Yorkshire Ripper, despite continued information from the public, interviews and elimination of suspects. That year, news came that the voice on the tape may have had a speech impediment. But the declaration by West Yorkshire Police that they were 'ninety-eight per cent sure' that the Wearside voice was the Ripper was never publicly revised, despite growing speculation by police officers, voice experts and the media that the letters and tape might actually be a hoax. Total realization for the police, press and public that the voice was not the Yorkshire Ripper would not come until eighteen months after the tape had first been released.

When Sutcliffe was finally arrested and made his confession, the horrible truth became abundantly clear to all. The author of the letters and tape was not the Yorkshire Ripper but a wicked hoaxer who had led the police on a wild goose chase away from the real killer, thus allowing Sutcliffe to escape detection and continue to kill.

On 11 August 1979 it was reported that George Oldfield had been taken ill. A statement from the police headquarters in

Wakefield announced that the chief was suffering from a chest infection. The truth was that, exhausted from working sixteen hours a day without time off and chain smoking sixty cigarettes a day, he had suffered a double heart attack and had been rushed to Pinderfields Hospital in Wakefield, where he remained for eleven days. Upon his release from hospital he was given strict orders by his doctors to rest until further notice. One of his last public statements before obeying these instructions was to once again push home the Geordie connection and warn: 'An innocent stranger is being condemned to death because someone in the north is protecting the Yorkshire Ripper.'

Less than six weeks later the Ripper struck again. This murder added credibility to the hoax because the voice on the tape said it would happen in 'September or October', and it did.

It is likely that Sutcliffe saw the 'prediction' as an opportunity to help perpetuate the hoax, as it was extremely beneficial to him for the police to think the man with the Wearside accent was the Ripper.

But, of course, it wasn't. The hoaxer managed to elude identification for over three decades. He may have been clever in making sure there were no fingerprints on any of his correspondence but he couldn't anticipate the advances of science. The simple act of licking the seal on an envelope may not have meant much in the 1970s but thirty years later it was pure forensic gold.

In 2005, West Yorkshire Police's Homicide and Major Enquiry Team decided to re-examine the Wearside Jack mystery. Buried in a dusty storage cage in the basement of the Forensic Science Service Laboratory were three tiny pieces of the original envelope. They were part of the gum seal and the sender of the tape would almost certainly have licked them.

Val Tomlinson conducted the tests. She said: 'We really only have one chance of this, there is no going back. The techniques we use will destroy any DNA traces left on the envelope flap and take away any DNA that we have left.'

A sterile swab was wiped over the samples to recover the DNA, then a sterile scalpel was used to remove the swab head, which was placed in a sterile tube, ready for examination. A DNA profile was found and the results were sent to the national police database, which holds profiles of convicted criminals. It was a long shot, but if the hoaxer had been convicted of a crime in recent years then chances were he would be in there. The results came back and it was a direct hit.

The DNA belonged to 50-year-old ex-bricklayer John Samuel Humble. Luckily for the police, he had a long career of petty crime and, after a 1991 conviction for being drunk and disorderly, his DNA was put on the database.

The voice that had terrified a nation was recorded by the then 23-year-old John Humble on a cheap cassette recorder he had purchased from Woolworths in the kitchen of his family home at 15 Halstead Square, a red-brick, semi-detached house on Sunderland's Hylton Lane Estate. At the time, he lived there with his mother Violet and 15-year-old-sister Jean.

All his letters were posted less than a mile away from the family home at the red letterbox outside the Ford Estate post office at 460 Hylton Road in Sunderland.

In the decades since the Yorkshire Ripper murders, Humble's life had been marred by crime and alcoholism. After his marriage break-up he went to live with his brother at 51 Flodden Road on the Ford Estate, close to their childhood home. They spent their days drinking cider in the run-down, poorly-furnished home. When police arrived to arrest Humble on 18 October 2005, both were in drunken stupors. Detectives had to wait almost a day until he was sober enough to be questioned. He reportedly, and perhaps understandably, went into shock when he came round and realized where he was.

Humble refused to speak during his first interview, nodding and shaking his head in response to questions, and he denied writing the letters or making the tape. However, later that evening his solicitor learnt that police had a DNA match so exact that there was a one in a billion chance of the hoaxer being someone other than Humble. The lawyer spoke privately to him before his second interview and it was then that he decided to come clean and confess all.

Asked directly if he was the hoaxer, he spoke for the first time to say: 'I sent the letters and tape' and indicated that he was prepared to give a full account. He said that he sent the first letter after 16-year-old Jayne MacDonald was murdered in Leeds in June 1977 and he didn't think the police were doing a very good job. Ironically, Humble claimed that he had wanted to focus the inquiry and make sure more resources were devoted to finding the Yorkshire Ripper. He admitted that he deliberately disguised his handwriting and that by the time he wrote the second and third letters he had wanted to increase his own notoriety.

Asked about his choice of wording, he said that he read the reports in *The Sun* and *Daily Mirror* and then went to Kayll Road Library in Sunderland and took out a green hardback book on the original Jack the Ripper murders, from which he copied out sections and phrases of the 'Ripper's' 1888 letters. At first, he claimed that he had been motivated to carry out the hoax because 'coppers were useless' but eventually admitted it was because he was bored. 'It was a stupid thing to do,' he said. 'I've regretted it ever since.'

Recalling the events that followed he said: 'I panicked when the coppers were raking all over Castletown', but incredibly, and quite unbelievably, the police failed to interview him during the hunt. 'They never came near me,' said Humble who grew up in the village. 'They checked the bloke next door, Ernie, but not me. I couldn't believe it.'

Eventually, the fact his prank had escalated and shifted the entire focus of a serial-murder inquiry began to take its toll on Humble. He knew that while the police were wasting valuable time and energy looking for him, they were not looking for the killer. He claimed to have phoned the inquiry team to tell them it was a hoax but this apparently did nothing to stop the chaos he had created.

Weeks later, apparently full of remorse and depression, he jumped from Wearmouth Bridge in a suicide attempt, but miraculously survived and was rescued by two police officers. Having sustained multiple injuries, he spent three months in hospital, where he also received psychiatric treatment.

In March 2006, Humble was convicted on four counts of perverting the course of justice and sentenced to eight years' imprisonment. He served half his sentence before being released in 2010 and has since disappeared into obscurity. Those that have known him can't believe he managed to keep his role in the Yorkshire Ripper manhunt a secret for so long.

It should be mentioned that in 2011, one year after John Humble's release, detectives working on the cold case inquiry into the murder of Joan Harrison in Preston in 1975 finally matched DNA from her body to that of 60-year-old Christopher Smith, a petty criminal with convictions for assault, theft and sex attacks. Unfortunately, Smith could not face justice as he had died in 2008. DS Graham Gardner, head of crime for Lancashire Constabulary told a press conference:

> 'The advances in DNA interpretation over the years have finally allowed us to identify Smith as the man at the scene of Joan's murder. That fact, coupled with other evidence we have gathered over recent months, has been sufficient to convince the Crown Prosecution Service that Christopher Smith would have been charged with her murder, had he been alive today.'

Learning the identities of both Wearside Jack and Joan Harrison's killer closes a chapter in one of the most important, frustrating, and ultimately tragic aspects of the Yorkshire Ripper investigation.

CHAPTER 17

Barbara Leach

'The consciousness of the Ripper has never been far from the surface around here for two or three years, but somehow no one ever thought of him striking in Little Horton – the student area. It's so friendly around here.'

Bradford student Paul Smith

Just two days into September 1979, Sutcliffe fulfilled the predictions of Wearside Jack by striking again in Bradford. It would leave the police totally convinced that the letters and tape were from the Ripper. They never entertained the idea that the real killer had simply listened to the tape and decided to carry out the murder as predicted. He knew very well that by doing so, the hunt, which had seen police knock on his door a number of times, would veer away from him and continue looking for the man with the Geordie connection.

It had been over a year and a half since the Ripper had struck in Bradford and once again he avoided the red-light areas of the city and targeted non-prostitutes. His next murder was described as having been done with 'breathtaking audacity' by the investigating officers because, not only would he claim his eleventh victim, but he would commit the murder within 700 yards of the city's central police station.

As you approach the bowl-like city centre of Bradford from any direction you eventually catch a glimpse of new Centenary Square, with its marvellous water feature and bars and restaurants. This recent regeneration has made the centre more attractive than before when bland office blocks lined the square.

One of the more recent changes has been the removal of the large concrete and glass building which was once Bradford's central police station and the city's police headquarters. It was located next to the petty court sessions building and the Victorian town hall. Opposite The Tyrls, as the police station was once called, stands the famous green-domed Alhambra Theatre and behind it is Great Horton Road, known locally in the 1970s as 'Little SoHo'. Today it's referred to as the 'West End'.

This area contains the university, the technical college and the art college. It's the student centre of Bradford with the Great Horton Road running through it. Off this road are many terraced streets comprising mainly student accommodation. Those that are not occupied by students tend to house Asian families, whose shops and restaurants, together with the late-night restaurants owned by Italians, Greeks and Chinese, lend the area the relaxed, rather sophisticated ambience that sets it apart from the rest of the city. A great spot for nightlife – bars and nightclubs are plentiful.

The red-light areas of Thornton Road and Sunbridge Road lie further to the east of the city but on Sunday, 2 September 1979, Sutcliffe avoided going there, knowing it would be full of police, and decided to make this popular student area his hunting ground.

Barbara Janine Leach – 'Babs' to her student friends – was a respectable 20 year old studying for a Bachelor of Science degree at the university. Two years earlier she had left her parents, David and Beryl Leach, in Kettering, where her father worked for Barclays Bank. They lived in a modest pre-war, semi-detached house close to the two schools Barbara was to attend growing up: Henry Gotch School and Southfield Girls' School. Her mother worked in the local telephone exchange until she took a higher education course and became a teacher. The extra income would help put Barbara and her brother Graham, who was two years older, through school and university.

With her A levels in English and Religious Education, she had a choice of several universities available to her and decided to study Social Sciences at Bradford University. She told her family she wanted to mix with 'real people'.

Dark and very pretty, she was a bright, lively and outward-looking young woman with a wide circle of friends. She enjoyed pop and classical music, horse riding, reading and growing indoor plants. She threw herself into university social life, which took up almost all of her time. She worked hard at her studies, taking time off only to go riding in the outlaying village of Tong, or to join friends for drinks at the Bradford Interchange, Shoulder of Mutton or The Mannville Arms. She shared a big house, which had been divided up into flats, with six other students, four men and two women. She had no specific boyfriend but loved mixing with others.

A few weeks before the start of her third year at university, she headed back to Bradford from her parents where she was spending the summer break because she wanted to put her flat at 20 Grove Terrace in order in time for the start of the autumn term.

Grove Terrace is one of seven quiet streets that run parallel to each other in the wishbone-shaped area between Great Horton Road and Morley Street which leads downhill to Centenary Square. It is directly opposite Bradford University.

Saturday, 1 September 1979, was her father's fifty-third birthday and Barbara telephoned to wish him many happy returns. She apologized for not having sent a card but promised that she would visit him and her mother the following Monday. Then she prepared to make the most of the weekend with the boisterous student crowd that had already returned to Bradford.

It was a warm evening when she set off with five friends to walk round the corner of the terrace to their favourite pub, The Mannville Arms, at 31–33 Great Horton Road. The Mannville was a typical West Yorkshire pub; noisy, busy and friendly, with a fine pint of hand-pulled bitter. It was popular with students as well as locals, or 'townies' as the more affected university types called them.

The start of the winter term was still weeks away but there were enough students who remained in the city throughout the summer to make it a typical Mannville Saturday night. The punks and the students competed good-naturedly for time on the jukebox. Cliff Richard's hit *We Don't Talk Anymore* and *Cavatina*, the haunting theme from *The Deer Hunter*, performed by Cliff's former group The Shadows boomed out over and over again.

Landlord, Roy Evans, had catered for several generations of students during his tenancy at the pub and they were his favourite customers. Sometimes, particularly on weekends, he would let a few of them stay behind for 'afters' – drinks after the legal closing time of 11pm – under the rule that allows a landlord to treat personal friends in his or her own time.

Tonight, he would do the same for Barbara and three of her flatmates, 20-year-old Lynn Johnson, 21-year-old Paul Smith and another 21 year old called Walter. More pints were pulled and the laughter from the small group, silhouetted against the bar lights, continued for another couple of hours.

They left about 1am and debated about whether to go for Indian food in one of the many nearby restaurants that normally stayed open until 2am, but then decided to call it a night and go home. Despite the mist-like drizzle that had started, at the corner of Grove Terrace Barbara announced to Paul Smith that she was 'just going for a little stroll.' She said she didn't have her front door key and asked him if he would wait up for her. 'I shan't be long,' she said.

She bade her friends goodnight and strolled off up Great Horton Road. Why Barbara went walking off by herself in the early hours is still a mystery. Those who knew her said it was something she often did with a friend from the flat, but never alone. One student, Stephen Raby, claimed that Barbara had friends living in nearby Ash Grove and was more than likely making her way to their house. Being Saturday night in student land, many a house party was in full swing.

Whatever the reasons, the rest of the group turned into Grove Terrace, catching their last glimpse of the dark-haired young woman in her red high-heeled boots, cheesecloth shirt and blue jeans – with the cheeky 'best rump' patch on the backside – and her khaki haversack bag hanging from her shoulder, as she passed into the shadows beyond the street lamp.

When, a little over an hour later, Barbara had not returned, her flatmates were not overly alarmed as there were plenty of parties nearby and she had many friends in the close-knit student community around Great Horton Lane. Perhaps, they reasoned, she had found a party and called in for a drink and a dance. One by one they went off to bed and when it reached 3.30am, Walter, who was the last awake, decided to leave the door on the latch and go to bed.

However, when morning came and it was discovered that the front door was still on the latch and that Barbara's bed had not been slept in, concerns were raised. Paul Smith and fellow flatmate, Steve Greenough, started to make enquiries. They contacted several of Barbara's friends and when The Mannville Arms opened at midday, they asked in there too. But there had been no sight of her. It now became apparent that something was wrong. It was unlike Babs to stay out all night; she had no steady boyfriend and she was not permissive. Thoughts turned to the worst and of course the ever-present shadow of the Ripper.

As Paul Smith would later recall: 'The consciousness of the Ripper has never been far from the surface around here for two or three years, but somehow no one ever thought of him striking in Little Horton – the student area. It's so friendly around here.'

By Sunday evening the police had been informed and they called the Leach family home in Hazel Road, Kettering and asked if Barbara had arrived there a day earlier than planned. She had not and, for the first time, her stunned parents heard the news that she had not returned after her early morning walk. Their agony can only be imagined as they waited in dread for information about their daughter who lived in the heart of Ripper territory.

By Monday afternoon, it was decided a search should be made of the streets and alleyways off Great Horton Road, starting with the ones closest to Barbara's home on Grove Terrace.

One of the streets on the search list was Ash Grove, but before you reach that, there was Back Ash Grove, a narrow alley-like lane serving as a rear approach to the houses in Ash Grove. Small and cobblestoned, unkempt and overgrown, it ran along the backs of the stoned terraced houses of Ash Grove, within sight of Bradford University and only a few hundred yards from the house where Barbara lived. Along the right-hand side of Back Ash Grove were small sectioned-off back yards, with access areas for the bin collections. At 3.55pm, Police Constable (PC) Simon Greaves entered the alleyway, checking each of the open yards and coal sheds that lined the route.

As he reached the rear of 13 Ash Grove he noticed a low brick wall, which stuck out from the back of the house. Between the wall and the house was a small recess, into which the bins would normally be placed. However, the bins had been taken out and in their place he saw a shroud of wet, rotting carpet draped over something that was wedged between the low wall and the house. Curiously, he moved around the wall and saw that several stones were placed on the carpet to hold down the edges, but in one spot the tip of a red high heel peeped out. The PC radioed for help and awaited backup. Within the hour, 100 officers had been drafted into the West End of Bradford.

The news was greeted with dismay and disbelief by the Bradford police. Despite all their efforts in keeping the red-light areas and back streets under constant surveillance, the killer had managed not only to strike again but do so within yards of the main police station.

The latest murder also came at a time when most of the Ripper team's top brass were 'off the patch'. George Oldfield was recovering from his heart attack, Dick Holland was in Scotland on a camping holiday and Jim Hobson was waiting anxiously in Chapel Allerton Hospital for news of his wife, Joan, who had fractured her skull after falling downstairs at home.

DS Holland, on his caravan site in Fife, heard the news on the radio and climbed into his car for the long drive back to Yorkshire. As he was speeding down from Scotland, DCS Hobson heard the results of his wife's brain scan – satisfactory. He too headed for Bradford and joined the man who had taken charge of the Leach investigation, DCS Peter Gilrain.

When CID lifted the carpet, they found the battered body of Barbara Leach. She was fully dressed but covered in blood. She had been posed in a jackknife position, with her booted feet resting against the low wall. Police believed it had taken the Ripper almost half an hour to manoeuvre her corpse into position and arrange it so that, even sixteen hours after rigor mortis had begun to wear off, it had not moved. What made it all the more remarkable was that he had done so only a few feet away from the kitchen window of a downstairs flat at Number 13.

The sheer audacity of the murder became even more apparent when it emerged that, a few feet away from the crime scene, there had been an open window behind which a party was underway at the time of the murder. A group of engineering students had been drinking in the ground-floor flat of 16 Ash Grove, directly opposite the murder scene.

John McGoldrick, a 22-year-old fourth year Chemical Engineering student from Glasgow, had attended the party and later, he recalled the night's events to *The Yorkshire Post*:

> 'I live in a flat a few doors away and a number of us had a bottle party at Number 16 in the early hours of Sunday morning. There was plenty of noise and the window was open. In fact, the guy who lives there was lying under the window as I sat talking to him. I remember glancing out a couple of times but I never saw anything unusual, but it was incredible to think that this girl was probably being murdered as we sat there enjoying ourselves and passing the night away.'

Within an hour of the body being found, DCS Jack Ridgeway, head of CID in Manchester, where two women had met their end at the hands of the Ripper, dropped what he was doing and travelled to Bradford.

As had become a grim routine, Professor Gee once again arrived on the scene and, after a preliminary on-scene investigation, had the body moved to Bradford Mortuary to begin his post mortem, which was to keep him busy until the early hours of Tuesday morning. However, from his initial examination at the crime scene, there was little doubt in his mind that his old adversary, the Ripper, was responsible. Barbara's massive head wounds which had covered her body in blood, were all too familiar.

At a press conference at Bradford police headquarters, DCS Peter Gilrain, who was in charge of West Yorkshire Police CID said:

> 'All I can tell you at this time is that at 3.55pm a patrolling police officer found the body of a young woman at the rear of Back Ash Grove. The body was covered in blood and I can't tell you what the injuries were at the moment but we are treating it as a murder inquiry.'

At the same time, Barbara's distraught parents were given the news they dreaded. The anguished family listened in horror and disbelief as police officers tried as gently as possible to tell them their daughter was dead. Mr and Mrs Leach were driven the 140 miles from Kettering to Bradford by police car, praying desperately that some awful mistake had been made and that the body waiting in the mortuary for their formal identification was not that of their daughter. But no mistake was made and a grieving Mr Leach blinked back the tears as he looked down at what was left of his daughter.

Task force officers began a fingertip search of Back Ash Grove in the falling evening light. Half a dozen men on their hands and knees stretched across the alleyway, searching the cobblestones for clues. Some were armed with scythes and every weed was cut down in the search for clues. Across from Back Ash Grove is the garden of 1 Claremont where the composer Frederick Delius was born, and that was searched too. Every resident of the seven-house block behind where the body was found was interviewed.

By Tuesday, 4 September it was all too clear that this was a Yorkshire Ripper attack. After discussion with Professor Gee, DCS Jim Hobson announced to the press: 'We are now satisfied that this murder is linked with other unsolved murders in Yorkshire and Manchester.'

We now know how the events of this night unfolded. Little Horton was not somewhere Sutcliffe frequented but on that fateful Saturday night, he had been cruising the streets in his dark brown Rover 3.5 registration plate FHY 400K. Presumably mindful of the police presence in his normal haunts of Lumb Lane and Manningham, he moved over to the West End of the city to try his luck there.

He had spotted Barbara Leach walking up the left-hand side of Great Horton Road, just up from the Mannville Arms and opposite the entrance to the university. He drove ahead of her and turned right into Ash Grove, parking a few doors away from Number 13.

He was about to exit the car when he saw Barbara turn the corner and walk towards him. He waited until she passed before he got out and followed her. In his hand, he had a ball-pein hammer and in his pocket was the large screwdriver that he had carefully fashioned into a point; it was the same fiendish weapon he had used on Josephine Whitaker five months earlier in Halifax, which left a distinctive 'Y' mark instead of the usual 'X' crosshead mark.

As she reached the front of Number 13, he swung the hammer down onto her head causing a large laceration. Barbara collapsed in a heap, moaning loudly. This all took place in full view of the living room window of 16 Ash Grove where the engineering students were holding a party. Sutcliffe had either not noticed the open window or not cared as the thrill of it probably stimulated him more.

He took hold of her wrists and dragged her up the driveway of Number 13 and round to the right side of the house, through the narrow walkway and into the bin area at the rear. She was still moaning as he pushed up her shirt and bra and undid her jeans, partly pulling them down to expose her crotch and stabbed her repeatedly with the screwdriver. In total, there were seven stab wounds in her trunk, four in the chest and three round her navel. The weapon had been reintroduced to the same wound in the chest fifteen to thirty times, replicating penile penetration while he masturbated.

Just as he had done with Jean Jordan, Yvonne Pearson and Helen Rytka, he hid Barbara's body. In each of these earlier murders, he had been disturbed by others arriving on the scene and in each case, he had very nearly been caught. Perhaps, during the attack on Barbara Leach, he had been disturbed once again, possibly by one of the residents in the neighbouring property looking out the window or walking out into the back yard for a smoke. It seems unlikely that we will ever know exactly what happened that night, but we do know that when he was finished, he moved the metal bins out of their place between the house and the low brick wall and put Barbara's body there instead. He took some time to manoeuvre it into a distorted jackknife position to make sure it was concealed in the small gap. Before leaving, he dragged over the discarded carpet, probably left in the overgrown alleyway, draped it over her body and weighed it down at the edges with stones found from the garden wall. Exiting via the front driveway of 13 Ash Grove, he got back in his car and drove straight home. Later he would dispose of the screwdriver by throwing it over the embankment on the westbound side of Hartshead Moor services on the M62 near Bradford.

On Tuesday evening, in the forecourt of the Catholic Chaplaincy, located at the end of the road at 1 Ash Grove, police set up mobile headquarters. Response was disappointing. Officers manning the mobile station reported no more than a couple of callers a day, 'and either they usually only come to ask what we are doing about it, or out of curiosity,' said one.

A weary Dick Holland, back after his long motoring trip from Scotland, immediately set about organizing a reconstruction of Barbara's doomed last stroll. Barbara Terry, a 24-year-old Woman Police Constable (WPC), volunteered for the task as she was of the same build and appearance as the dead woman. Dressed in similar clothes, she began the walk, followed by Dick Holland and Peter Gilrain. Other officers flanked the route, just in case the Ripper himself should turn out to watch the reconstruction which had a considerable amount of advance publicity. Afterwards, WPC Terry said:

> 'I was scared. It was very weird. When I was asked to do the reconstruction, I accepted without thinking. When it came to wearing the clothes and actually doing the walk I began to feel a little nervous. I had a funny feeling that the Ripper may be lurking in the background, watching me. I know the way women are reacting to these murders. There is real fear hanging over almost everyone.'

WPC Terry's photograph, with Barbara Leach's face superimposed, was printed on thousands of posters appealing for information from the public. There were notices printed in Urdu to appeal to the city's large Asian community. This was followed by an appeal, made in Hindi and Gujarati, by WPC Jagjit Dahele, a 26-year-old Kenyan Asian who came to Britain with her family eleven years earlier and had been in the force for seven years. Her appeal, broadcast on local radio, asked for help 'in catching this monster'.

With the murder of Josephine Whitaker five months earlier in Halifax and now Barbara Leach in Bradford, neither of whom were prostitutes, ordinary women across West Yorkshire felt at risk for the first time. It was with a sense of shock, gradually turning to outrage and anger, that they realized nobody was immune. Warnings for women to keep off the streets and to beware of the dark came from all sides.

Rather unwisely, DCS Peter Gilrain, who was heading the Bradford inquiry, said:

> 'For a woman to take a walk late at night was a very foolish thing to do, bearing in mind the killer had already claimed eleven victims.... No woman in this part of the world should go out at that time. These are extremely brutal attacks, and he is now picking them at random, not just concentrating on prostitutes. In fact, no woman in the north of England is safe until he is caught. The police can't protect every one of them.'

Bradford University's Deputy Student President Kevin Ball said a campaign had been launched warning students of the dangers and that they were trying to strike a deal with local taxi firms to take students home from union events.

Student Union Treasurer Jules Offord gave a statement to the press regarding the safety of those living on the campus and surrounding Great Horton:

> 'We are drafting a letter to send to all new undergraduates and other students. We are going to advise students to use transport provided by the union after all late-night functions at the university. We are also warning them not to walk alone, unless they feel capable of defending themselves against an attack. We are all horrified at this killing. There is a small group of women at the university who have been campaigning to arm themselves as protection against attacks.'

The sentiment was echoed by Trisha Calvert who had joined the recently formed Women's Right to Self Defence campaign. The group was formed in protest when a local woman was charged with possessing an offensive weapon, which she claimed she carried in case of a Ripper attack. Questionnaires compiled by the group and given out in the town centre showed that many women were scared to go out alone and either carried some means of protection or wanted to.

Standing by the front door of the university and facing a crowd of reporters, she said: 'The police can't provide twenty-four-hour protection for every woman in Bradford and we want the right to defend ourselves against attacks. The answer isn't just more police patrols in red-light areas, every man is a potential attacker – day or night.'

In the midst of this student uprising, at 5pm on Friday, 14 September, just twelve days after the body of Barbara Leach had been found, PC Keith Mount was manning the police incident room in Sunderland when the telephone rang. With pad and pencil at the ready to take notes, he picked up the receiver.

'Hello police incident room Sunderland.'

There came a chilling reply in the voice that had gripped a nation. He had no doubt who the caller was. It was Wearside Jack.

Caller: 'Tell him it's a fake.'

Officer Mount: 'Can you repeat that? I can't hear you it's a bad line.'

Caller: 'Tell him it's a fake.'

Officer Mount: 'What's a fake?'

Caller: 'The tape recording.'

Officer Mount (desperately trying to keep the caller on the phone): 'What one is this? The one he's just received?'

Caller: 'The Ripper tape recording.'

Officer Mount: 'How do you know that?'

Caller: 'Just tell him…just tell him…the one in June.'

Officer Mount: 'Pardon?'

Caller: 'The one in June.'

Officer Mount: 'I'm sorry it's a bad line. You're going to have to repeat it.'

Then the line went dead.

PC Keith Mount reported the call, which added weight to the view supported by a growing group of officers that the tape was almost certainly a hoax. However, his report was dismissed by West Yorkshire Police, or at the very least brushed under the carpet.

A few days later, over forty officers from eight forces across the north of England gathered in Bradford for a top-secret conference out of which emerged Project R.

Launched a fortnight later, Project R was a joint effort by the police and Leeds-based advertising agency Graham Poulter and Associates, designed to ensure that everyone in Britain who could read, see or hear would know about the Ripper in the hope that someone, somewhere, would hold the clue to his identity.

Every designer, photographer, writer and distributer involved in the project gave their services for free. Tony Handley, joint managing director of the company said: 'When you are asked to do something like this you don't say no. If we can use our expertise to catch him that's all we can ask.'

Mobile exhibitions were set up across West Yorkshire – multilingual Ripper roadshows barnstormed pubs, clubs, factories, shopping centres, town squares and village greens. Bradford's Arndale Centre – later renamed the Kirkgate Centre – held one of the largest pop-up exhibitions. Hundreds of shoppers were bombarded with information outlining key details of the investigation; they could read through the letters sent to the police and the *Daily Mirror*, gaze over the transcripts of the 'I'm Jack' tape recording and be invited to play detective.

Two million copies of a four-page newsletter highlighting the murders were distributed door to door. Inside were samples of the handwriting from the three Ripper letters and a transcript of the tape recording. The tape was broadcast several times a day on radio and TV and a Ripper poster replaced the normal transmission card of ITV, which was then on strike.

Gas bills sent to every house carried a plea for help in finding the Ripper stamped on the envelope.

Billboards were erected in 600 towns and villages. Each one read: 'THE RIPPER WOULD LIKE YOU TO IGNORE THIS. THE MAN NEXT TO YOU MAY HAVE KILLED 12 WOMEN.' Pictures of these billboards were printed onto flyers and posted through every letterbox in West Yorkshire. On some of the flyers, the opening paragraph urged the reader not to consider the Ripper as heroic or on some grand crusade. To the modern reader this may seem a bizarre thing to say, but it was felt by some at the time, especially among religious communities, that the women were murdered as a direct consequence of their lifestyles and they had somehow brought it upon themselves. Some saw the Ripper as being on a one-man crusade to rid the streets of vice and sin.

So when it came to the flyers, nothing was left to chance. Everyone, no matter what their beliefs, must do their bit to help the police.

Project R attempted to turn the entire nation into valuable informants and I believe the police totally underestimated the effect their campaign would have on the amount of information they now received.

Over 18,000 phone calls were taken in the first couple of weeks and the police were left with a daunting list of 17,000 suspects. All these suspects now had to be cross checked against school and birth records and entries on the DHSS computer, an invasion of privacy that was sanctioned by the government as a one-off.

The global publicity brought news teams to Bradford from as far away as Japan. A story about the Ripper appeared on the front of its daily newspaper, *The Mainichi*, which had a circulation of one million. The Japanese were interested because they'd had a similar series of prostitute murders just after the Second World War. The man was eventually captured and turned out to be a member of the armed forces.

Newspaper reporters and TV crews from America, Australia, Canada, Brazil, Israel, Germany, Italy, Holland, Belgium and France descended upon West Yorkshire to report on Britain's biggest ever manhunt.

By January 1980, almost a quarter-of-a-million people had been interviewed, over 25,000 statements had been collected, 26,000 houses were visited and over 175,000 vehicles had been checked. Such a system could no longer be controlled or contained. Stories tell of the paperwork becoming so big that the floor of Leeds Police Station had to be reinforced to take the weight.

Despite its good intentions, Project R had created chaos. Officers couldn't clear their workload fast enough before the next batch of information poured in. By the end of January, the sheer volume of information ground the inquiry to a near halt. Within weeks the billboards would start coming down and the roadshows would fade away.

The 'I'm Jack' tape was no longer played and cooperation between the press and the police started to dry up. It seemed that someone had quietly pulled the plug on the whole Geordie investigation. Silence descended upon the Yorkshire Ripper inquiry and many people felt it was now time to call in Scotland Yard.

In fact, Scotland Yard was already involved. On 20 September 1979, the headline in Bradford's *Telegraph & Argus* read: 'Crack Yard Chief Joins the Ripper Squad.'

The move was announced by West Yorkshire Police, despite previous denials from Chief Constable Ronald Gregory that 'the Yard' would be brought in.

Commander Jim Nevill, a top anti-terrorist expert had arrived in Wakefield to be briefed on the progress of the murder hunt. During his five years as head of the anti-terrorist squad, Nevill had led hunts for the international terrorist known as Carlos the Jackal and for the killer of Georgi Markov, who was assassinated at a London bus stop by a poisoned pellet fired from an umbrella.

Often the first senior officer on the scene of terror attacks, Nevill was the man who took charge and talked to the media. During the tense Balcombe Street siege in 1975, he appeared in television news reports night after night – unruffled and immaculate – as one of the two senior detectives negotiating with the cornered gang of renegade IRA gunmen.

As a young Flying Squad officer, he had been part of the investigation into the Great Train Robbery of August 1963 and over the years had developed into a seasoned, old-style detective, firm and authoritative. He was a tenacious investigator and interrogator but fair-minded and likeable.

Now, in 1979, he was being asked to come to Leeds to help find the most notorious serial killer of modern times. This generated mixed feelings among the West Yorkshire forces as the thought that the inquiry would now be handed over to more competent officers was considered a 'kick in the teeth' to those who had spent the last four years working insane hours, knocking on thousands of doors and interviewing thousands of potential suspects.

The question of Scotland Yard being brought in to help had been brought up by reporters at press conferences and, during one, attended by George Oldfield and other high ranking officers, one of the most famous replies was given: 'Scotland Yard? They haven't caught their own Ripper yet!'

Professional pride was at stake, so any announcement that the Yard was being called in had to be handled delicately. A reluctant Ronald Gregory faced the cameras and said: 'Last week I saw [Metropolitan Police Commissioner] Sir David McNee and discussed with him the Ripper inquiry. I asked him if he would send one of his senior investigators to West Yorkshire to help with the inquiry. He agreed to send Commander Jim Nevill.'

Gregory was quick to reassure the public and, more importantly, his own force, that Nevill would not be taking over the inquiry but would have an advisory position only.

Playing down the significance of Scotland Yard being involved he added: 'There's always been a certain charisma attached to the Yard but since its amalgamation, its staff are not called in for inquiries by the bigger forces. We would still not call in Scotland Yard to take over this inquiry.'

Nevill's arrival in Leeds, alongside a colleague from the Yard, was described as the deployment of 'fresh eyes and minds' in the four-year hunt for the man who had, by that stage, murdered twelve women.

However, Nevill would return to London empty handed a month later, and it would be another year before Sutcliffe was arrested, purely by chance.

Another sad twist to the tale of Barbara Leach came when her parents went to collect her personal belongs from her flat. Among her items was a birthday present for her father. On the day of her phone call home, when she had apologized for not sending a card, she had bought him a half-pint mug emblazoned with the words: 'Life's too short not to live it up a little.' She had intended to give him it during her visit on the Monday but, sadly, never got the chance.

On 20 October 1980, students at Bradford University planted a tree as a memorial to Barbara Leach, in the grounds of the university, next to the Shearbridge halls of residence. Her family were in attendance as the purple sycamore tree was planted by Vice Chancellor Professor John West, President of the Student Union Reg Bull and Barbara's father David. A plaque to mark the occasion was fixed beside it. Barbara had been a conservationist; she loved trees and had joined the Plant a Tree Society a month before she was murdered. Afterwards, Reg Bull said the idea to plant the tree had come from the students' union. He added: 'We would like to epitomize the affection which the students had for Barbara. We hope that it will symbolize life and that the plaque will be a constant reminder that she was a student here.'

Today, forty years later, the purple sycamore continues to grow with successive generations of students walking past it every day. Next to it, the small stone plaque still stands, dedicated to fellow student Barbara Leach.

The Mannville Arms, where Barbara and her friends drank the night of her death, closed its doors in 2010 and, at the time of writing, is a convenience store. As for the surrounding area, with the exception of the university, which continues to grow in size to accommodate the increasing number of students, nothing much has changed.

The front of the houses on Ash Grove remain generally well-kept, despite the surrounding area falling upon hard times in terms of crime and disorder. Not much has changed with the rear of the properties – they are still reached via narrow passageways running along the sides of the houses and remain overgrown dumping grounds for household rubbish and abandoned furniture. Following years of burglaries and illegal drug use, green security gates now restrict public access to the laneway and yard where Barbara Leach was brutally murdered.

CHAPTER 18

Marguerite Walls

'I am satisfied the woman's death was in no way connected with the Ripper killings.'

DCS Jim Hobson

D uring the final months of 1979 and the beginning of 1980, Sutcliffe would be interviewed for the sixth, seventh, eighth and ninth time and still manage to evade capture.

On 23 October 1979, Sutcliffe was seen by two detective constables for the second time about his Sunbeam Rapier being spotted over thirty-six times in red-light areas. Unfortunately, at this point, the report PC Andrew Laptew had filed was missing from the system, more than likely discarded and written off.

On 13 January 1980, Manchester Police returned to Bradford for a second attempt at tracing the owner of the five pound note. In order to reduce the number of people who could have received the note from over 8,000, an innovative re-enactment took place. They recreated the counting out of the same amounts of money using the same bank staff as September 1977. Using experienced bank employees and the ledgers, they where able to establish more clearly where the money had been distributed and reduce the number of firms that could have received the note down to three – Clark's, Butterfields, and Parkinson's. They also reduced the number of people who could have received the note down to 241 (including Sutcliffe).

Sutcliffe and his wife, Sonia, were interviewed at their home by a detective sergeant from Yorkshire and a detective constable from Manchester. Sutcliffe was asked about his work, and also for an alibi for the night of the murder of Barbara Leach four months earlier. He was unable to provide one. The officers searched Sutcliffe's house, and examined his boots and the tools in his garage. Incredibly, due to a failure in the incident room indexing, either through missing or misplaced cards, the officers were unaware of Sutcliffe's more recent interviews. Of the 241 suspects that were to be interviewed from the original five pound note investigation, only seven had been flagged in the index as having additional information. It was later discovered that Sutcliffe was one of eighteen others who should have fallen into this category, but who had been missed in the initial search of the index.

On 30 January 1980, at the Kirkstall Forge Engineering works in Leeds, Sutcliffe was again interviewed while loading his lorry. He was asked again about his car travelling through red-light districts, and he said that he was home at the time of the Leach murder, which his wife could confirm.

The policemen also had a photograph of the boot print left at the scene of the murder of Josephine Whitaker, but failed to notice that Sutcliffe was wearing the exact same boots when interviewed. Sutcliffe would later recall: 'I stayed dead calm, and as I got into the wagon I realized I was standing on the steps, which were mesh, and they could look up and see for themselves that I was wearing those boots. But they didn't. They couldn't see what were in front of their own eyes.'

The final interview on 7 February 1980 happened as a result of the incident room inspector not being satisfied with the action report from the previous interview. He ordered a more in-depth interview concentrating on Sutcliffe's vehicles, his vehicle sightings in red-light districts and his alibis. Sutcliffe was interviewed at T. & W.H. Clark by two detective constables, where he gave alibis for some of his car sightings, as well as an alibi that he was home on the night of the Whitaker murder, which again Sonia would confirm.

On 25 June 1980, a special 'Ripper Patrol' unit in Bradford spotted his Brown Rover 3.5 driving fast and erratically through the red-light district of Grosvenor Road in Manningham. Two plain clothes officers, PC Bob Doran and PC Graham Melia, clocked the time of the incident at 11.30pm and the location as just past the Royal Standard pub on 22 Manningham Lane. They promptly gave chase and although Sutcliffe had no intention of stopping, he didn't try and lose them either and led them straight back to his home at 6 Garden Lane, parked the car and ran inside. When the officers finally got him to come out there followed a massive argument, which was witnessed by a couple of neighbours. He was arrested there and then and charged with being drunk in charge of a vehicle. The officers were, however, highly suspicious and made a call to the Ripper incident room at Millgarth Police Station in Leeds to gain details on their captured suspect. Word came back that Sutcliffe had been interviewed and eliminated from the inquiry based on handwriting comparisons with the Wearside Jack letters.

It's probably no exaggeration to say Sutcliffe must have felt invisible to the police investigation and reassured that he could continue his murderous campaign.

He would strike again in August 1980.

Of all the murders committed by the Yorkshire Ripper, I find the killing of Marguerite Walls the most puzzling. At the time, the police didn't believe she was a victim of the Ripper, due largely to the fact a rope was used to strangle her. However, there were several similarities to Ripper crimes, such as trauma to the head caused by a blunt instrument (possibly a hammer) and some of the clothing was removed and scattered about the crime scene.

Even after he was arrested and gave detailed confessions to the police, he denied killing Marguerite Walls but after several weeks he came clean and admitted that he was responsible. At the time, the explanation for this murder was flimsy at best. Excuses such as, 'I didn't like the term Ripper, so I used a rope' can hardly be believable, considering he went on to attempt to kill two more women and succeeded in killing a third using his usual Ripper trademark method.

He also claimed he didn't confess to her murder because it might have led investigators to look at more unsolved killings using a rope, which he didn't commit. This could be possible and a fantastic argument is made for this in Chris Clark's book *Yorkshire Ripper: The Secret Murders*.

For now, let's examine the events of 20 August 1980 as history records them. Then I will offer a new explanation, never considered at the time and which, to me, would explain not only why he used a rope but why he first denied the murder and later confessed it to the police.

It had been almost a year since the murder of Barbara Leach and rumours were rife that the Ripper had finally gone away or committed suicide or been locked in an asylum by his horrified family, or had simply given up his crusade.

But all these rumours were proved wrong when he decided to venture back to the streets, choosing once again a non-prostitute as his victim.

Marguerite Walls, known as Margot, was a 47-year-old unmarried woman and former Women's Royal Army Corps sergeant. She worked as a civil servant at the Department of Education and Science office in Richardshaw Lane, Pudsey.

Pudsey is a small town that sits neatly between the western outskirts of Leeds and the eastern fringes of Bradford. It doesn't have a red-light district or any known association with prostitution.

Margot was described as quiet and introvert and was a first-class executive officer; hard-working and conscientious but a total enigma. To her work colleagues she was kind and polite but distant. She seemed to live mostly for her work.

Dark haired and attractive, she lived alone in her detached house at 7 New Park Croft, Farsley, a twenty-thirty minute walk from her work. She wasn't known to have many friends. She nursed her privacy and beyond revealing to her co-workers that she had been born in Lincolnshire, that her family lived in the Midlands and that she served with the Army in Northern Ireland, Margot pretty much kept herself to herself.

On Wednesday, 20 August 1980, she was working extra hours at the office, perhaps getting as much work done as possible before her ten-day holiday, which started the following day. She was a keen member of the Leeds and Bradford Fell Walking Club and had planned to go walking in the Lake District.

She left the office around 10.30pm. The walk home to Farsley, a suburb in Leeds, would take up to half an hour. A cautious woman, she always avoided the short cut that would take her home ten minutes quicker and opted for the safety of the brightly lit main streets. Her preferred route would now take her down the hill of Richardshaw Lane and left onto the main Bradford Road. A quick few minutes towards Bradford and she could cross over the road and turn right into New Street. From there it was only a matter of minutes before she was home. Sadly, she would never make it home. The false illusion that the bright street lights would somehow make her safe proved the opposite as she was now illuminated and alone and, by a misfortune of timing, spotted quite clearly by the Yorkshire Ripper who just happened to be driving past.

On that night, Sutcliffe had decided to venture out and claim another life. He had a perfect opportunity as Sonia was working the night shift at the Sherrington Nursing Home in Heaton. He had originally been intending to journey back to his old hunting ground in Chapeltown in Leeds. With the police apparently eliminating him from their enquiries, he felt it was safe to kickstart his reign of terror once more.

But after leaving his home in Garden Lane and cruising down the Bradford Road towards Leeds, he spotted Margot walking along the pavement to his left. He slowed down as he went past her and from the rear-view mirror he saw her turn the corner into New Street. He parked his car in a nearby road and went after her on foot, a hammer concealed inside his coat.

He walked 300–400 yards quickly and caught up with her as she was passing the stone pillars which marked the large sweeping driveway entrance to Claremont House. At the time this was, ironically, home to local magistrate Peter Hainsworth whose son Richard was one of *The Yorkshire Evening Post* reporters who would soon be covering the killing. She was just 400 yards from her house.

He hit her with the hammer and screamed, 'You filthy prostitute!' Margot stumbled and fell to the pavement. All this took place in full view of the surrounding houses and windows of New Street. Despite the fact that several teenagers claimed to have heard a scream around this time, nobody had heard it outside their window or if they had, they had chosen to ignore it.

Sutcliffe didn't have a knife on him but instead had brought a length of blue and pink cord, around 60 centimetres in length, with knots tied in it to aid his grip. He pulled it from his coat, looped it round her neck and used it to try and drag her through the gates of Claremont House. But Margot had no desire to go quietly.

Despite being quiet and reserved in public life, she put up one hell of a fight. She lashed out at Sutcliffe, punching and clawing at him, swinging wildly with her black suede handbag. She was fighting for her life as the hammer blow had opened up her head and she was losing blood and strength. The wildly scattered bloodstains were a grim testimony to Margot's determination and courageous final fight with the Ripper. To this day, when I read the reports, I find it incredible that nobody saw or heard a thing.

I'd like nothing more than to write about how neighbours came to her rescue or she succeeded in fighting him off, escaping to join the small handful of survivors who would later tell their tale. But in the end, she was, sadly, overpowered and dragged into the gardens which lay to the left of Claremont House. Here she was felled by another hammer blow, then strangled with the rope.

When Margot was quite dead, her killer stripped off her black coat, purple skirt and blouse so she was naked except for her tights. He flung her clothes aside before dragging her body further into the garden and crudely burying it beneath a mound of grass cuttings.

When he had finished he made his way back to his car on Bradford Road. I'd like to think he was left bruised and battered by the woman who refused to lay down and die.

Revisiting the crime scene today, there aren't any real changes to New Street or the surrounding houses since 1980. There is, however, a dramatic change to the area where Margot died. The eighteenth-century Claremont House still stands but it is no longer privately owned and is no longer surrounded by trees and greenery. It is now the refurbished and extended Claremont Care Home. The stone pillared gates, which once marked the entrance to the rough and ragged driveway leading up to the house, have been removed and a wider, stoned driveway now leads the way to the nursing home.

The land, which was once the front gardens of Claremont House where Margot's body was discovered, was sold off to housing developers who built eight houses on the site. They lie to the left of the driveway and now form part of the cul-de-sac known as Claremont Gardens. I doubt that the present occupier of 3 Claremont Gardens knows that a victim of the Yorkshire Ripper was found directly in front of their living room window.

One thing that is noticeable about the crime scene location is how different the area was to the Ripper's usual lairs. Farsley is an upper middle class area, inhabited mainly by professionals. It was certainly no Chapeltown, Moss Side or Manningham. It was also well lit with houses lining both sides of New Street. Anyone looking out of any of the windows could get a good view up and down the entire length of the street. The grounds of Claremont House provided cover and the privacy Sutcliffe needed to carry out the murder without being seen, but the initial attack was very public.

It's also odd that, if Sutcliffe was indeed going in the direction of Leeds to commit another murder, he took a longer and more awkward route to the city by avoiding the much quicker and easier motorway at the recently built Stanningley Bypass.

Can we take his confession seriously? Can we believe that he caught site of Margot Walls as he drove past on the back road to Leeds, decided to park and go after her down the street and managed to catch up with her at the only convenient spot on the street for privacy? Or perhaps Sutcliffe was already there in the grounds of Claremont House, concealed by the bushes and waiting to pounce on an unsuspecting victim. But why would he be there, in a respectable area of Leeds, without a knife? Let's look at a possibility.

On Monday, 11 July 1977 the *Telegraph & Argus* reported the brutal Ripper attack on 42-year-old Maureen Long. It said that Professor Gee had linked her attack and injuries to those of other Ripper victims. At last the police had a survivor who was definitely attacked by the Ripper and was now the most important eye witness in the investigation. But in a bizarre and foolish act of journalism, the paper printed her address as 22 Donald Street, Farsley.

Number 22 Donald Street was directly opposite the garden of Claremont House. Farsley was not a known red-light area; it was certainly not an area near any of the attack zones of Chapeltown or Bradford, yet here we have Sutcliffe prowling about in the gardens of a house a mere 30 yards from Maureen Long's home. Is it possible that Sutcliffe was stalking or keeping watch on Maureen's house? He may have got a morbid kick out of being so close to her, or perhaps, in a more sinister twist, he was waiting for the opportunity to find her alone and finish the job by silencing her forever.

On 4 January 1981, after Sutcliffe had been arrested, he said: 'I saw Maureen just a couple of weeks ago. I was in the Arndale Shopping Centre with my wife when I came face to face with her. I recognized her immediately. She seemed to look at me, but she obviously didn't recognize me.'

This statement was taken just four months after the Marguerite Walls' murder. It's more than possible his encounter with Maureen came before 20 August and 'a couple of weeks ago' could just be a figure of speech. Seeing Maureen in the shopping centre obviously had an impact on him and possibly shook him up a bit. The fact he mentioned it to officers after his arrest shows it was on his mind.

He said she didn't recognize him but maybe it brought home to him that, as long as she was walking around, they might see each other again and next time she might be able to place him. He couldn't have been comfortable knowing a woman who could potentially identify him was walking the same streets as him, and it would only be a matter of time before he bumped in to her again. He would have known where she lived thanks to the newspaper printing her address, so maybe he decided to stalk her house. Perhaps he planned to wait for her to come out by herself but this time change his method of attack or, as some have suggested, converted back to a method that he may have used in the past but which, had so far, not been linked to him.

Following Margot Walls' death, several papers reported that at 8.30pm on the night of the murder, a suspicious looking man aged around 35 had been spotted lurking around the bushes of Westroyd Park, Farsley, less than 50 yards from the crime scene. He was described as 'acting strangely' as he was caught by passers-by popping in and out of the bushes several times. Was this Sutcliffe lurking near Maureen's house?

It's worth pointing out that Maureen Long and Margot Walls were of similar height and both had short dark hair. Both wore black the night they were attacked, and both carried a similar large brown handbag. Is it possible that Sutcliffe had been waiting in the gardens of Claremont House, saw Margot coming down the dark street and mistook her for Maureen? After failing to kill Maureen when he attacked her, was he stalking a possible witness with the premeditated aim of killing that witness so she couldn't identify him? If true, it would seriously diminish his chances of claiming to be on a 'mission from God to rid the streets of prostitutes'. As there is no record of Maureen being a prostitute, it would also dismiss his claims that the non-prostitutes he killed were simply mistaken for prostitutes. Now it starts to make sense.

Fast forward to his interviews and confessions:-

> **Officer:** 'Did you kill Margot Walls?'
>
> **Sutcliffe:** 'No. You've got a mystery there.'

Maybe he denied killing her because he feared that once police linked Maureen's address to the murder site, it would be obvious that Sutcliffe was stalking a non-prostitute in the hope of killing her. If so, there could be no defence of mistaken identity or mission from God plea with this one. But look what happens after a short while, when no police officer links the addresses together – Sutcliffe freely admits to the murder and claims he was mistaken in thinking Margot Walls was a prostitute. I doubt we will ever know the real events of that night but there is certainly a series of bizarre coincidences which shouldn't be ignored. Whatever the circumstances, it looks like Sutcliffe would attempt to use the rope again in another attack before reverting back to his Ripper trademarks.

The body of Margot Walls was found around 9.30am the morning after her murder by two gardeners hired to maintain the grounds. As they arrived they noticed her beige-coloured shoes lying 30 yards up the driveway. Curious, they had a quick look around and found a torn purple skirt, leather shopping bag and chequebook close to a rockery which bordered the garden area. The police were summoned and a search of the gardens soon revealed the body hidden in the undergrowth, next to a small stone garage and covered with lawn trimmings. The rest of her clothing, including a cardigan and blouse, was nearby, also concealed with grass cuttings. Her body was battered and bruised with two lacerations to the skull. No stabbings or mutilations had taken place but a ligature mark around her neck was visible. Three of her ribs had been fractured as her killer had knelt hard on the chest while strangling her. There were also scratch marks around the vagina, most probably caused by the killer's fingernails.

DCS Jim Hobson arrived on the scene to take charge and, with Professor Gee on annual leave, called in Professor Alan Usher, a Home Office pathologist based in Sheffield. Formal identification of the body was conducted by Margot's brother, Robert John Walls, a university information officer from Beacon Rise, Stourbridge.

While the post mortem was being conducted, more than 100 police officers were drafted into Pudsey to begin exhaustive house-to-house enquiries. Over the next five days, twenty-five officers on their hands and knees searched every inch of the garden in a desperate hunt for clues. A photograph taken at the time shows officers combing through the leaves and grass cuttings. In an attempt to jog people's memories, WPC Liz Ross 31, took part in a reconstruction of the murdered woman's walk home, using the actual bag Margot carried the night of her murder.

By the end of the week DCS Hobson told the press: 'I am satisfied the woman's death was in no way connected with the Ripper killings.' It was an understandable response. In an age when criminal profiling was in its infancy, detectives were all too quick to rule out any victim that didn't have the trademark hammer blows and stabbings, which usually accompanied a Ripper attack. There were obvious Ripper-like elements, such as the trauma to the head, clothing rearranged and discarded, but the use of a ligature and the lack of stab wounds, appeared to suggest a different killer. It's doubtful whether they ever realized Maureen Long lived within sight of the crime scene. If they had, perhaps they may have thought differently.

CHAPTER 19

Upadhya Bandara

'She was walking slow like a prostitute, I followed her down the narrow road. I hit her on the head with a hammer. I didn't have any tools on me to finish her, so I used that rope to strangle her.'

Peter Sutcliffe 1981

Upadhya Bandara was a 34-year-old doctor from Singapore who had arrived in England in August 1979. She had won a scholarship from the World Health Organization and was studying a postgraduate course in Health Service Studies at the Nuffield Centre for International Health and Development at Leeds University.

On Wednesday night, 24 September 1980, after visiting friends she started to walk home in Headingley, Leeds, an area popular with students. It was just after 11pm but it would only be a ten-minute walk to her room in the large Victorian semi-detached property of 5 St Michaels Villas, just off Cardigan Road. Here she lived with five other students from the nearby university. At the time, the 5ft 4ins graduate was wearing brown trousers, a red crew neck T-shirt and a beige cardigan.

As she passed by the Kentucky Fried Chicken takeaway at 2 Otley Road, with the Arndale Centre to her right, she noticed a man inside staring at her. She continued on her way and crossed over the main street and up to the junction of St Michael's Road. At this junction is the famous student pub the Skyrack, which had closed for the night, and the adjacent area was quiet and deserted. She turned down past the pub and crossed over the road and into St Michael's Lane. She was now less than 250 yards from her front door. Had she looked behind her she would have seen the same man was now following her. Sutcliffe had found a new stomping ground outside the red-light district and any woman was a target. Only a few hours before, he had driven Sonia to her part-time job at the nursing home before making the short twenty-minute journey to Leeds.

Her failure to notice that she was being followed resulted in her taking the quicker route of Chapel Lane, a narrow, dark and deserted cobblestoned alleyway, which ran down the back of the large terraced houses of St Michael's Crescent and came out again at Cardigan Road. When I visited the area a few years ago it struck me as a place I would not want to walk down after dark. The lane is lined with high walls and fences that lead to the back yards of the houses. It's still badly lit and, no doubt at the time, most of the back gates would have been locked and any back porch lights would have been turned off. There really was nowhere to run to, had you found yourself in trouble there.

If she had just kept walking along the slightly longer, but brighter and more open St Michael's Road, Sutcliffe may not have taken a chance on the attack. But that's all very well in hindsight.

Instead, Upadhya had turned left into the dimly lit Chapel Lane and had walked about 60 yards until she was adjacent to the rear of 4 St Michael's Crescent. It was here that she suddenly heard footsteps approaching from behind. Thinking it must be someone in a hurry home, she moved to the side to allow them to pass. But they didn't pass her by.

Instead Sutcliffe struck her on the back of the head with a hammer, which stunned the poor woman. As she turned to fall into the wall he lunged again, this time striking her on the front of the head. She collapsed onto the cobbles and, although dazed, she remembered the feeling of rope being looped around her neck and suddenly restricting her air supply and constricting her wind pipe. It was the same rope Sutcliffe had used on Margot Walls just over a month before in Farsley. He used it to drag Upadhya to a secluded bin area that serviced the adjacent properties. Her shoes were scraping along the floor as he dragged her but he felt they were making too much noise, so he stopped and tried to pick her up, holding her under the armpits and moving her towards the bins. But with two arms now carrying the woman, he couldn't hold the rope properly and this allowed Upadhya enough time to push her fingers between the rope and her neck and give her a small but precious amount of air. Despite this, she was dazed and bleeding and losing consciousness fast.

Now I said earlier that there was very little help if you found yourself in trouble in Chapel Lane, but there was one item there which we don't have in our modern age. Today, we have plastic wheeled bins with attached swing lids. In the 1980s there were only large metal bins with detachable lids. As he dragged her into the bin area he knocked over one of the metal containers. The lid fell off and hit the cobbles with a smash and clatter, effectively alerting those in the nearby houses that someone or something was in their back yard. Two such residents were Valerie Nicholas and her husband Hugh at 5 St Michael's Crescent. Having heard the commotion, they decided to investigate.

In the meantime, Sutcliffe removed Upadhya's shoes and handbag and threw them over a wall. But when he saw the porch light of Number 5 come on, he abandoned his attack and fled back up Chapel Lane to the safety of his car, which he had parked round the back of the Arndale Centre.

Valerie and Hugh Nicholas had heard the sound of Sutcliffe's footsteps as he ran off, and when they opened the back gate they found the battered and unconscious Dr Bandara lying among the bins. Valerie attended to her wounds while Hugh phoned for an ambulance and the police. An officer patrolling nearby was alerted to the scene and promptly arrived by car to take over first aid treatment. He checked her and, despite her wounds and a large pool of fresh blood on the ground, she was still alive.

Upadhya was still unconscious, but started to come round once the ambulance arrived on the scene. According to Valerie Nicholas, 'She was concussed and when she came to in the ambulance she had no idea who she was or what had happened to her.'

Later in hospital, when she had regained her senses, she described her attacker as aged 25, around 5ft 4ins in height, with black hair and a full beard and moustache. Once again, the police were faced with another assault on a lone woman at night, with head injuries caused by a blunt instrument and another similar description of a young man with dark hair and a beard. This was an almost identical description given by Marcella Claxton, Marilyn Moore and Tracy Browne.

You would think by now it was fairly obviously the work of the same man, but you would be wrong. Due to the lack of any stab wounds, and the use of a ligature, it was not considered to be a Yorkshire Ripper attack. It was, however, linked to the murder of Marguerite Walls and, rather than consider the fact it could be the same man, police now believed there was a second killer on the loose.

Upadhya had recently successfully completed her course and was due to go on holiday. However, she cancelled her ten-city European trip to recover from her attack, assist the police with their enquiries and take part in a police reconstruction. If she could save another poor woman from the same fate as her own, she felt it her duty to do so.

Incredibly, back in Singapore, Upadhya's family were unaware of her ordeal as she forbade her employers at the Singapore Health

Ministry to tell her them what had happened. She eventually returned home in December 1980 and, when quizzed about the scar on her forehead, explained it away as a minor accident. It wasn't until February 1981, after Sutcliffe had been arrested, that she broke her silence and told her loved ones.

CHAPTER 20

Theresa Sykes

'I couldn't run, I couldn't do half the things you always think you would do in this situation... . When you're 16, you don't think about it. I just thought, oh it won't happen to me...but it did.'

Theresa Sykes

On Bonfire Night, Wednesday 5 November 1980, Sutcliffe returned to Huddersfield. He had killed there almost three years earlier when he brutally murdered prostitute Helen Rytka in the red-light district on 31 January 1978. This time he would choose an ordinary housing estate and his victim would be a teenage mother.

He drove down New Hey Road towards Huddersfield town centre for about a mile and a half, then turned left up Acre Street at the roundabout. He parked his car in the car park of the Bay Horse pub at 1 Acre Street and got out to prowl the area on foot.

At the same time, less than ten minutes' walk away at 35 Willwood Avenue, 16-year-old Theresa Sykes was arguing with her boyfriend, Jimmy Furey, over which one of them was going to get some cigarettes from the nearby shop. Jimmy was adamant that he couldn't be bothered to make the walk in the cold, so Theresa stormed off and left him in charge of their three-month-old son Anthony.

Theresa was the daughter of Raymond and Margaret Sykes, landlords of the Minstrel pub in Cross Church Street in Huddersfield. After she had fallen pregnant in September 1979, she left her home at the pub and dropped out of school to set up home with Jimmy.

In May 1980, Anthony was born and the young couple, who planned to marry the following year, moved into their two-bedroomed, semi-detached house shortly after. It overlooked the playing fields between Willwood Avenue and New Hey Road, connected by a dark, narrow path running up the front of the houses. A short walk down this path would bring Theresa to the Jeco Off Licence at 22 Acre Street.

As she made her way out onto the main road she noticed a man standing in a telephone box, close to the police station at 80 New Hey Road. She thought it odd that he was just standing in there without using the phone and carried on to the shop.

On her way back, she passed the phone box and noticed the man was no longer there. She briskly turned left into the playing fields and started to walk back to her house via the same narrow path she had just come up. Her journey would take her past the cul-de-sac endings of Bay Close, Peckett Close, Millfield Close and Raynor Close. As she got half way down the path she became aware of footsteps behind her. Glancing back, she noticed the man she had seen in the phone box about 10ft behind her. She turned round further and their eyes met before he veered off to the left and into Raynor Close.

Relieved that the stranger had disappeared, she carried on walking and was under the light of the path's final lamp post and just 20 yards from the safety of Willwood Avenue when she looked down at the ground, saw her own shadow and, to her horror, a second shadow behind it. 'When I saw the shadow that's when I became really frightened,' she would recall years later.

She turned left and tried to open the gate of the garden opposite but as she grabbed it, she felt a blow on the top of her head and she collapsed. She was, however, still conscious and managed to grab the hammer and wrestle with her assailant in a desperate bid to survive. A few yards away, her boyfriend Jimmy was watching the Bonfire Night fireworks that flared and boomed, admiring the rockets with their multi-coloured trajectories and dazzling starbursts. He was also mindful that Theresa should be home at any minute and was keeping an eye on the path. He saw the commotion but thought it might be kids fighting. He ran downstairs and shouted up the street.

By the time Jimmy had got downstairs, Sutcliffe had seized control of the hammer and delivered two more blows to the back of Theresa's head but, miraculously, she still hadn't lost consciousness. Perhaps it was hearing Jimmy's shout and sensing that he was about to be disturbed that made Sutcliffe back off and look about but then, horrifically, he came back to have another go at her.

'He walked away then stopped and came back again,' recalled Theresa later. 'I screamed then.' This time Jimmy ran barefoot to where she was. Sutcliffe took off but was only walking at first, probably because he didn't want to attract too much attention.

As Jimmy reached the stricken girl, he shouted 'Theresa!' At that point, Sutcliffe began to run and Jimmy gave chase. Sutcliffe ran into Millfield Close and down to the junction of Reinwood Road, all the while pursued by Jimmy who was shouting, 'I'll fucking kill you!' Eventually Sutcliffe scrambled over a wall into a garden where he hid behind a bush.

Jimmy came to the end of Millfield Close and stared into the darkness of Reinwood Road. He looked up and down the street but couldn't see a soul, muttered under his breath and realized his bare feet were cut from the chase. He hunted about for a short while before turning back to help Theresa.

When he got back, a neighbour, Rita Wilkinson, who had also come out to investigate after hearing noises, was attending to Theresa's wounds. Rita had taken her inside and Theresa sat in a chair with blood flowing furiously from her head; clearly panicked, the teenager became hysterical and once again started screaming.

Within minutes of the ambulance being called, police were swarming all over the area, hoping to catch their nemesis who in all likelihood was still hiding nearby. A dog handler arrived and as the trail was still hot, the Alsatian quickly picked up the attacker's scent following it along Raynor Close to Reinwood Road, down Adelphi Road and then to a small dirt track, where, to the dismay of the investigators, the trail went cold.

Theresa was rushed to Huddersfield Royal Infirmary and then transferred to Chapel Allerton Hospital in Leeds where she underwent neurosurgery on her head wounds. On 1 December, she had further surgery on her injuries at Pinderfields Hospital, Wakefield and eventually, over five weeks after Sutcliffe's attack, she was allowed home.

Police refused to publicly link the attack with the Ripper and insisted they were looking for a local man. When asked about a connection with this crime – and similar crimes in the area – to the Yorkshire Ripper, DCS Hobson said, 'They have found no indication of a connection yet.'

Theresa's parents, Raymond and Margaret Sykes did not agree with the police. Raymond believed there were too many similarities between the attack on his daughter and other known Ripper victims and claimed that Theresa was the monster's latest victim. 'I know it was him,' ran the headline in the *Daily Mail*. However, police refuted these claims with DS Tony Hickey repeating the official line: 'This was a local incident.' Raymond Sykes would eventually be proved correct, although not for another month.

Theresa was lucky to be alive and doctors believed that not losing consciousness probably saved her life. Unfortunately, the relationship between Jimmy and Theresa wouldn't be so lucky.

Traumatized by what happened, Theresa shut herself off from anything to do with the attack and in a way blamed Jimmy for the fact she went out that night. It also didn't help that gossiping neighbours had started rumours that it was Jimmy who assaulted her, and this put a lot of stress on their relationship. Within a short time, Theresa was back living with her parents and Jimmy was barred from Raymond's pub, the Minstrel, for assaulting two customers who claimed he was behind the attack. He eventually lost contact with his son.

Theresa Sykes is now a divorced mother-of-four in her mid-fifties, but the physical and mental scars are still there. She still has a table-tennis-sized ball dent at the top of her head from when Sutcliffe first hit her with his hammer and she suffers from memory loss. However, in recent years she has made peace with Jimmy and said, 'After the attack me and Jimmy split up but I know I owe him my life.'

That cold November night back in 1980 was as close as Sutcliffe had ever come to being caught in the act. It would also help lead to his downfall eight weeks later when, for the first time, his alibi for this attack and Sonia's recollection of the night did not coincide.

CHAPTER 21

Jacqueline Hill

'I'm reluctant to get involved in criticism of the police, but Scotland Yard are the best in the world. West Yorkshire Police have done all they can. They should recognize the greater experience and expertise of Scotland Yard. Now is the time to call them into the case.'

Arthur Bottomley, Labour MP for Teesside, Middleborough

Around 9.28pm, Monday, 17 November 1980, the Yorkshire Ripper killed for the thirteenth and final time. His victim was a 20-year-old Leeds student called Jacqueline Hill. The circumstances surrounding this murder would be considered a breaking point for the patience of both the press and the public. It would call into question the competence of West Yorkshire Police, leave public confidence in the authorities at an all-time low and, for the first time in British history, have a prime minister threatening to personally take charge of a police investigation.

At 9.22pm that evening, 19-year-old Andree Proctor, a second-year English student, left a friend's house in Headingly to make the five-minute walk back to Lupton Flats, the student halls of residence on Alma Road. Had she left the house three minutes earlier, it's highly likely she and not Jacqueline Hill would have been the Ripper's next victim. Her journey home would take her along Otley Road, past the shops at the front of the Arndale Centre, whose windows were already lit up with Christmas decorations. She would then make a right turn at the corner and come into Alma Road which would incline for 200 yards until reaching Lupton Flats.

As she turned into Alma Road at 9.26pm, something caught her eye no more than 50ft in front of her. The road was poorly lit and she couldn't make out what it was, but it seemed to move quickly off the footpath and into the shadows to her right-hand side. She paused and later she would say: 'I just did not realize what I had seen. I knew it was suspicious… . It was creepy, I had to do a double take and saw something move.' Cautiously, she carried on up the road and kept an eye on the area where she saw the movement – it was a dark piece of waste ground beside the rear of the Arndale Centre. Due to the low street lighting, it was impossible to see further into the unlit patch of ground and not wanting to hang around, she moved off the footpath into the centre of the road and hurried past quickly, continuously glancing over her shoulder for the next 100 yards until she reached the safety of the halls of residence. She went to bed, thinking nothing more about what she had seen.

Twenty-five minutes later, another student and resident of Lupton Flats, Amir Hussain, made the same journey home along Alma Road. The 33-year-old Iraqi post-graduate engineering student at Leeds University, reached the same spot Andree Proctor had been at nearly half an hour earlier but, unlike Proctor, he stayed on the footpath and in doing so, noticed something lying on the ground. It was a woman's cream-coloured handbag. He picked it up for closer inspection. It was a raffia-type bag with two red vertical stripes and a red strap. Inside the bag was a Barclaycard with the name Jacqueline Hill on it and a small amount of money. He thought it unusual the handbag would still contain money if it had been discarded by a thief, so he assumed one of the students must have dropped it on their way home to the halls.

Back at Lupton Flats, he was unable to find anyone to hand the bag over to so he took it back to the block where he lived. In the kitchen he and fellow students, 49-year-old archaeology postgraduate Tony Gosden, 20-year-old Paul Sampson and 19-year-old Paul Dinsdale, examined the bag again and, in the bright light, saw spots of blood on it. Gosden was a former Hong Kong police inspector and knew the significance of what had been found. After a brief discussion, it was decided that Paul Sampson would call the police. The call was logged at Headingly Police Station at 12.03am on Tuesday 18 November.

Two young officers were dispatched to investigate the claim and within a short time had arrived at the hall of residence and examined the bag. It was decided they would take the bag back to the station with them, but this didn't rest easy with the students who insisted that some attempt should be made to try and find out if Jacqueline Hill was in her room somewhere on the campus. The officers were reluctant to take up the search, claiming it was far too late to go around knocking on people's doors. They did, however, agree to go to where the handbag was found and conduct a search. Amir Hussain, accompanied by Paul Dinsdale, led the officers to the spot where he had discovered the bag but, to the frustration of the students, the officers only conducted a three-minute torchlight search of the grounds of a house on the other side of the road from where the bag was found. After a brief look round they said they were busy and had to go on another call.

Now it's easy, with hindsight, to say a thorough search should have been conducted at the time, but surely a bloodstained handbag in Yorkshire Ripper territory would warrant more than a three-minute look around? Certainly both sides of the street should have been checked. It was a police blunder that would come back to bite Chief Constable Ronald Gregory in the coming weeks.

If they had conducted a more thorough search along the side of the street that the handbag was found, they would probably have noticed a knitted mitten and a pair of glasses on the footpath. A further search of the overgrown waste ground next to this would have resulted in the discovery of the Yorkshire Ripper's thirteenth victim lying next to the Arndale Shopping Centre. No one knows for certain but, had a proper search been conducted, it is possible Jacqueline would have survived, just as Maureen Long did three years earlier. Their injuries were very similar.

It wasn't until 9am that morning that a passer-by spotted the mitten and glasses on Alma Road. An hour later, Donald Court, one of the managers from the Arndale Centre, was taking the previous day's takings to the bank. His journey took him along Alma Road and up the service ramp located at the back of the building. This ramp led up to the shopping centre's car park.

After walking half way up the ramp, he stopped to switch the heavy bag of change into his other hand. At this point, he looked directly onto the waste ground below and saw what he first took to be a tailor's dummy lying in the undergrowth. As he stared, he realized to his horror that it was a woman and he ran to fetch help from a nearby shopkeeper. Jacqueline Hill's lifeless body was lying amid a clump of small saplings by a large ash tree. The body was naked except for a pair of woollen, blue, knee-length socks and it was partially covered by a check-patterned coat.

Within twenty minutes, a dozen police cars had descended upon Alma Road, sealing off the street. The waste ground was taped off and officers awaited the arrival of the mobile headquarters, followed by DCS Peter Gilrain, head of the Ripper Squad in Leeds and Detective Superintendent Alf Finlay, head of the Eastern area CID.

A trail of wooden duckboards snaked its way across the grass from Alma Road to the body so detectives could examine Jacqueline without disturbing any evidence. Dozens of workers in a six-storey office block pressed themselves up against the glass to gaze down on the police investigation and watched as several large sheets of black tarpaulin were brought in to conceal the body from public view. Professor David Gee, an all too familiar face for

West Yorkshire Police, arrived on the scene. In his company was another Leeds pathologist Dr S. Siva. The main focus was whether the Yorkshire Ripper had struck again.

Up until this point, the discovery of the handbag the night before was unknown to the crime scene investigators, and it wouldn't be until later in the day when Paul Sampson, one of the students involved in the previous night's discovery, was on his way to Otley Road and saw the police cars and taped off crime scene. He approached one of the stationed officers to inform him of the events the night before. The handbag was eventually traced to a lost property office in the police station.

It didn't take long for Professor David Gee to determine that this was indeed a Ripper killing and a sullen-faced George Oldfield confirmed as much to the public in a press conference twenty-four hours later.

Jacqueline 'Jackie' Hill was a young and gifted third-year student. Those that knew her say she was gentle and caring, a selfless person who was loving towards others, a genuine good Samaritan who had planned to devote her life to the community but never got the chance. She had high hopes of becoming a probation officer after leaving Leeds University. Her father, Jack, had retired early from his job as a plant mechanic when doctors found he was suffering from lung cancer. Her mother Doreen, 46, was an arts and crafts teacher. The Hills lived comfortably in a four-bedroom detached house in Lealholm Crescent, Ormesby, Cleveland, with their two younger children, Adrian, 16 and 15-year-old Vivienne. When she wasn't in Leeds studying, Jackie taught children at Sunday school at the family's local village church. Sadly, she would be buried there following her murder.

Tragically, all the hard work and dedication Jackie put into her studies, along with a series of unfortunate decisions and events, would come together to play a cruel hand in her death. On the night of her murder she decided to put in extra study time by journeying into Leeds city centre to attend a seminar in Cookridge Street for probation officers. At 9pm, after the seminar was over, Jackie would normally have walked back to her flat in the city centre, but she had recently moved out of that accommodation at the wishes of her parents. They were concerned about all the Ripper attacks that had taken place in Leeds and, following the Barbara Leach murder, they felt the students' halls of residence near Otley Road would be a much safer option. They convinced her to move into Lupton Flats. All the blocks there were secure and contained nine flats across three floors with five people per flat. Jackie's flat was in the middle of the ground floor with four other female students.

She seemed to enjoy her time there and frequented several of the student pubs along Otley Road, namely the Skyrack and the Original Oak.

From Cookridge Street, it would normally take forty minutes to walk to Alma Road, but as it was wet that night, Jackie decided to take the Number 1 bus from Beeston to Holt Park. This would drop her off opposite the front of the Arndale Centre. From there it was only a two-minute walk to Lupton Flats. The bus wasn't particularly busy that night, with only fifteen passengers in total, and within twenty minutes she had reached her stop.

Unfortunately, that same night Peter Sutcliffe had decided to take another life.

Earlier that day, he had made a delivery to Kirkstall Forge in Leeds and clocked off at the Clark depot between Shipley and Bradford at 7pm. He phoned Sonia and said he was in Gloucester making a delivery and would be home very late. It was then that he decided to take his brown Rover V8 and head over to Headingly in Leeds. It had been seven weeks since his last visit, when he had attempted to murder Dr Bandara but had to flee before he could complete the kill.

Arriving in Otley Road just before 9pm, Sutcliffe parked his car and bought some Kentucky Fried Chicken from the outlet attached to the Arndale Centre. He returned to the car a short while later and ate his meal while scanning the street ahead for passers-by.

At 9.23pm, the green and white Holt Park bus pulled up in front of him and Sutcliffe watched as five people disembarked, going off in different directions. One of them was Jackie Hill. He watched her cross over by the lights and go in the direction of Alma Road. The 5ft 6ins student with short dark brown hair was wearing a two-tone checked grey duffle coat with a detachable hood and plastic toggles. She was wearing dark blue jeans, brown shoes and an off-white fluffy woollen scarf and Fair Isle patterned mittens. She carried a cream handbag.

Sensing his opportunity, Sutcliffe fired up the ignition, drove up past the bus stop and turned right into Alma Road. As he did so, he overtook Jackie who had just turned the corner, and stopped about 40ft in front of her on the left-hand side of the street. He sat and waited for her to draw level with the car, a ball-pein hammer in his hand. Within a minute Jackie passed the car. Sutcliffe jumped out and quickly crossed over to the other side of the road to position himself behind her.

As she passed by the opening of the waste ground next to the Arndale Centre, he struck her on the back of her head and, like so many of his victims, she crumpled to the floor. He bent down to drag her off the path and into the undergrowth, but he had only got her half way in when a car turned onto Alma Road and drove towards him. He ducked down and, amazingly, the occupants of the vehicle failed to see him or if they did see him, they failed to comprehend exactly what was going on. After the car had gone, Jackie began to move and moan. Sutcliffe bent down and hit her again with the hammer, then he picked her up into a standing position, grabbed her under her armpits and dragged her into the waste ground. It was at this moment student Andree Proctor had entered Alma Road and caught a fleeting view of Sutcliffe dragging Jackie Hill into the darkness. As Andree paused to consider what she had seen, Sutcliffe had managed to move the body a full 30 yards into the undergrowth and was now hidden by trees and shrubs, just below the car park ramp of the Arndale Centre. From the darkness he was able to see out onto the much brighter street, and he remained silent as he watched Andree Proctor walk past. He must have thought she hadn't seen him as he continued with his evil deed.

He began stripping off Jackie's clothes and tossing them aside. He pushed her bra up and her knickers down before producing a yellow-handled screwdriver from his pocket and thrusting it repeatedly into her chest and lungs. As he did so he stared at her face and noticed the poor woman's open eyes staring back at him. This angered him for some reason and he stabbed the screwdriver into her eye, piercing part of her brain. When he was finished he left her lying on her back with her head pointing towards the car park ramp, legs spread open and feet pointing towards the entrance to the waste ground. He draped Jackie's checked coat partially over her body.

After leaving the scene he got back into his car and made a U-turn before driving back down to Otley Road. As he got to the bottom, a passer-by signalled to him that he was going the wrong way on a one-way street. He ignored the man and drove on. Unfortunately, the passer-by wouldn't remember anything about the car other than it was box-shaped.

The killing of yet another 'respectable' victim, particularly in the heart of Headingley, which was full of young, female students, living away from home for the first time, caused an eruption of public fury and indignation. Terrified women started demanding police action to protect them and, following reports that the police failed to react to the discovery of Jackie's handbag, the press thundered that Chief Constable Gregory should call in Scotland Yard immediately.

Five years of frustration was vented not only on the front pages of every newspaper in the country, but by the public and the politicians as well. The reputation of West Yorkshire Police was being battered by three sides.

A tired and beaten looking George Oldfield, who had been attending a senior officer conference in Derbyshire, confirmed what most people realized: the Yorkshire Ripper had taken his thirteenth victim. 'The man is obviously very mentally ill and has got this sadistic killer streak in him. He can flip at any time,' said Oldfield. He appealed to women, in particular, to look at their husbands, boyfriends, brothers and fathers and ask themselves if he could be the man police wanted.

But the public had heard the same statement many times before after other Ripper murders. This time they weren't listening. Scores of frantic parents began phoning Leeds University demanding their daughters be sent home immediately. In the week following the murders, the grounds of Lupton Flats were virtually empty of all women apart from a WPC who was stationed there to gather information.

The student union piled pressure on the local council to guarantee student safety and made it perfectly clear that the Ripper was no longer interested in killing only prostitutes. They demanded the university scrap single-sex residential buildings and dormitories as having a dorm with just women in it would only encourage the Ripper to stalk those areas. They wanted security fencing around the perimeter of the grounds of the halls of residence and compulsory transport to take students home at night from seminars and lectures.

The feeling that West Yorkshire Police were ill equipped to catch the Ripper was now being repeated publicly by local MPs. Sir Donald Kaberry, Conservative MP for Leeds North West suggested it was time to reintroduce the death penalty: 'Let's all help to get this dastardly man caught – and I would say hanged,' he said.

Tom Torney, Labour MP for Bradford South said it was now time for Scotland Yard to take over the investigation. He told the *Telegraph & Argus*:

'I have every respect for the West Yorkshire Police but this incident over the handbag was a very bad mistake…. Previously I thought the Ripper hunt should be left in local hands, but this has made me change my mind. I shall wait to see what I get from the Home Office then decide whether or not to put down a parliamentary question or something of that order.'

Arthur Bottomley, Labour MP for Teesside, Middleborough, where Jackie Hill's parents lived, said: 'I'm reluctant to get involved in criticism of the police, but Scotland Yard are the best in the world. West Yorkshire Police have done all they can. They should recognize the greater experience and expertise of Scotland Yard. Now is the time to call them into the case.'

All eyes were now focused on Chief Constable Ronald Gregory and what he was going to do next. The press and the public could not be ignored any longer.

On 24 November, Ronald Gregory arranged a press conference to confirm that Scotland Yard would not, under any circumstances, be brought in to lead the Yorkshire Ripper manhunt. He repeated the fact that two senior Scotland Yard officials had already been to see the investigation and had confirmed West Yorkshire Police were doing all they could to bring the perpetrator to justice.

Gregory spent almost an hour fighting off criticism regarding the disastrous decision not to conduct a proper search of the area after Jackie's handbag had been found. He agreed that a full investigation into the handling of the search would be undertaken to see if anything had been mishandled. He came close to losing his temper as he faced the angry culmination of five years of public, police and media frustration about the Ripper murders. In an attempt to defend his officers Gregory said:

'It is easy to say, with hindsight, that the officers should have found the body. There were three spots of blood on the handbag. At this stage, the girl had not been reported missing. So here was a report of a handbag with one or two spots of blood on it. This was not significant. Property is found every day with bloodstains on it. With hindsight you could say that every time there is a handbag found we should organize a search.'

Returning to the issue of Scotland Yard, he also dismissed suggestions that the case needed to be looked at with fresh eyes. He said:

'Statements have been made criticizing police action…before the full facts can be known. They can only undermine the morale of the force and unnecessarily intensify public concern. It is not my intention to recall the Metropolitan Police. Two of their most experienced officers, Commander Jim Nevill and Detective Superintendent Joe Bolton, spent several weeks with the investigating team last year. Apart from certain useful advice to the West Yorkshire officers, they were satisfied everything possible was being done.'

He was backed by PC Rod Thomas, branch secretary of the Police Federation, who said:

> 'There is nothing they can do which is not already being done. People who talk about bringing in the Yard are living in the past, when small borough forces did not have the facilities or expertise for murder inquiries. Since amalgamation of the little forces we have just the same back up as Scotland Yard. I do not think it will be any good to bring them in. We have every confidence in the officers in charge of the case and all that is needed is a little bit of luck.'

The press conference painted the police as tired, desperate and out of ideas. Even more so when it was suggested a curfew be put in place for women after the hours of darkness. This suggestion caused uproar among the female community, who rightly pointed out that the Ripper was a man and so all men should have a curfew placed on them. Some women's rights groups put forward the idea of an identity badge or licence for men who had to be out after dark and God help any man who stepped outside without one. They also pointed out that women couldn't even defend themselves from attack by going out armed with a knife as the police had repeatedly threatened to arrest and charge anyone carrying an offensive weapon, regardless of why they were carrying it. Women improvised by making sure they carried items in their handbags such as sharp (or discreetly sharpened) steel combs and long sharp hat pins.

It was apparent that very soon anger would turn to violence.

A two-hour march through Leeds city centre was organized by 'Women Against Violence Against Women' and they were joined by other women's liberation organizations from around the north of England. In a defiant act aimed directly at the suggested curfew, it was arranged as a night-time protest.

Over 500 women gathered in the city centre and it was clear from the atmosphere in the crowd and the police presence, that things could turn violent at any moment as they marched along Boar Lane and into Briggate. At the Odeon cinema, the X-rated Brian De Palma film *Dressed To Kill*, starring Michael Caine and Angie Dickinson had been running since July. As the march passed by, around seventy protesters broke off from the main group and rushed the front doors of the cinema. The screaming, chanting and banner-carrying crowd struggled with police and around fifty got into the foyer. They tried to break into the projection room but the quick-thinking projectionist saw them coming and barricaded the door. In frustration, some of the protestors turned their attention to the main auditorium where the film was being shown. They shouted insults and abuse to the audience before throwing cans of red paint over the screen.

One of the cinema staff, Carol Getliffe, later told *The Yorkshire Post*:

> 'It was like a riot in there and I was terrified. So were some of our customers – about 200 were watching the film and most of them were just stunned. It happened so quickly. Eventually more officers arrived and the remaining protestors were taken out and the front doors locked.'

One of the march organizers, Betty Power, later explained to the same newspaper the motives behind attacking the cinema:

> 'The film is sexist and exploits the sexual aspect of killing. That's bad enough but how dare they show it in Leeds at this time? It depicts Ripper-style killings. The whole idea is abhorrent and women have a right to be angry and to react violently when they are confronted with this kind of sheer exploitation.'

From Briggate, the march moved into Merrion Street and Woodhouse Lane. All the while, the women were screaming at passing men, 'Get off our streets!' and 'What were you doing last Monday?' (the night Jackie Hill was murdered). They stopped buses and cars, pounding them with their fists and banner staves. Eventually they reached the BBC studios where they stopped and three dozen officers formed a cordon across the entrance.

Directly across the street was the Fenton pub, where a small crowd of men had come out to watch the protest. Probably the worse for drink and sensing the opportunity to wind the women up, they started singing, 'There's only one Yorkshire Ripper!' Minutes later, about thirty women broke away, crossed Woodhouse Lane and tried to get into the Fenton but were prevented from doing so by officers who beat them to the doors.

There were further violent scenes at the Parkinson entrance to the university campus. Police lost their helmets as they struggled with scores of women shouting obscenities and trying to get into the Science and Technology compound. When that failed, they tried to get into the refectory where the rock band Iron Maiden was playing. A window was smashed as they struggled with stewards who manged to fend them off and get the doors closed.

The protest continued through the campus into Clarendon Road where about fifty halted near Leeds Grammar School and prevented the traffic from passing.

Explaining the reason for the march, one woman said: 'The country should know women are no longer being passive.'

The social unrest eventually reached 10 Downing Street and Prime Minister Margaret Thatcher. She was so outraged at the apparent lack of progress in the case that she decided she would come to West Yorkshire to personally take charge of the police investigation. Many of the senior cabinet and her advisers had to talk her out of it. Not only would it be a PR disaster for the police force and the public's trust in the law but politically (and probably more accurately) should Thatcher be unable to make a difference, it would reflect badly on the Conservative Government.

In late November 1980, Ronald Gregory announced the formation of a new 'Super Squad' to take on the Yorkshire Ripper. The team, unprecedented in police history, brought together the cream of British police officers. 'They are probably the most experienced group of officers who could be mustered to assist this investigation,' said Gregory.

The team consisted of Commander Ronald Harvey, recently appointed adviser to the Home Office Chief Inspector of Constabulary; Assistant Chief Constable David Gerty of the West Midlands force; Deputy Chief Constable Leslie Emment of Thames Valley; Assistant Chief Constable Andrew Sloan of Lincolnshire, who was national coordinator of Britain's Regional Crime Squads and Stuart Kind, one of the country's leading forensic scientists and director of the Home Office Central Research Establishment at Aldermaston. Speaking of the line-up, Gregory said:

> 'It is a unique squad. This inquiry and these murders have reached such proportions that we have to think of involving men other than our own officers. It is an acknowledgement of the public concern and our concern. I am hoping for new ideas from this team. We cannot carry on in the same groove because we have had no success so far.'

George Oldfield was still technically head of the Ripper investigation, but following his heart attack his health was not good, so the decision was made to promote Jim Hobson to temporary assistant chief constable, the same rank as Oldfield. In a further blow, Ronald Gregory put Hobson in overall charge of the new Super Squad. Oldfield was still considered by many to be in charge but it was in name only. Hobson now had the power to appoint his own detectives. In certain circles his promotion was regarded as a criticism of the way Oldfield had conducted the investigation.

By the end of November, several members of the West Yorkshire Police Committee pronounced themselves unhappy about the way the new Ripper Super Squad would work. One, Michael Parkinson, told *The Yorkshire Post* that he and the others had been misled into believing the team would remain in situ until the killer was caught. 'I was most surprised to learn from the newspapers that the team would only be advisers and would be staying here for only a short time,' he said.

It would appear that the formation of the Super Squad was nothing more than elaborate window-dressing to stifle the growing public clamour for Scotland Yard to be called in. If the squad was formed for its cosmetic effect, it didn't take long for the paint to wear off.

On 19 December 1980, Jackie Hill was buried in the small village church near her family home in Cleveland. Over 200 mourners joined her parents, family and friends as her coffin was carried to the grave. As they stood in the rain, bidding farewell to the bright young student, her favourite song, *Bridge Over Troubled Water* by Paul Simon and Art Garfunkel, played out.

Around this time an anonymous letter arrived at the Millgarth incident room in Leeds. The letter, which was one of many received from the public, suggested the police should focus their attention on a man called Peter Sutcliffe of Garden Lane, Bradford. The writer of the letter was Trevor Birdsall, the close friend who had been with Sutcliffe during three of his previous attacks. Despite previously put off from coming forward because the hoax tape from Wearside Jack made him think the culprit had a North-Eastern accent, this time his conscience and his suspicions had got the better of him. But for so many women it was too late.

By the time he came forward with his letter, there was a backlog of 36,000 documents waiting to be read and filed. It was estimated that it would have taken the existing staff nine months to go through every one, and only providing no new murders occurred.

Today the waste ground where Jackie Hill was dragged to her death has been converted into an overspill car park for the staff and management of the Arndale Centre. A metal boundary fence has replaced the wire mesh that once lined the perimeter. The service ramp that leads to the customer car park can still be accessed and from here it's easy to see how her body was discovered by Donald Court on that cold Tuesday morning in November 1980. The ramp still offers a complete view of the now thirty-two-space car park where the investigation into the Ripper's final victim was conducted. The murder site is between car park space number thirty and thirty-one.

The surrounding area is now extremely popular as part of the famous Otley run pub crawl, which, on any given weekend, sees students, stags, hens and birthday parties don fancy dress to take part in a sixteen-pub drinking competition from Woodies in Far Headingley, past the Arndale Centre down to the Dry Dock pub at the edge of the city centre. Although many of the pubs have changed since 1980, a few have stayed the same, namely the Skyrack and the Original Oak where Jackie socialized with friends. Across the road, the Kentucky Fried Chicken sits in the same spot where Sutcliffe bought his meal, minutes before he attacked and killed her.

Further up Alma Road, Lupton Flats is still home to hundreds of Leeds University students, who come and go at all hours of the morning. They continue to walk past the spot where the Ripper claimed his last victim and through the halls of residence via security gates, probably unaware that the gates were only added as a result of a fellow student being murdered less than 100 yards away.

CHAPTER 22

The Ripper Unmasked

*'Do you understand what I am saying? I think you are in trouble,
serious trouble.'*

Detective Inspector John Boyle, 4 January 1981

On 2 January 1981, the Yorkshire Ripper's reign came to an end in the driveway of a large Victorian house in Sheffield. His capture was all down to two police officers on routine patrol, but they had no idea at the time.

Earlier that day in Bradford, staff at the Heaton Royds Hospital on Cottingley Cliffe Road had seen a prowler lurking around the back of the main building, just behind a stone wall that divided the hospital grounds from the Northcliffe golf course.

After seeing Sutcliffe's picture in the newspaper, three nurses and a doctor would all later claim that the mysterious prowler was definitely him. They said he was hiding behind the 4ft stone wall, watching staff walking from the main building to the mortuary. One of the female nurses who confronted him said he was putting his socks and shoes on. The sighting in broad daylight was barely a mile from where Sutcliffe lived on Garden Lane in Heaton. The time of the incident was not recorded so it remains unknown, but it had to be before 4pm for it to be broad daylight in the beginning of January.

The staff had been on the alert ever since Thursday, 20 November 1980, when a phone call was made to the switchboard of Leeds General Infirmary from a man claiming to be the Yorkshire Ripper. He warned that his next victim would be a member of the female staff. At first this was regarded as a crank, but when further calls were made the next day and again on the following Monday, police were informed, and although it is unknown what details were given during the calls, they were taken seriously because all the hospitals in West Yorkshire were put on red alert for a possible Ripper attack.

Warning posters were put up around the wards and staff quarters advising women not to go out in the dark by themselves and to make sure all doors leading to the wards were kept locked after visiting hours. Should a member of staff have to journey outside, they were advised to keep to well-lit areas and report anything suspicious.

Commenting on the incident at Heaton Royds, the nurse who spotted Sutcliffe told the *Bradford Star*:

> 'He was just watching me going over to the mortuary. There were two of us and he was watching us through a hole in the wall. There was something fishy going on. I ran over to him and he was in the process of changing his socks and shoes and he claimed that he was just playing golf. He put his socks on quickly and he was screwing his hands together all the time. He then tried pulling his lip over his teeth and I realized he was hiding a gap.'

The medical staff who had seen the prowler described him as having dark short hair, a beard and a wild look in his eye. Police were called but by the time they arrived he had disappeared into nearby Heaton Woods.

This sighting of Sutcliffe was finally reported in the *Bradford Star* on 11 June 1981 but seems to have been missed by the national press. Heaton Royds Hospital eventually closed its doors at the end of the 1990s and since 2001 has been a residential property. Now known as Chak Gardens, it is the family home of Mohammed Aslam, owner of the West Yorkshire-based Aagrah restaurants.

If it was Sutcliffe prowling about the grounds of the hospital, what was he doing there that day and why was he changing his socks and shoes? I will suggest a few ideas later but for now we should explore the next set of events.

Sometime between 3pm and 4pm that day, Sutcliffe told Sonia that he was going to collect the key of his sister's car which had broken down again. However, he didn't drive to her home in Bingley but instead drove to a spare car parts scrap yard near Cooper Bridge Road in Mirfield Leeds. In 1981, the yard was a branch of the famous Doncaster Motor Repairs but today it's known as Motorhog and its address is listed as Wakefield Road by the Cooper Bridge Road roundabout.

He picked up two number plates from a Skoda, one which had fallen off the vehicle and the other he pulled off. At 9pm he called Sonia from a service station (location unknown) and told her he was having car trouble. An hour later, having used black electrical tape to fix the stolen plates over those on his Rover, he was cruising around the Hanover Square area of Sheffield, a red-light district 30 miles from his home. This would be the first time he would visit Sheffield with the intention of murder. He knew very well the police presence would be minimal as they were all preoccupied in Leeds, Bradford and Manchester. He would cruise around the area for thirty minutes before selecting a potential target.

Denise Hall, 19, was one of the prostitutes working in Hanover Square when Sutcliffe pulled up in his brown Rover 3500 with black vinyl roof. He asked her if she was 'doing business' and as Denise bent down to look through his car window she noticed his eyes were dark, almost black, and appeared to pierce through her own. This frightened her so she said 'Sorry' and began to walk away. Sutcliffe drove off, but as he brought his car out of Hanover Square and turned right into Broomhall Street, he saw another working girl and decided to choose her instead.

Birmingham-born Olivia Reivers was 24 and of Jamaican descent. She had moved to Sheffield seven years earlier and had been working the red-light district for the last four years. She was the mother of two children and had a live-in boyfriend named Joe. They seemed to have an arrangement when it came to her working as a prostitute, although he preferred her to have regular clients than risk the danger of strangers on the street. She knew Denise Hall well. Earlier that night, she had made the short journey from her house in Wade Street to call for Denise who lived in Brunswick Street. They had walked to their usual patch together and conducted business as normal, but unlike Denise, Olivia wasn't as cautious. When Sutcliffe pulled up looking for business she had no hesitation in going with him. In later interviews Olivia would say:

> 'I don't know why Denise was suspicious, but she turned him down. Obviously something must have warned her off. You might think you can judge people's characters by looking at them, but I can't look at a person and decide what sort they are. We were all worried about the Ripper but no one knew what he looked like, so we wouldn't have known him if we saw him. Anyway, you can't afford to turn down the chance of ten pounds in this game… . I was walking on the pavement when the car stopped. The driver asked me if I was doing business and I said I was. I told him it was ten pounds in the car with a rubber. He said that it was OK.'

Olivia got in and the pair drove towards Broomhall Road and she directed him up Park Lane and then left onto Glossop Street. After taking another left, they were now in Melbourne Avenue. A lot of the women working the Hannover Square area took their clients to this quiet tree-lined avenue. Situated in the upmarket residential area of Broomhill and with big stone Victorian and Georgian properties with large shaded driveways, most of the houses had been converted into business premises. Number 3 was a large, three-storey Victorian property with a long sweeping driveway that curled round the back of the building. Visiting the scene today it's easy see why it was a popular choice for prostitutes seeking privacy with their clients. The driveway was set back from the avenue and the high walls and bushes either side afforded considerable cover. It was also close enough to the boundary of the red-light district so the women could be back quickly for another client.

In 1981, the building was home to the Federation of British Engineers Tool Manufacturers, and was better known as Light Trades House. Sheffield still teemed with hundreds of small businesses and workshops producing goods from locally made special steels, including cutlery and handmade tools such as drills, slit saws, scythes and sickles. Light Trades House represented these businesses. In its heyday, more than thirty different associations were based there.

Its decline came when global companies became less interested in maintaining an involvement in national trade associations and by the time it closed its doors in 2002 most of the groups had already gone their separate ways, linking up with larger umbrella organizations from their sector.

Today Light Trades House is home to LabLogic Systems, manufacturers of medical machinery. They do not want to be associated with the Yorkshire Ripper story and refuse to discuss the building's connection to the case.

Back in 1981, Sutcliffe drove Olivia through the gates but instead of going all the way to the back of the building, he swung the car round in the driveway so he was now pointing towards the entrance gate. He then reversed it further up the drive so his back bumper drew level with the doorway of the house. No doubt he did this so he could make a quick getaway.

Meanwhile, a local routine patrol car was making its journey from nearby Hammerton Road Police Station to Hanover Square. The driver was 31-year-old Probationary Constable Robert Hydes and his supervisor, 47-year-old Police Sergeant (PS) Robert Ring, a man with many years' experience in policing the city. Both officers were working the night shift, which was 10pm to 6am. PC Hydes had been assigned to Hammerton Road station after completing his seven months' South Yorkshire police training. As part of his mentoring of the young constable, PS Ring would accompany him on a routine patrol of the red-light district to show the new officer how to handle the issue of kerb crawlers operating in the area. They cruised around the usual sites of Broomhall Street and Hanover Square before deciding to journey up to the well-known prostitute hangout of Melbourne Avenue.

Meanwhile Sutcliffe and Olivia were parked in the driveway of Light Trades House and once the engine was turned off Olivia asked, 'Would you like to pay first, please?' Later she would say:

> 'He gave me a ten pound note and I took a rubber out and had it in my hand putting the money into the packet. He asked: "Do you mind if I talk to you a bit?" I said: "No." He said that he had had an argument with his wife. He did not say what about or what the result of the argument had been. He asked me my name and I said Sharon. He said his name was Dave. He then took off his car coat and put it on the back seat.'

Olivia went to work unbuttoning his trousers and trying to arouse him. Ten minutes later nothing was happening. Olivia would later state:

> 'When we were parked in the drive in Melbourne Avenue I tried to arouse him but he was cold as ice; he didn't respond at all, so he said we would try again later... . He spoke about his wife quite a lot. He seemed worried about her... . He mentioned something about not being able to go with her.'

Sutcliffe suggested getting into the back seat and trying again, but Olivia refused and said she preferred to stay where she was. It was a wise move as Sutcliffe would no doubt have used the locked door method on her as he had done on Vera Millward, Marilyn Moore and Yvonne Pearson. He already had the ball-pein hammer lodged down the side of his seat, along with a knife he had taken from his kitchen drawer. The coat he had just placed on the back seat contained another knife and the length of knotted rope he had used on Marguerite Walls and Dr Upadhya Bandara.

'It looks like you aren't gonna make it tonight luv,' said Olivia sympathetically. Sutcliffe mumbled something and sank back into his seat. Later she said:

> 'It was then that I began to sense something was wrong. Drunks who don't measure up to it get angry with themselves, but this was the first guy I'd come across who couldn't manage it when he was stone cold sober. Then I noticed he became tense, frightened like, though I don't know what of. For some reason,

which I still can't explain, I began to get nervous myself. He was
showing no signs of wanting to drive off and I began thinking
that he never intended to have sex with me in the first place.
I was trying to work out why he had paid me ten pounds.'

Suddenly the front of the windscreen was illuminated by headlights
as a police car turned into the drive and parked nose-to-nose with
Sutcliffe's Rover. PC Hydes and PS Ring had made their way into
Melbourne Avenue at around 10.50pm, and spotting the brown
Rover had decided to go and investigate.

When PC Hydes approached the car, Sutcliffe told Olivia:
'Leave it to me. You're my girlfriend.' After winding down the
window, he said as much, as well as saying it was his car and that
his name was Peter Williams. Meanwhile, the more experienced PS
Robert Ring made his way to the back of the car and noted down
the licence plate as HVY 679N.

He then went back to talk to Sutcliffe himself. In his police
report that was read at Sutcliffe's trial, he stated: 'He said that she's
my girlfriend and I asked what her name was. He said: "I don't
know, I have not known her that long." I said: Who are you trying
to kid? I haven't fallen off the Christmas tree. To which Sutcliffe
said: "I'm not suggesting you have."'

Ring returned to the police car and, via his pocket radio, checked
the registration number with Sheffield Police Headquarters
Control Room who did the check on their Police National
Computer terminal linked to the national system. He was soon
joined by PC Hydes, who had been openly sceptical about the
information Sutcliffe had given him. While the two officers waited
for the results of the check, Sutcliffe asked Olivia: 'Can't you
make a run for it?' She replied: 'No, I can't,' and explained that
she was a well-known prostitute.

When the information came back that the plates were registered
to an Aslam Khan and actually belonged to a Skoda not a Rover,
the two officers returned to Sutcliffe. After informing him that the
number plates were not for his car, PS Ring removed the car keys
from the steering column. PC Hydes, meanwhile, had discovered
that the false plates were only held on by black electrical tape.
The two officers then escorted Olivia to their police car.

Sitting alone in his car, Sutcliffe recognized the seriousness of
the situation and seized the opportunity. He grabbed the ball-pein
hammer and the single-bladed knife he had concealed under his
car seat, got out of the car and headed for a stone porch at the front
of the building behind his car. In his haste, he left his jacket folded
on the back seat. Walking twelve paces to the corner of the building

and out of view of the officers, he saw an oil storage tank. He took both weapons and placed them onto some leaves on the ground behind the storage tank and against the wall, hoping the officers wouldn't hear the clinking sound.

He may have also tried to jump over the bordering wall and into the next garden but had not managed it and this may have been what caused the thud that led the officers to look back and shout at him to ask what he was doing. Sutcliffe emerged from the shadows and replied, 'I've just fallen off that bloody wall,' and that he was 'busting for a wee'. He was told to 'come round and go for a piss in the corner' where they could see him, but he said it didn't matter. He returned to his car where he was arrested on suspicion of stealing the licence plates. Before leaving in the police car, he grabbed his coat and put it on. His brown Rover was left in the driveway and both Sutcliffe and Olivia were taken to Hammerton Road Police Station were they arrived at 11.25pm.

Once there, Sutcliffe asked to use the bathroom. He still had the knife in his jacket, which he needed to get rid of. He said later: 'I went there straight away as soon as I got to the police station. I dropped it [the knife] in the top of the water cistern so it wouldn't be found in my possession.'

Whilst writing this chapter it occurred to me that I should try and get a picture of the toilets where Sutcliffe hid the knife. Unfortunately, Hammerton Road Police Station no longer exists. The building that Sutcliffe and Olivia Reivers was brought to that night closed its doors in 2014, partly due to lack of funding. It was demolished in 2016. At the time of writing, it is a waste ground being used as an unofficial car park by local residents.

After he returned from the bathroom, Sutcliffe was questioned further and admitted his real name was Peter William Sutcliffe and that he had stolen the licence plates because he had been caught drink driving the previous year and would no doubt be banned from driving once he had gone to court. He felt there was no point in renewing his car insurance, which was up shortly, and so he stole the plates. It seemed a fairly plausible story and under normal circumstances he would have been booked and released on bail to appear at a petty sessions court in the future. The whole process could have lasted ninety minutes and Sutcliffe could then be free to go. But the desk sergeant wasn't happy and knew that West Yorkshire Police would want to be informed of anyone from Bradford being caught with a prostitute.

A phone call to Leeds confirmed that Sutcliffe had already been interviewed by the Ripper Squad, that he worked in the mechanical trade and that his alibis seemed to have come only from family.

Furthermore, he had denied ever being with prostitutes. It was now 2.30am on Saturday morning and it was decided to lock Sutcliffe in the cells for the night, contact Dewsbury Police Station, inform them of the arrest and ask if they could send someone in a car to pick him up and question him further. Sonia was informed via telephone that her husband would not be home that night. At 5.12am it was established who would be handling the theft charge. Dewsbury police informed Sheffield police that, after the new shift came on duty at 6am, they would send somebody to collect Sutcliffe.

At 8am that morning, 3 January 1981, the desk sergeant at Dewsbury informed the Ripper incident room at Millgarth of Sutcliffe's impending arrival. In the past, the stealing of licence plates might not have warranted an officer to contact the Ripper Squad but, two weeks earlier, a mass briefing of 500 sergeants by Ronald Gregory himself had emphasized the need for diligence and forwarding of all information to the Ripper Squad, no matter how unimportant. This was a direct result of the botched search conducted during the Jackie Hill murder when officers had found her bloodstained handbag but not followed it up with a proper investigation of the area.

At 8.55am Sutcliffe arrived at Dewsbury Police Station in the back of a West Yorkshire Police car. He was accompanied by three officers; two were in the lead car with Sutcliffe and the third was driving his brown Rover. His jacket pockets were searched, a standard police procedure which, unbelievably, was not carried out in Sheffield. In his pockets, detectives found some money, a pair of his underpants and a piece of blue and red plaited nylon rope about 3ft long. Asked what the rope was for he said it was to lift things such as car engine parts. This rope was knotted, with two knots at each end and two additional knots a few inches apart near the middle. When asked what these were for, he replied it was to make it easier to grip the rope. (When the house, garage and car searches were conducted later on, further pieces of rope were seized including one about 4ft long, which was found in Sutcliffe's bedside cabinet.)

He was asked to remove his clothing so it could be examined thoroughly. This was one of the most bizarre and shocking revelations in the case, yet nobody seemed to pick up on its significance. When he took off his trousers, the officers found that he was wearing a rather odd garment underneath. They appeared to be special leggings, which he said were leg-warmers. They consisted of two sleeves of a jumper made of a silky material, crudely sewn together, upside down, and pulled up to his waist with a leg fitting in each arm. There was a large gap in the leggings, which exposed his private parts. More revealing was the fact that he had sewn in extra padding around where his knees would go. Such a bizarre garment could only have one obvious use. The large gap was for easy access to his penis and the padding was to protect his knees while kneeling on the ground. The only reason he would have use for such an item would be to kneel over an unconscious, dying or dead person lying on the ground. He could masturbate over his victim while killing them to satisfy his necrophilia – the sexual gratification he gained while performing sex acts on dead women.

Incredibly, no mention was made about this attire at his subsequent trial, nor was he identified as Marcella Claxton's attacker, who masturbated over her after attacking her in 1976 but failing to kill her. Both pieces of information would have been vital to the prosecution in proving that Sutcliffe killed simply for sexual kicks. He was a man sexually obsessed with the dead, whose erotic thoughts were those of a necrophilic sexual deviant obsessed with having power over an unresisting and unrejecting partner.

My question is, at what point did Sutcliffe put on these murder trousers? Where did he hide them this whole time? It's not the kind of garment you could easily explain away if found by a loved one or friend. He must have arrived in Sheffield with them on but he must have changed into them after he left home, hence why his underpants were in his coat pocket.

I want to put forward the theory that the earlier sighting of Sutcliffe lurking behind the wall at the grounds of Heaton Royds Hospital was the moment he was changing into his new clothing. Was he really stalking the nurses or was he removing his underwear and slipping on his leggings? To do so he would have to remove his shoes and put them back on again, which is exactly what he was doing when the nurse caught him by the wall.

It's worth bearing in mind that the wall is about 3ft high. A person would have to be crouching or kneeling down to be looking through a gap in that wall. Had Sutcliffe been kneeling down to look at the nurses going in and out of the mortuary while masturbating? To my memory no mention of this incident has been written about before except in that small article in the *Bradford Star* months later. I'd hazard a guess that no proper searches of the area were conducted by the police following this article and if you consider they never found the purse belonging to Wilma McCann, and the fact that some serial killers keep trophies, it's just possible there are more secrets out there by that wall. It's an intriguing thought.

At 9.10am that morning, Sonia Sutcliffe telephoned Dewsbury Police Station for the first and only time to enquire about her husband and she was told he was being questioned about an offence in relation to his car. By then CID officers had begun to interview him. Within the first hour Sutcliffe, who did not appear surprised at such attention for such a minor offence, told police officers he was a lorry driver from Bradford and had made regular deliveries to Sunderland in his 32-ton artic. He talked about his interest in cars and said that he had been interviewed as part of the five pound note inquiry and as a result of the surveillance operations in red-light areas.

At 10am detectives in charge of the interview contacted the Ripper incident room at Millgarth to say they might be interested in this Bradford lorry driver called Sutcliffe. He had told them he had already been interviewed about the Jean Jordan murder and the five pound note as well as by West Yorkshire Police after being recorded in the red-light area surveillance operations. He was a size 7 shoe and had a gap in his teeth. One of his cars had been a white Ford with a black roof. Hadn't the one driven by Maureen Long's attacker been similar? Alarm bells had started to ring in the minds of the interviewing officers.

At 12.30pm, DS Desmond O'Boyle arrived at Dewsbury Police Station. He was attached to the Ripper Squad and had once been a detective in Manningham. He had seen the files on Sutcliffe, which showed that he was already known to the Ripper Squad and had been seen a number of times by police during the Ripper investigation, firstly in regard to the five pound note, then because of surveillance when his registration plate was noted in Bradford's, Leeds', and Manchester's red-light areas, and because he worked for an engineering firm. Samples of his blood and hair were taken and the interview continued. He was asked about his car being seen in Manchester and he said he'd never been there. He gave the usual excuses about how his job took him home through the red-light districts and how he had already been interviewed and given the police his handwriting samples. He discussed his alibis and the fact he had been at home with his wife on Bonfire Night when Theresa Sykes was attacked.

It was near 5.30pm on Saturday evening, and by this point DS O'Boyle felt it was probably a false alarm and Sutcliffe was unlikely to be the Ripper. He didn't have a Geordie accent and his handwriting didn't match the Wearside Jack letters. When his blood test came back, it was indeed a rare blood group B but, unlike the sender of the tapes and the killer of Joan Harrison in Preston 1975, Sutcliffe was a non-secretor (meaning little or none of his saliva and semen would contain antigens to reveal his blood type). O'Boyle was prepared to recommend that Sutcliffe be released. However Chief Superintendent John Clark, who was in charge at Dewsbury, was not convinced and still considered Sutcliffe a major suspect in the Ripper case. He ordered DS O'Boyle to express his 'displeasure' to the duty officer at the Millgarth incident room at the lack of rank of the officer sent to interview Sutcliffe. Probably not wanting to get a hard time from his superiors, O'Boyle decided to stay on when his shift finished at 6pm to help out his replacement, Detective Inspector (DI) John Boyle, who had been sent down to take over. The interview continued into the night, pretty much repeating all the things that had been asked previously. At one point in the interview it was decided to send out for fish and chips. Sutcliffe joked that he would go and get them, but they would be cold by the time he got back.

It was now 10pm on Saturday night and over in Hammerton Road Police Station in Sheffield, PS Robert Ring had clocked on once again for another nightshift. Checking up on the previous night's proceedings, he was amazed to find the man he had arrested in Melbourne Avenue was still being held for questioning by the Ripper Squad. It was then he made the most important decision of his career. In the back of his mind, he recalled that he had seen Sutcliffe go to the side of the house on the night he was arrested. The police had been busy putting Olivia Reivers into the car but he remembered Sutcliffe had disappeared for a few moments.

He decided to return to the Light Trades House and explore the area where Sutcliffe had gone.

At around 11pm, PS Ring arrived back in Melbourne Avenue. With torch in hand, he walked to the spot where Sutcliffe's car had been parked and then moved over to the stone porch area where Sutcliffe had gone. He walked round to the back of the porch where he saw the oil storage tank. He shone his torch along the side of the tank and there, to his disbelief, he found the ball-pein hammer and knife lying on the leaves. I can only imagine what a moment that must have been for him to realize he had arrested the Yorkshire Ripper.

He radioed back to the station where he was given a rather frantic answer of: 'Don't touch anything, a photographer is on the way.' As Ring waited for back up to arrive, DI Slack, who was stationed at Hammerton Road station, remembered that when Sutcliffe had first been brought in, he had asked to go to the toilet. Slack and another officer made a check of the toilets and in the cistern above the urinals they found a wooden-handled knife. The game was up.

At 12.10am on Sunday morning, 4 January 1981, DI Boyle telephoned his Ripper Squad superior, DSI Dick Holland at his Elland home in Leeds. This was it, the moment he had waited five years for. Sutcliffe had been arrested sixteen hours earlier and only now, for the first time, did there seem to be a real breakthrough. On the orders of Dick Holland, an officer was immediately assigned to sit with Sutcliffe in his cell.

At 9am Dick Holland was briefed at Bradford Police Station. DI Boyle and DS O'Boyle had been sent back to Sheffield to re-interview Olivia Reivers. Holland would now go personally to 6 Garden Lane and confront Sonia Sutcliffe. Taking Inspector George Smith and DC Jenny Crawford-Brown they arrived at 9.30am. They interviewed Sonia about her husband's whereabouts on the key nights of the murders and attacks. It transpired that out of all the nights in question, Sonia only remembered Bonfire Night and the fact Sutcliffe had come home around 10pm. This revelation blew apart his claim of being at home at 8pm when Theresa Sykes was attacked. Sonia identified the kitchen knife found in Sheffield as one she had bought in a set years ago.

Dick Holland then moved to the garage and ordered his officers to start bagging up various tools, including screwdrivers, chisels, hammers and a hacksaw. Holland knew the hacksaw was a key piece of evidence because the Ripper had tried to cut Jean Jordan's head off with a hacksaw; a fact purposefully withheld from the press, public and most of the ground detectives. This may or may not have been a good idea considering several past interviews had resulted in Sutcliffe's house and garage being searched by officers. The hacksaw that hung in his garage was the same one that had been used on Jean Jordan, yet no detective searching the garage knew about it. When Holland and Crawford-Brown left the house, they took Sonia with them for further questioning.

Now they had the weapons and they had a lot of circumstantial evidence to go with it, but in 1981 DNA evidence was unknown and there was no way of knowing if they were the weapons that had been used in previous murders. Could they really prove Sutcliffe had committed all the Yorkshire Ripper murders? Could they get him to crack under questioning?

Inspector Boyle had all the information he needed and this time he was joined by DC Peter Smith, who was requested by Dick Holland because of his long service on the Ripper Squad and intense knowledge of the case.

At 12pm, the interviews continued, gradually building up speed and pressure. Officers went through all the details Sutcliffe had provided before, only this time they were tying him up. He was pressed about the amount of times his car had been logged in red-light areas in Leeds, Bradford and Manchester. How could he explain his car being seen in Manchester if he'd never been there? He said it must be a mistake. The detectives called his bluff and told him they had double checked all the records and it was definitely his car. Sutcliffe began to get rattled and started mumbling that his car had broken down in Bradford city centre and he had left it in the car park at Bradford City Library, and that 'someone must have used it to go to Manchester and put it back on that spot.' It was quickly pointed out to him that the person would have had to fix his car first then take it to Manchester only to bring it back again and park it in the same spot. Sutcliffe knew his excuses were unravelling fast.

By 2pm Boyle and Smith were pressing Sutcliffe hard, particularly about the night of Theresa Sykes' attack on 5 November 1980. His alibi had been shot down by Sonia admitting he hadn't been at home at 8pm but that he came in around 10pm. They now felt the time was right to ask him about his movements that night.

Boyle: 'Why did you go to Sheffield that night?'

Sutcliffe: 'I gave three people a lift to Rotherham and Sheffield from Bradford. They stopped me on the M606 and offered me ten pounds to take them home, so I did.'

Boyle: 'I don't believe that. I believe you went to Sheffield on Friday night with the sole purpose of picking up a prostitute.'

Sutcliffe: 'That's not true. It was only after I got to Sheffield and had declined an offer to go with a prostitute that I decided to use the money I got from the hitch-hikers and go with one.'

Boyle: 'When you were arrested in Sheffield, you had a prostitute in your car which had false plates on it. I believe you put them on to conceal the identity of your vehicle in the event of it being seen in a prostitute area.'

Sutcliffe: 'No, that's not true. To be honest with you, I've been so depressed that I put them on because I was thinking of committing a crime with the car.'

Boyle: 'I believe the crime you were going to commit was to harm a prostitute.'

Sutcliffe: 'No, that's not true.'
Sutcliffe was clearly rattled and it was now time for Boyle to drop the bombshell.

Boyle: 'Do you recall that before you were put in a police car at Sheffield you left your car and went to the side of a house?'

Sutcliffe: 'Yes, I went to urinate against the wall.'

Boyle: 'I think you went for another purpose.'
There was no response from Sutcliffe. He just sat there looking at the floor. Boyle waited a moment to let it all sink in before continuing.

Boyle: 'Do you understand what I am saying? I think you are in trouble, serious trouble.'
There was another long pause before Sutcliffe finally spoke, this time with a sense of defeat.

Sutcliffe: 'I think you have been leading up to it.'

Boyle: 'Leading up to what?'

Sutcliffe: 'The Yorkshire Ripper.'

Boyle: 'What about the Yorkshire Ripper?'

Sutcliffe: 'Well, it's me.'

Both officers leant back in their chairs, glancing towards one another as the gravity of what they had heard sank in. Five years had seemed a lifetime and here it was, finally over. The most notorious serial killer since Jack the Ripper was sitting right in front of them.

Outside the interview room Dick Holland had decided it was time to make a phone call to the man he regarded as his superior officer and it wasn't going to be DCS Jim Hobson, the man officially in charge of the Ripper Squad. The phone call went to his old boss, George Oldfield, who was having his Sunday dinner at the time. He shouted down the phone: 'George, we've got the bugger! Get over here fast before Hobson does!'

Over the next twenty-four hours – apart from a break when Sutcliffe was returned to his cell to rest from 3.30am to 8.30am on the Monday morning – Boyle and Smith took perhaps the most incredible statement ever given by a killer. DS Smith sat at the desk and wrote down the words while Sutcliffe sat in front of the desk but sideways, resting one arm on it. DI Boyle paced about the room while asking the questions. Sutcliffe's detailed accounts left no doubt in the minds of the detectives that this was indeed the Yorkshire Ripper. As he would chillingly state, all the details were locked in his head, 'reminding me of the beast that I am.'

After five years the Yorkshire Ripper investigation had resulted in two-and-a-quarter-million police man hours, 250,000 people interviewed, 157,000 cars checked, 28,000 official statements taken and 27,000 houses visited.

It was the largest murder inquiry in the history of the British police and the ultimate irony was that it was solved almost by accident.

CHAPTER 23

Mad Or Bad?

'I'm gonna do thirty years or more unless I can convince people I am mad and maybe then ten years in a loony bin.'

Sutcliffe to Sonia in Armley Prison, Leeds

By 4pm on Monday, 5 January 1981, Dewsbury Town Hall had attracted a crowd of more than 2,000 people waiting to see the Ripper being brought to court. As the police van pulled up, an angry mob cried: 'Hang the bastard!' and 'Killer!' But they were deprived of seeing him as Sutcliffe was ushered into court under a blanket. Fifty officers rushed in to form a human wall between the baying crowd, some of whom had clambered on to car roofs hoping to catch a glimpse of the accused as he entered the side door of the hall. Pebbles and stones thrown at the police van flew over their heads.

The oak-panelled room on the first floor was packed with more than 200 reporters. At about 5pm, Sutcliffe was led into the court, handcuffed to a guard. Court Clerk Dean Gardener asked: 'Are you Peter William Sutcliffe of 6 Garden Lane, Heaton, Bradford?' After an affirmative response, he continued: 'You are accused that between 16 November and 19 November 1980 you did murder Jacqueline Hill against the peace of our Sovereign Lady the Queen. Further, you are charged that at Mirfield, between 13 November and 2 January, you stole two motor vehicle registration plates to the total value of 50p, the property of Cyril Bamforth.'

He was then ordered to be remanded in custody at Armley Prison in Leeds. Here he would be assessed by doctors and further police interviews would take place.

Meanwhile over in Bradford, Peter and Sonia's house in Garden Lane was besieged by reporters and onlookers all hoping to get a scoop on the Ripper's arrest. It became so bad that residents petitioned the council to block off the street from the public. Sonia had rather wisely moved out to stay with her parents. When she eventually returned she found her windows had been smashed and an attempt had been made to burn the house down.

On 20 February, Sutcliffe was charged with the Yorkshire Ripper murders and, fearing a fair trial would be impossible if held locally, it was decided his case should be heard at the Old Bailey in London.

Sixteen weeks later, Sutcliffe appeared in the Old Bailey's Number 1 Court. He took his place in a dock that had been occupied by some of the country's most notorious serial killers including Dr Crippen and John Christie. Now it was the turn of the Yorkshire Ripper.

However, by this point Sutcliffe had been given plenty of time to think about how his trial might pan out. Until this point, his only reason for carrying out his crimes was to exact revenge. But now he offered a different explanation; one which seemed to be readily accepted behind closed doors by both prosecution and defence.

He claimed that the murders had been part of a divine mission after hearing the voice of God while working in the Catholic section at Bingley Cemetery. According to Sutcliffe:

> 'I was digging and I just paused for a minute. It was very hard ground. I just heard something – it sounded like a voice similar to a human voice – like an echo. I looked round to see if there was anyone there, but there was no one in sight. I was in the grave with my feet about 5ft below the surface. There was no one in sight when I looked round. I got out of the grave. The voice was not very clear. I got out and walked – the ground rose up. It was quite a steep slope. I walked to the top, but there was no one there at all. I heard it again, the same sound. It was like a voice saying something, but the words were all imposed on top of each other. I could not make them out, it was like echoes. The voices were coming directly in front of me from the top of a gravestone, which was Polish. I remember the name on the grave to this day. It was a man called Zipolski. Stanislaw Zipolski.'

He was shown a photograph of Bingley Cemetery and pointed at the grave he claimed the voice was coming from. He was mistaken in his recollection, for the name on the grave is Bronislaw Zapolski.

From this point on, he said he would hear the voice of God when he was feeling depressed, advising him to rid the world of prostitutes.

This somewhat convenient excuse was taken up willingly by the Crown Prosecution, Defence Counsel and the Attorney General. Even before he was formally charged with the murders, they had discussed and agreed that Sutcliffe was mentally ill and suffering from paranoid schizophrenia. A lot of figures in authority were only too happy to brush it under the carpet quickly and quietly. After all, a long, drawn-out trial might expose the calamitous way the police had handled the investigation, especially in relation to the Wearside Jack hoax.

The Old Bailey appearance was supposed to be a routine hearing at which his guilty plea of manslaughter on the grounds of diminished responsibility would be accepted. After five years of terrorizing women in the north of England, it looked as if the Yorkshire Ripper would be quietly put away.

This would have almost certainly been the case, had it not been for the judge, Sir Leslie Boreham. Barely concealing his irritation with both counsels, he threw out their suggestion of accepting Sutcliffe's plea of manslaughter, adding that, 'The only reason this man is mad is because he has told you so.' He ordered the court to reconvene in five days' time and made it clear that a jury would listen to the evidence of both sides and decide for itself whether Sutcliffe was a madman or a callous murderer.

Among those who gave evidence during the two-week trial were Sutcliffe's drinking pals Ronnie and David Barker, who said they often visited red-light districts with him; Trevor Birdsall, who revealed that he had suspected his friend of being the Ripper; and Olivia Reivers, who had been Sutcliffe's intended victim on the night he was arrested.

Whilst the evidence was given and the full horror of the crimes became apparent, Sonia sat quietly opposite her husband in the dock. Following his arrest, she had sat for fifteen hours straight in a cold interview room while five of the most brutal police interrogators went at her, delving into every inch of her life. At the end, they were convinced she knew nothing of her husband's night-time activities. The alibis she had provided for him in the past were explained quite easily due to the fact the couple rarely went out together and when detectives came calling, often weeks and sometimes months after a murder or attack, she would simply agree with her husband when he said that they were both indoors watching TV at the time. She, like most people, simply couldn't remember one particular night that far back. What should have sent alarm bells ringing was the fact Peter always could.

Sonia had already come to terms with the fact that her life and reputation was now forever smeared by his deeds and she would always be known as the wife of the Yorkshire Ripper. He was, however, her husband and in her mind, mentally unwell. She agreed to stick by his side and support him through his trial.

The prosecution was led by Sir Michael Havers, who did an amazing 'reverse ferret' and showed that, contrary to the previous claim that he was on a mission from God, there had been a deviant, sexual aspect to many of Sutcliffe's attacks. He had stuck a sharpened screwdriver into Josephine Whitaker's vagina, had scratched Olive Smelt's buttocks and had sex with Helen Rytka as she lay dying. The job of the prosecution would have been made so much easier if they had offered up the crude, crotch-exposing leggings that Sutcliffe was wearing when arrested.

Prison officer Anthony Fitzpatrick testified that he had heard Sutcliffe boasting in the hospital ward of Armley Prison that a deal had been done between defence and prosecution that he would be sent to a mental hospital. Prison hospital officer John Leach testified that, during a visit by Sonia to Peter six days following his arrest, he said: 'I'm gonna do thirty years or more unless I can convince people I am mad and maybe then ten years in a loony bin.'

Much of the trial was taken up with the examination and cross-examination of forensic psychiatrists, Dr Hugo Milne of Bradford, Dr Malcolm McCulloch of Liverpool and Dr Terence Key of Leeds. Each had interviewed Sutcliffe and provided the basis for the defence, led by James Chadwin QC, that Sutcliffe was suffering from paranoid schizophrenia. But under cross-examination it became clear that their diagnoses might not be altogether sound. Sutcliffe's defence team had tried to dissuade him from giving evidence under oath, but he refused to follow their advice.

On Monday, 11 May 1981, Sutcliffe stepped into the witness box and began to give evidence that would last nearly two days. His soft-spoken voice hardly faltered as his defence counsel accompanied him through his recital of death. He even laughed when he recalled that when questioned about the boot prints found on Emily Jackson's thigh and Patricia Atkinson's bedsheet, the policeman interviewing him had not noticed he was wearing the very boots at the time.

Sutcliffe calmly explained his divine mission and the voices he had heard. He claimed that God had told him to clean up the streets and had protected him from the police for so long. 'They had all the facts for a long time. But then I knew why they didn't catch me – because everything was in God's hands,' he said. Even under cross-examination he remained unshaken. He also conceded that he had been planning to do 'the Lord's work' on Olivia Reivers when the police finally caught him.

Mr Justice Boreham summed up the case and the jury was led out to make its decision. It had heard the evidence of the psychiatrists and seen their convictions waiver under cross-examination. And it had heard the words of Sutcliffe himself.

Was this a man who was mad pretending to be sane or a sane man pretending to be mad? After five hours of deliberation, the jury of six men and six women returned to the court to notify the judge that it could not come to a unanimous decision. It was told a majority decision would suffice and fifty-five minutes later, late in the afternoon of 22 May 1981, the jury returned to the court. Sutcliffe rose to his feet to hear the verdict. The jury found him guilty of thirteen murders and seven attempted murders by a majority of ten to two.

Peter William Sutcliffe was sentenced to life imprisonment, with a recommendation that he should serve at least thirty years for the 'cowardly' and brutal nature of the killings. His new home would be a top-security wing at Parkhurst Prison on the Isle of Wight.

Epilogue

There were two reports made following the arrest and conviction of Peter Sutcliffe in 1981: a Home Office-appointed public document, the Byford Report, and an internal West Yorkshire Police inquiry, the Sampson Report. The main part of the Byford Report was released to the public in 2006 following a Freedom of Information Act request. On 30 June 1983, the Sampson Report, led by former Assistant Chief Constable Colin Sampson, since promoted to Chief Constable, was released amid press and TV news coverage. As expected, the report was highly critical of those in charge of the inquiry. Heads would roll and the four main players would all leave their jobs before long.

First in the firing line was Chief Constable Ronald Gregory. The police inquiry concluded that the bungled Ripper investigation may have cost the lives of Sutcliffe's last six victims. However, Gregory responded by saying Sutcliffe had been 'extremely lucky and very clever. The truth is that we never had sufficient evidence to charge Sutcliffe.' Gregory added: 'He was interviewed several times at home. His wife gave him alibis and nothing was found in his garage or car.'

In January 1982, Home Secretary William Whitelaw told Parliament that Gregory would not be sacked for the 'major errors of judgement' uncovered by the various reviews. Nevertheless, over dinner at the Garrick Club a month later, when the Conservative MP Alan Clark asked Whitelaw why he had not fired Gregory for making 'such a balls-up of the Ripper case', Whitelaw hinted that Gregory's departure was imminent. In the event, he remained in the post for a further year, retiring in June 1983.

In his final annual report in 1983, Gregory wrote: 'The Ripper is a thorn in my career. I wish we could have caught him earlier. But I know the men on the case could not have worked any harder.'

After his retirement, Gregory moved to Cyprus where he came under fire once more for selling his story to the *Mail On Sunday* for £40,000. Relatives of some of the Ripper's victims accused him of taking 'blood money'; the then Home Secretary Leon Brittan called him 'deplorable' and – particularly hurtful to

Gregory – a police review branded him 'disloyal' and a 'hypocrite'. Ronald Gregory died on 9 April 2010 aged 88.

Jim Hobson, the officer who replaced George Oldfield for the latter part of the Yorkshire Ripper investigation, announced his retirement shortly after Sutcliffe's arrest. He went on to become head of security for Stylo Barratt Shoes Limited at their head office in Harrogate Road, Bradford. At the time of writing I don't know if he is still living. I have checked the police obituaries but cannot find any record of his death. If alive today he would be in his nineties.

Dick Holland, George Oldfield's right-hand man during the Ripper inquiry, retired in 1983 and became a security guard at Huddersfield Royal Infirmary. Over the years, he appeared in several documentaries and books about the Ripper case. Each time, he said his biggest regret was ignoring the police suspect report drafted by PC Andrew Laptew, which could have saved the lives of the three final Ripper victims. He died from pancreatic cancer on 17 February 2007, aged 74.

Assistant Chief Constable George Oldfield, at one time the most famous detective in the UK, stayed in his position for two years following the Ripper trial. Dogged by ill health, he announced his retirement in July 1983. He was heavily criticized by press and public alike for getting too personally involved in the case and for the next two years refused to acknowledge any fault behind his decisions. On 5 July 1985, he passed away from chronic heart disease at Pinderfields Hospital in Wakefield. He was 66 years old.

PC Andrew Laptew is still regarded by many as the man who originally nailed the Ripper, even though his report was ignored by his superiors at the time. He continued to serve with West Yorkshire Police until his retirement in 2001. He later returned as a civilian investigator compiling financial profiles of drug dealers and money launderers. He managed to reconcile his differences with his old boss Dick Holland, thanks largely to author Michael Bilton who brought them together whilst writing his book *Wicked Beyond Belief: The Hunt for the Yorkshire Ripper*. The two became friends and Andrew delivered the eulogy at Dick Holland's funeral in 2007. Today Andrew Laptew is a volunteer at Bradford Police Museum and a regular face on documentaries regarding the Yorkshire Ripper investigation.

Sonia Sutcliffe continues to live at 6 Garden Lane and until 2015 had been a regular visitor to prison to see her former husband, whom she finally divorced in 1994. There were rumours that she was going to move out of the three-storey detached property after the trial but she decided to keep the house. No doubt if she ever did sell it, the local council would snap it up and, in all likelihood, demolish it. We've seen this in other criminal cases – the Gloucester home of serial killers Fred and Rose West was demolished in 1996 and the house belonging to Soham double killer Ian Huntley was flattened in 2004.

Part of her reluctance to dispose of the property may well be financial. The house the Sutcliffes bought in 1977 for £16,000 is now worth around £250,000 but, should Sonia sell it, the Legal Aid Trust is likely to claim her ex-husband's share to regain compensation paid out for his victims and their families.

In May 1989, Sonia was awarded a record £600,000 damages from *Private Eye* for libellous claims that she was aware her husband was the Ripper. This was later reduced to £160,000. A further bid to sue the *News Of The World* failed as she lied about her financial resources. She was ordered to pay huge costs, which nearly bankrupted her but further successful lawsuits brought her in another £200,000.

She married hairdresser Michael Woodward in a low-key ceremony in 1997 but so far, Michael has refused to move into Garden Lane, perhaps due to its history. He lives alone in a flat in a converted mill in Saltaire, a fifteen-minute drive away.

As for Peter Sutcliffe, he has rarely been out of the press. Within a short period of arriving at Parkhurst Prison, he convinced some doctors that he was suffering from schizophrenia.

On 13 December 1982, Home Secretary William Whitelaw ruled that Sutcliffe should stay in Parkhurst Prison despite reports recommending he be transferred to a psychiatric hospital. Both the prison psychiatrist, Dr David Cooper, and Professor John Gunn, a psychiatrist called in by the Home Office, have certified that Sutcliffe is mentally ill in accordance with the Mental Health Act.

On 10 January 1983, while in Parkhurst, he was seriously assaulted by James Costello, a 35-year-old career criminal with several convictions for violence. Costello had followed Sutcliffe into the recess area of the hospital wing and twice plunged a broken coffee jar into the left side of his face, creating four wounds requiring thirty stitches.

In November 1983, he was declared bankrupt after solicitors for murder victim Jayne MacDonald applied to Bradford County Court for damages. Several of Sutcliffe's surviving victims, including Maureen Long, Marilyn Moore and Theresa Sykes, also won substantial damages against him.

Also in November 1983, the mother of murder victim Jacqueline Hill took out a writ against West Yorkshire Police accusing them of 'negligence and incompetence' in the hunt for the Yorkshire Ripper. Her case failed in December 1985.

On 27 March 1984, at the direction of the Home Secretary Leon Brittan, Sutcliffe was sent to Broadmoor Hospital for the criminally insane.

In November 1992, Sutcliffe finally admitted responsibility for the 1975 attack on Tracy Browne to Keith Hellawell who was then Chief Constable of Cleveland. He has never been charged with her attack.

In December 1994, it was reported that Sutcliffe would be notified by Home Secretary Michael Howard within six weeks that he will never be released. He had been sentenced in 1981 to a minimum sentence of thirty years.

On 23 February 1996, Sutcliffe was attacked in his room in Broadmoor Hospital's Henley Ward. Paul Wilson, a convicted robber, asked to borrow a videotape before attempting to strangle him with the cable from a pair of stereo headphones. Two other convicted murderers, Kenneth Erskine and Jamie Devitt, intervened after hearing screams.

In 1996, Keith Hellawell revealed that he had examined seventy-eight unsolved murders and attacks that could possibly have been Ripper attacks. Eventually, he reduced this number to twenty, which he believed may have been the responsibility of Sutcliffe. These offences were linked by a number of factors including similar descriptions of the offender, the use of a hammer as a weapon, and similar head injuries.

In 1997 Sutcliffe was attacked in Broadmoor again, this time by fellow inmate Ian Kay who stabbed him in both eyes. Sutcliffe lost the vision in his left eye, and his right eye was severely damaged. Kay admitted trying to kill Sutcliffe and was ordered to be detained in a secure psychiatric facility.

In 2001, police officials finally learnt of the existence of Sutcliffe's murder trousers; the strange attire fashioned from a silk shirt, with the knee pads sewn in. He had been wearing them when he was arrested. A detective for West Yorkshire Police who had been the exhibits officer at the Old Bailey, had been given instructions after the trial to incinerate all Ripper exhibits. However, fearing that potential evidence would be destroyed, which might at some future date link Sutcliffe to other unsolved murders and attacks, the detective secretly hung on to the leggings and, once retired, handed them back to West Yorkshire Police in the hope they could be tested for DNA evidence.

In November 2002, the law lords prevented Home Secretary David Blunkett from being able to increase the minimum life sentencing tariff recommended by the judiciary. A few months later in 2003, fearing that Sutcliffe might be released, the retired detective who had handed the murder trousers to police contacted *The Yorkshire Evening Post* and informed them of the existence of Sutcliffe's leggings. He said he could not understand why no mention was made of the leggings at Sutcliffe's trial. Other newspapers took up the story but to this date it is unknown if any tests have been carried out on Sutcliffe's 'killing kit'.

However, the revelations about the leggings reopened public debate about whether Sutcliffe was mentally ill or a cold and calculated sexual serial killer. On 24 March 2003, David Peace wrote a long article for the *New Statesman* which asked: 'Should the Yorkshire Ripper really be in Broadmoor?'

Sutcliffe's father, John, died in 2004 and was cremated. On 17 January 2005 Sutcliffe was allowed to visit Grange-over-Sands where his ashes had been scattered. The decision to allow the temporary release was initiated by Blunkett and ratified by Charles Clarke when he succeeded him as Home Secretary. Sutcliffe was accompanied by four members of hospital staff. Despite the passage of twenty-five years since the Ripper murders, his visit was the focus of tabloid headlines.

On 22 December 2007, Sutcliffe was attacked by fellow inmate Patrick Sureda, who lunged at him with a metal cutlery knife while shouting, 'You fucking raping, murdering bastard, I'll blind your fucking other one.' Sutcliffe flung himself backwards and the blade missed his right eye, stabbing him in the cheek.

In early 2010 Sutcliffe, by now calling himself by his mother's maiden name Coonan, made an application to have a minimum term set to give him a chance of parole. It was a frightening prospect for the families of his victims and naturally they fought against it. Their prayers were answered in July 2010 when the High Court ruled that he will never be freed. Sutcliffe appealed against this decision but on 9 March 2011 his appeal was rejected. Mr Justice Mitting said:

> 'This was a campaign of murder which terrorized the population of a large part of Yorkshire for several years. The only explanation for it, on the jury's verdict, was anger, hatred and obsession. Apart from a terrorist outrage, it is difficult to conceive of circumstances in which one man could account for so many victims.'

On 29 June 2015, *Yorkshire Ripper: The Secret Murders* was published by Chris Clark and Tim Tate. It identified a further twenty-three murders in the UK, which they believe were committed by Sutcliffe. Despite the strong evidence put forward for each case, Sutcliffe has not been charged with any more crimes.

In August 2016, it was ruled that Sutcliffe was mentally fit to be returned to prison, and that month was transferred to HM Prison Frankland in Durham. Doctors had confirmed Sutcliffe was no danger to anyone as long as he continued to take his medication. By coincidence, at the same time it was reported that he would finally be leaving the comfortable life of Broadmoor, it was also reported that he was claiming to hear voices again, telling him to kill. These have, thankfully, fallen on deaf ears this time and he is back behind the bars of a proper prison, where the jury decided he should be in 1981.

So, is this the end of the Yorkshire Ripper story? Sadly not. In 2017, West Yorkshire Police launched Operation Painthall to determine if Sutcliffe was guilty of unsolved crimes dating back to 1964. This inquiry also looked at the killings of two sex workers in southern Sweden in 1980. As Sutcliffe was a lorry driver, it was theorized that he had been in Denmark and Sweden, making use of the ferry across the Öresund Strait. West Yorkshire Police later stated that they were 'absolutely certain' that Sutcliffe had never been to Sweden.

Despite the volume of evidence pointing to many more crimes committed by Sutcliffe, he continues to be vague and not forthcoming. Perhaps he's desperate to cling on to some eminence of power he feels he has over the authorities. There are still hundreds of files locked away, which the public have yet to see, and despite numerous requests through the Freedom of Information Act these files are still being withheld. Time will tell if we will ever get to see them, but with the promise of new evidence still to come, it seems the trail of the Yorkshire Ripper may have only just begun.

Bibliography

Beattie, J. (1981). *The Yorkshire Ripper Story*. Quartet/Daily Star.

Bilton, M. (2012). *Wicked Beyond Belief – The Hunt for the Yorkshire Ripper*. Harper Press.

Brannen, K. *The Yorkshire Ripper*. execulink.com/~kbrannen

Burn, G. (2004). *Somebody's Husband, Somebody's Son*. Faber & Faber.

Byford, L. (2006). *The Byford Report*. gov.uk/government/publications/sir-lawrence-byford-report-into-the-police-handling-of-the-yorkshire-ripper-case

Clark, C., Tate, T. (2015). *Yorkshire Ripper: The Secret Murders*. John Blake Publishing.

Cross, R. (1981). *The Yorkshire Ripper – The In-Depth Study of a Mass Killer and His Methods*. Granada.

Great Crimes And Trials Of The Twentieth Century. (1992). *The Yorkshire Ripper*. Nugus/Martin Productions Ltd.

Jones, B. (1994). *Voices From An Evil God*. Blake Publishing.

Lavelle, P. (1999). *Wearside Jack – The Hunt for the Hoaxer of the Century*. Northeast Press.

Murder Casebook. (1991). *The Yorkshire Ripper*. Marshall Cavendish.

Nicholson, M. (1979). *The Yorkshire Ripper*. Star.

Rumbelow, D. (2004). *The Complete Jack the Ripper*. Penguin.

Yallop, D. (1993). *Deliver Us from Evil*. Corgi.

Archives

Bradford Police Museum
City of Bradford Libraries
City of Leeds Libraries
West Yorkshire Archive Service, Wakefield (The National Archives)
West Yorkshire Police

Index